PHENOMENOLOGY AND SKEPTICISM

Northwestern University
Studies in Phenomenology
and
Existential Philosophy

PHENOMENOLOGY AND SKEPTICISM

Essays in Honor of James M. Edie

Edited by Brice R. Wachterhauser

Northwestern University Press
Evanston, Illinois

Northwestern University Press
625 Colfax
Evanston, Illinois 60208-4210

Printed in the United States of America

ISBN cloth 0-8101-1387-2
paper 0-8101-1388-0

Library of Congress Cataloging-in-Publication Data

Phenomenology and skepticism : essays in honor of James M. Edie / edited by Brice R. Wachterhauser.
p. cm.—(Northwestern University studies in phenomenology and existential philosophy)
Includes bibliographical references.
ISBN 0-8101-1387-2 (cloth : alk. paper).—ISBN 0-8101-1388-0 (pbk. : alk. paper)
1. Phenomenology. 2. Skepticism. 3. Relativity. 4. Husserl, Edmund, 1859–1938. I. Edie, James M. II. Wachterhauser, Brice R., 1953– . III. Series: Northwestern University studies in phenomenology & existential philosophy.
B829.5.P4532 1996
142'.7—dc20 96-25587
CIP

The paper used in this publication meets the minimum requirements of the American National Standard for Information Sciences-Permanence of Paper for Printed Library Materials, ANSI Z39.48-1984.

Contents

Acknowledgments

I would like to thank Professor Calvin Schrag for extending permission on behalf of *Man and World* to reprint James M. Edie's essay "On Confronting Species-Specific Skepticism as We Near the End of the Twentieth Century." It originally appeared in *Man and World* 25 (1992), 313–39.

Also, I want to express my appreciation for the excellent work in manuscript preparation that Susan Donahue and Joanne Devlin did for this volume. With their able technical and editorial assistance this volume has been able to see the light of publication in a much more timely fashion. I owe them a great deal for their tireless, behind-the-scenes labor.

Lastly, a word of thanks to all the contributors for participating in this project and to James Edie for suggesting its theme. Without your enthusiasm and encouragement, I would not have undertaken it. My hope is that this volume will bring us and others to more philosophical conversations, guided by the ever-present hope of truth. If it does so, I think all our efforts will be amply repaid and James Edie's legacy rightly honored.

James M. Edie. Photograph by Bachrach

Introduction: The Shipwreck of Apodicticity? Phenomenology's Journey "beyond" Skepticism

Brice R. Wachterhauser

When one raises the issue of the relation between phenomenology and skepticism, one raises at the very least two very large issues: the first is Husserl's relation to skepticism in all the phases of development his philosophy underwent; the second is the relationship of Husserl's disciples and successors to skepticism, all of whom consider themselves "phenomenologists" of one stripe or another, all of whom consider themselves deeply indebted to Husserl, but all of whom also work out their version of phenomenology in terms of a sharp critique of some aspect of Husserl's monumental work.

Obviously an essay, let alone an introductory essay to a volume of essays on this theme, is not the place to attempt a systematic overview of either of these issues. To undertake a thorough examination of Husserl's relation to skepticism we would have to offer detailed analyses of all of Husserl's major works from his *Philosophy of Arithmetic* in 1891 to his *Crisis of European Sciences and Transcendental Phenomenology*, worked on by Husserl until shortly before his death in 1938. It is well known that during this time span Husserl not only produced prodigious quantities of texts but that he was, to his lasting credit, a philosopher of consummate integrity, who repeatedly examined and revised his own efforts to introduce the new philosophical method of phenomenology. Although

Husserl's inspiration to establish "philosophy as rigorous science" might be plausibly seen to be constant throughout most of his career, his understanding of "philosophy," "rigor," and "science" undergoes considerable change during this time. Needless to say, any survey of these changes would be in constant danger of oversimplification. On the other hand, a sweeping survey of Husserl's disciples and successors and their reaction to skepticism is similarly precluded. One would have to discuss such figures as Scheler, Heidegger, Sartre, Merleau-Ponty, Gadamer, Ricoeur, and perhaps Derrida as well. And this only lists the greatest luminaries of the tradition; lesser lights would make the list even more impossible to manage.

Nevertheless, when all caveats about the dangers of oversimplification and generalization have been prudently pointed out by the editor, it remains the business of editors of volumes on such themes as "Phenomenology and Skepticism" to give general introductions to the field. Fortunately, I think it is possible to give a general overview of both Husserl's relation to skepticism, as well as that of his successors, which while schematic and doubtlessly oversimplified, nevertheless captures some of the important truth about phenomenology's relation to skepticism. What I will offer is the broad outlines of an existential-hermeneutical critique which will, I think, provide a framework broad enough to illuminate many of the important issues implicit in our theme.

I would begin by pointing out that Husserl understands the deepest form of skepticism to be the denial of apodicticity or necessary and universal truths. He takes such skepticism to be absurd because it denies the very conditions of necessary truth which are requisite for *any* theory to make sense.[1] Thus he set out to defend all necessary and universal truths as truly indubitable in the Cartesian sense of being beyond *all possible doubt.* But this radical Cartesian demand to defend the foundations of knowledge beyond *all possible doubt* leads Husserl to up the ante, as it were, by introducing the additional criterion of presuppositionless grounding. Not only must the foundations evince necessity with compelling self-evidence but even self-evidence itself and its conditions in the ego must be analyzed regressively to such a point that their every presupposition has been made transparent and justified beyond any conceivable doubt. Husserl accepts this challenge with such seriousness and radical thoroughness that he is determined to leave no possible doubt unexamined in order to put it to rest definitively. This leads him to intense self-examination and self-criticism. Again and again he points out the most difficult problems confronting his own position and attempts to overcome them honestly and with definitive rigor. This captures something of the true sense in which Husserl could refer to himself as a "perpetual beginner" in phenomenology. It is the true beginnings or "roots" of phenomenology, no matter how difficult to unearth or deal with once they are uncovered, that spur Husserl's radical methodological reflections to the unprecedented depths they achieve.

In the same radical spirit of no-holds-barred reflection, Husserl's students ask themselves if Husserl succeeds by his own radical criterion of apodicticity and presuppositionlessness and many decide, unfortunately, that he fails.[2] Their critique of Husserl's search for ultimate foundations generally turns on two issues, freedom and finitude. The proper understanding of each allegedly shows that Husserl's search for apodicticity and presuppositionlessness cannot possibly succeed. But Husserl's critics also point out that such alleged failure on Husserl's part does not lead us back to skepticism but supposedly beyond skepticism. It is argued that skepticism's allure is not overcome by Husserl's success but ironically by his failure. What this failure shows is that skepticism, as Husserl understands it, as well as Husserlian antiskepticism, the flip-side of the same coin as it were, is the result of an inadequate understanding of the conditions of human knowledge.[3] Far from being an ordinary language critique of skepticism in the tradition of J. L. Austin, a critique which attempts to point out that the skeptic's dilemma is a function of the skeptic's misuse of everyday language, this critique of skepticism claims that the "things themselves"—human knowing and its conditions—show skepticism as well as Husserl's antiskepticism to be untenable.

Thus it is said that Husserl's opposition to skepticism is justifiable, not in terms that Husserl himself envisaged, but in terms for which he nevertheless laid the groundwork. He laid the groundwork for the overcoming of skepticism, as well as for the overcoming of his own demand for apodicticity and presuppositionlessness because he fearlessly and ruthlessly pursued the conditions of human knowledge to such a point that his program of discovering an Archimedean point for all cognition allegedly collapsed under its own weight, and along with it skepticism as its inverted image. What Husserl made it possible for these disciples to see (but which he himself perhaps never saw the full implications of) was that both freedom and finitude are each in their own way factual conditions of human understanding. As *factual* conditions of understanding they are inherently contingent and as such they can never be grasped with apodicticity. Moreover, freedom and finitude can never be grasped with the indubitable clarity and distinction or the transparent presuppositionlessness such principles must evince if they are to function as unshakable starting points on which all truths can somehow be built up. Instead, freedom and finitude are "facts," and even though they are conditions of knowledge they are not truly ultimate first principles but contingent, factual conditions whose existence and role in knowledge can always be questioned just like any other contingent fact. Thus it is argued that in one sense at least Husserl's program of discovering the indubitable foundations of knowledge is wrecked on the rocks of finitude, because these foundations never present themselves as necessary and presuppositionless. Instead what they show is that all knowledge contains within it both an inescapable element of contingency and doubt and unclarified depths that can never be put to rest without perhaps undermining the possibility of human understanding itself.

So it is that this critique of Husserl would claim that a proper understanding of knowledge moves us beyond skepticism, but not beyond doubt and the need for further inquiry. Knowledge remains possible within the parameters of this critique, but it is a knowledge inherently open to question; it is fallibilistic in principle. Thus one might say that while this account of knowledge precludes certainty at the deepest level of analysis it nevertheless seeks to preserve truth. In this way the skeptical problematic is supposedly supplanted by an account of knowledge which does not equate knowledge with either certainty or presuppositionlessness. Thus, the denial of certainty and presuppositionlessness does not lead to skepticism because the possibility of knowledge as such is not denied when certainty and presuppositionlessness are denied. Thus, this account of knowledge might very well reject dichotomies like apodictic versus inherently doubtful truth-claims, necessary and contingent truths, a priori and a posteriori knowledge-claims, etc., but nevertheless say that there is an important difference between truth and falsehood. What this difference amounts to is an important point of dispute and inquiry today. Some, following Nietzsche, wonder if this is the last dichotomy that needs to be overthrown. Can it be said, perhaps, that this dialectical development within phenomenology has changed the face of skepticism but not supplanted skepticism as such? This is an important question but one which we cannot answer here. First we must try to understand more clearly how it is that the problems of freedom and finitude supposedly "shipwreck" Husserl's project.

It is well documented that Husserl's search for the final and ultimate justification (*letzte Begründung*) for knowledge, his search for the *fundamentum absolutum et inconcussum* leads him in Cartesian fashion to the indubitable evidence of the *ego cogito,* which Husserl understands in light of his views on intentionality as the *ego cogito cogitatum.* In his more idealistically motivated writings, like *Cartesian Meditations,* Husserl understands this *ego cogito* as a first truth which can be grasped without contingent presuppositions. If it is the case that this ego can be grasped presuppositionlessly, then it can function as the ultimate foundation for knowledge. Only such a noncontingent presuppositionless starting point will satisfy the demand for a final, definitive, justification of the possibility of human knowledge.

This radical search for an ultimate justification for knowledge (and of all our life activities which presuppose knowledge) is motivated ethically by a principle of ultimate self-responsibility (*aus letzter Selbstverantwortung*) which aspires to take control of one's life by making the foundations of life transparent to the knowing self. This ethical attitude leads to a refusal to leave any naive belief unexamined and unquestioned. Only if we can discover truly indubitable and presuppositionless starting points for all our most important endeavors can we take on this final responsibility for ourselves.

To assure that this goal of radical questioning is met, Husserl proposes his famous epoché or bracketing of the "natural attitude"—i.e., a suspension of all belief in the real world with its infinite variety of brute, impenetrable facts, in order to make it possible to focus on the experience of meaning, which can be made the *ego cogito*'s proper object, if only the ego learns to adopt the right attitude. It is Husserl's conviction that whereas facts and their ontological conditions are ultimately opaque and impenetrable in their contingency, meanings have an essential or ideal being which all apprehension of fact presupposes. Just as important, these meanings are not opaque but can be made transparent objects of the thinking ego, which is capable of grasping these meanings apodictically in their essential, necessary truth. Thus, Husserl proposes to transform a contingent grasping of the foundations of knowledge, an epistemological program which claims that knowledge *is* such and such to one which declares that it *must* be such and such. This transformation from "it is so" to "it must be so" is necessary for Husserl's ethical imperative of *letzte Selbstverantwortung.* Only if these meanings and their conditions can be made fully transparent, only if they can be fully surveyed and their necessity finally established beyond all question, can we be assured that our life as rational beings has been firmly secured. Only then can we adequately fulfill philosophy's demand to "know thyself" and thus escape the flux and turmoil of shifting belief. Making these meanings transparent means making them an object of the ego's knowing, a knowing which can be made apodictic or certain in every respect, a knowing in which the object and its conditions presents itself fully without any residue of contingency or brute fact that cannot be traced back to presuppositionless or transparent principles known with apodicticity.

Unfortunately for Husserl's project, it would seem that freedom is just such a contingency. If we reflect on the founding act of the phenomenologist, i.e., *the decision* to take up ultimate self-responsibility for one's life by engaging the phenomenological epoché so that the essential, necessary foundations of all experience can show themselves in the immanence of the ego's intentional structure, what we find is that the decision itself is not capable of becoming the type of object of the ego's knowing that presents itself with either apodicticity or presuppositionlessness.[4] The decision qua decision is a free act and hence it is never necessary but always contingent. This means that as a *free* act it is not necessary but could have been otherwise. Moreover, this freedom is itself a brute fact whose opacity cannot be transcended by an apodictic insight which would secure it from all doubt once and for all. Nothing is quite as dubious and fraught with obscurity as the idea of freedom. For this reason, Kant "deduces" the idea of freedom from that of responsibility or duty and offers no further claim to make it transparent. To the extent that phenomenological thinking rests on freedom its roots are metaphysically obscure and problematic; they are anything but apodictic or presuppositionless.

If we turn from the mere contingency of this founding act of freedom and inquire into its motivation, another problem for Husserl's project presents itself—finitude. "Finitude" or dependence on factors that cannot be brought under our complete knowledge and control has shown itself in the very contingency of the founding fact of freedom. Hence "finitude" is the more general term employed by all "hermeneutical" critiques for the problem to which Husserl's transcendental idealism succumbs. But the issue of the motivation of this free act shows us another way in which Husserl's search for apodictic and presuppositionless starting points is preempted by contingent particularities that will not yield to the transcendental reduction.

The ideal of *letzte Selbstverantwortung* is not a self-evident, necessary ideal but one which has contingent roots in a philosophical ideal of humanity stretching back at least as far as Socrates's appropriation of the Delphic oracle's maxim to "know thyself." We do not choose this ideal on the basis of *apodictic* or presuppositionless insight but on the basis of a *practical* insight into what is the best life for us, an insight which is by no means necessary and certain but at best "proximately and for the most part" true. In Aristotle's words "we must be content, then, in speaking of such subjects and with such premises to indicate the truth roughly and in outline, and in speaking about things which are only for the most part true and with premises of the same kind to reach conclusions that are no better" (*Nichomachean Ethics*, Bk. I, 3, Ross translation). If this is so the attempt to introduce apodicticity and presuppositionlessness at this very basic level of analysis seems doomed to failure from the start.

Finitude manifests itself, however, not just at the beginning of Husserl's approach but also in the "middle" as it were, in the central

Husserlian doctrine of constitution of the known object. Without going into all the subtle intricacies of Husserl's doctrine of constitution it can be said that Husserl's idealism leads him to emphasize the active role of the thinking subject in "constituting" the known object. Leaving aside the controversial issue of the extent to which the doctrine of constitution implies the "creation" or "production" of the object qua known object, Husserl's theory of the perceptual object well illustrates the subject's *active* role in knowing the object. It is this *activity* of the ego in knowing that seems to defy a regressive analysis that comes to rest in transparent apodictic insight. Husserl's insight into the nature of perception illustrates the problem well.

Husserl reminds us that when we perceive any physical object we always do so "*abschattungsweise*" or perspectively.[5] In other words, we only see one side of the object at any given time and we never have the whole object, the object as it is from all perspectives or *Abschattungen,* before us all at once. Instead our view of one side shades into or merges with our view of another side as we gradually move around the perceived object and change our perspective. This "merger" takes place by the activity of the ego, which holds together the various perspectives and "constitutes" them into a single, unified known object. This act of "merging" or constitution has a distinct temporal structure to it; it is the ego's task to hold the object together, with the help of memory, by linking past perspectives of the object to the anticipated, not yet seen sides of the object. This "linking" takes place "via" or "through" the immediate act and object of perception, the present link as it were between past perspectives and future anticipated ones. According to Husserl, past and future present themselves as "horizons" or a more or less implicit, unthematic framework for our explicit, thematic present awareness of the object. This means that past and future, memory and anticipation, do not accidentally enter into the constitution of the object now and then but are, for us, de facto conditions of its cognition. This allows finitude to enter the dynamic of constitution in that the object can only be known as we know it, because, in the act of constitution, it is remembered and anticipated in a certain, contingent way. In remembering previously given perspectives on the object the ego has no a priori controls over what elements it remembers and carries over into its ongoing act of perception. Moreover, other elements of its life, other "interests" the ego may have, can influence the constitution of the object. We cannot circumvent these influences via a second-order reflection, because an analysis of memory itself yields no apodictic first principles that control its operations. In fact, making the act of memory itself a thematic object itself depends on memory and so would involve us in an infinite regress. Similarly, the anticipation of the perceived object is subject to analogous qualifications. There are no pure, disinterested anticipations of the object any more than there are pure, disinterested memories. In fact, anticipations depend in part on memory for their character. It is always through the past that we anticipate the future, even when we imagine genuinely new possibilities. Just as interest can enter the field of memory without announcing its presence or effects to consciousness, so anticipation is similarly "out ahead of itself" in the sense that the ego does not know in advance what it will anticipate but must wait to see what it in fact does before it has a sense of how it has projected itself into its own acts. Thus it has been frequently pointed out that both the "retentional" and "protential" character of perception allows the historical contingencies of the past to enter via the doors of memory as well as the historical surprises of the future to enter by way of anticipation.[6]

If history in all its contingency contributes to the constitution of perceptual objects it seems even more true that it contributes to the constitution of cultural objects. Even more than perceptual objects, cultural objects are "products" of the thinking self, constituted via memory and anticipation and never "purely" given in themselves, apart from our contribution to them.

If this critique is correct it can be seen how it is that the appeal to finitude has undercut Husserl's quest for apodictic and presuppositionless starting points. Husserl's own insights into the "horizonal" nature of constitution make this critique of one version of his quest for secure foundations possible. Because we cannot go beyond the "finitude" or contingent dependencies that make our knowing possible, the ego, the knowing self, can never be the "sovereign master of its own house"; it can never secure its knowing beyond all possible doubt, because at least some of its foundations are neither apodictic nor presuppositionless but inherently contingent and opaque. Thus, there is no "final justification" of knowing; as knowers we are cut off from both absolute origins as well as our final historical telos. We can neither know where we really come from as knowers nor can we know where we are going until we get there. As Heidegger puts it, we are "being-in-the-world" existing "out ahead of ourselves" or as Ricoeur would have it, we exist *in media res*, in the middle of things (*HHS*, 106) belonging to the world and always having an understanding of things without having access to either the "bottom" of things, the ultimate "ground" on which we stand, or the final end point of our historical trajectory as knowing subjects. Perhaps this is why Husserl confessed in one of the appendices to the *Crisis* that "philosophy as science, as earnest, rigorous, indeed, apodictically rigorous science—the dream is spent."[7] If this critique is valid then skepticism as the denial of a fully transparent knowledge collapses along with this Husserlian model of knowledge which is founded on it. In this view, these two positions are two sides of the same coin, the one just the inverted image of the other. If this critique is valid, knowledge and truth as such have not been denied but a certain, unique model of knowledge and truth—Husserl's and arguably that of European rationalism from Descartes through Kant and Hegel to the Neo-Kantians—has been shown to be untenable. And along with it its mortal adversary, skepticism, collapses as well because this kind of skepticism equates knowledge with transparent and certain truths.

This newly vacated space must now be filled by a new model of knowledge and truth, the exact contours of which are still largely unclarified, even though it has been the subject of much work and debate. With regard to skepticism, however, I think it is premature to say that as a result of Husserl's confrontation with skepticism and its supposed failure we have moved beyond skepticism. Instead, skepticism in our day will, at the very least, take on another form; we will see, as it were, another face of skepticism, which instead of defining itself as a denial of apodicticity and presuppositionlessness will define itself as the denial of all knowledge and truth.

But there is also a possible Husserlian response that should be pointed out here. While a Husserlian could admit that the search for truly presuppositionless starting points in the ego runs aground on the problems of freedom and finitude, the necessary, logical conditions of knowledge still evince apodicticity or necessity and universality. The phenomenologist would argue that there is a distinction between *ontological* conditions of knowledge and *logical* conditions of knowledge that the hermeneutical critic is in danger of ignoring. Early in his career Husserl drew a distinction between *noetic* and *logical* conditions of knowledge. This distinction is implicit in the distinction between noetic and logical skepticism touched on above. The noetic conditions of knowledge have to do with the necessary conditions of knowledge in the structure of subjectivity as such. The logical conditions have to do with conceptual necessities, necessities for the coherent meaning of any theory whatsoever. While this critique shows that Husserl's analysis of the noetic conditions of knowledge do not yield the kind of presuppositionlessness his own search for justification called for, the logical conditions of knowledge nevertheless remain untouched. Even if the noetic or ontological conditions of knowledge remain open to question and create occasions for doubt, the logical conditions like the law of noncontradiction are still necessary for any meaningful theory whatsoever. Even if one suspects that the laws of logic are not completely transparent and presuppositionless, they are nevertheless necessary and universal. In Husserl's language they are given apodictically but the evidence for them may not be adequate or complete.[8] Moreover, the status of logic as a necessary presupposition of knowledge does not as such presuppose freedom as recent advances in artificial intelligence make very clear. No one argues that the computer's freedom is a necessary condition of its deducing valid truths. Even if Husserl's idealistic attempt to find a truly presuppositionless starting point for all knowledge in the transcendental ego succumbs to this critique of freedom and finitude—and I think it does—it does not follow that the laws of logic are contingent and can be applied relatively. However inescapable finitude in the form of historicity may be in the constitution of all knowable objects this doesn't change the fact that all *real* acts of knowing presuppose *ideal* structures, like the law of noncontradiction, whose validity is not historically constituted but whose presence makes any *meaningful* historical constitution possible in the first place. What the Husserlian would insist is that although Husserl's idea of a *presuppositionless* foundation may have failed, there are nevertheless still apodictic or necessary foundations to be discovered and vigorously defended. This can be done by not confusing, to begin with, noetic or ontological conditions with logical conditions, and by similarly not confusing the demand for apodicticity with the demand for presuppositionlessness. If these distinctions are valid, the hermeneutical theorist could accept this rejoinder but simply point out that it is an idealistic philosophy of transparent starting points that her critique challenges, not the indispensability of logic. It is Husserl's transcendental idealism with its rationalistic demand for truly presuppositionless beginnings that succumbs to this critique and not logic or phenomenology as such. Thus, Ricoeur can claim with compelling plausibility that Husserl's idealism must bow to this hermeneutical critique but "phenomenology remains the unsurpassable presupposition of hermeneutics" (*HHS*, 101).

It would be misleading in the worst way if my analysis of the "shipwreck of apodicticity" were taken to imply that Husserl and phenomenology have nothing more to contribute to the dialogue. Husserl's own contribution regarding the "horizonal" character of our experience shows how misleading a facile dismissal of phenomenology would be. Nevertheless, it must be admitted that the hermeneutical critique shows us that phenomenology's legacy is mixed. On the one hand, Husserl's most radical idealism succumbs to this critique, but skepticism is not its necessary outcome. In fact, such a skepticism as the counterimage of Husserl's search for transparent starting points collapses along with this strand of Husserl's thought. On the other hand, necessary conditions of knowledge, like the laws of logic, remain untouched by this critique, but the exact nature of knowledge and truth is still up for grabs and the ontological conditions of knowledge create their own problems which must be addressed.

This is where *Phenomenology and Skepticism* enters the conversation. In light of the quest for new models of knowledge and truth (or revivifications of old models, as the case may be) the contributors explore various facets of the relationship between phenomenology and skepticism as we understand it today. It is to these contributions that we now turn.

James M. Edie, in whose honor this collection has been assembled, leads off the discussion. It is appropriate that Professor Edie be singled out to begin this collection on phenomenology and skepticism because throughout his career he has not only dedicated himself to expounding, defending, and expanding phenomenological thought, but because in his effort to promote Husserl's ground-breaking achievements Edie has always placed Husserl's confrontation with skepticism at the center of his contributions.[9] I remember as a graduate student the passion and rigor with which Professor Edie impressed on us the importance of Husserl's confrontation with the skeptical consequences of psychologism. Again and again, he attempted to move us away from our half-hearted skepticism and awaken us to the relevance of Husserl's insights for combatting the many skepticisms of our day. In these efforts, Professor Edie was never the authoritarian graduate professor, but he always played the phenomenologist, the protagonist who drove us to "the things themselves," because he thought that only "the things themselves" would be sufficient to prove the skeptic wrong and in the process give our uncertain philosophical longings a firm direction. Many of us remained finally unconvinced by the idealistic turn that Husserl eventually took, but all of us also went away from Professor Edie's classes with a sense that Husserl's importance was real and that his thought would continue to repay careful study.

In his contribution to this volume, "On Confronting Species-Specific Skepticism as We Near the End of the Twentieth Century," Professor Edie argues for the ongoing relevance of Husserlian ideas for coming to terms with contemporary sources of "species-specific skepticism"—i.e., the claim that fundamental norms of logic and truth are merely relative to the human species. Edie begins by focusing on the "decentering of the subject" and the "deconstruction of subjectivity" carried out by such thinkers as Heidegger, the Frankfurt School, Derrida, and Rorty. He wonders whether the repudiation of the search for secure foundations of knowledge and the substitution of "conversation" for such foundations can really suffice. Either the conversational context seems so wide as to be meaningless or it pushes us toward a renewed foundationalism, i.e., a renewed awareness of the common conditions of any conversation whatsoever. Edie writes:

> it is certainly a practical as well as a theoretical postulate of all anthropological science within our own species of homo sapiens, just on this planet, that however diverse, and, on the surface level, "incomprehensible" other cultures we may encounter may be, at the limit, it its always possible for us, ourselves, just as humans, to put ourselves in their place, to experience the world from their perspective, and at least ideally, to be able to communicate with them. We describe their languages, we describe their social structures, we in fact communicate with them and they with us, and each can come to see the common world of experience through the eyes of the other. The objectivity, universality and validity required of "scientific" (and therefore of "rational") laws *requires* that all humans experience the world as the other does. And in fact this is accomplished, perhaps not totally—given the ineffability of individual difference—but sufficiently for scientifically rational discourse to continue to take place.

The ability to make this kind of significant contact with other people from other times and cultures presupposes, Edie argues, the presence of the "eidetic" or a priori element in all thought, "which leads to apodictic insight into the formal structures of reason itself." These structures of reason itself show that logical laws, like the law of noncontradiction, are not relative to our species. They show us "not that we cannot *believe* two contradictories to be true at the same time and in the same respect"—in fact, we know we often do believe and act on such contradictory beliefs—but what Husserl showed and Edie reminds us of is that two such contradictory beliefs "cannot both *be* true." Similar apodictic results can be had for the concept of truth. According to Edie "if species-skepticism were true, we would have to conclude that what could be true for one species of thinking being could be false for another. But whenever the words 'true' and 'false' are used in *their proper meanings*, this possibility is ruled out a priori." This leads Edie to a reconsideration and defense of Husserl's account of transcendental consciousness or those elements of any consciousness necessary for any meaningful experience. This shows us that Husserl's foundationalism is not species-specific at all but transcendental with its emphasis on the conditions of experience for *any* consciousness. Edie concludes, with an eye to recent discussions of "textuality," that "there is solid reason for distinguishing what happens on the level of the surface strings of ordinary conversation, from the logical and a priori constraints on meaningfulness, noncontradiction and possible truth, on the level of the depth grammar (or what Husserl called 'pure logical grammar') necessary to the structure of any possible natural language, discourse or text." Agreeing with Merleau-Ponty, Edie argues that "our life is essentially universal" because "the least use of language implies an idea of truth."

Robert Sokolowski's "Thoughts on Phenomenology and Skepticism" argues that Husserl's relation to skepticism is deeper and more complicated than first meets the eye. Beyond Husserl's nearly lifelong opposition to skepticism,[10] there are historical similarities between Husserl and skeptics like Sextus. Not only does Husserl borrow the term *epoché* from the skeptics, but like them, Husserl too wishes to "assent to none of the things that are nonevident." But of course there are profound differences too. For Sextus, the appearances (*ta phainomena*) never point beyond their own immediate givenness to a categorical presentation by virtue of which Husserl argues the *identity* of things is presented to us in their truth. Ultimately, "truth is what skepticism is skeptical about" and the possibility of truth is precisely what phenomenology shows to be possible. But this does not necessarily make phenomenology the dogmatic antipode to skepticism. Rather, phenomenology insists on a subtle, detailed analysis of the various degrees of evidence with which different types of things present themselves. So it is that phenomenology incorporates the skeptic's concern with the grounds of evidence and warrantable assent into their working attitude. Thus, phenomenologists avoid dogmatism because they insist on the "moderation of philosophy, which acknowledges, contemplates, and describes the evidences that things give to us, but only within the limits that are proper to them." In this way phenomenology puts the critical attitude of skepticism to its proper use and thereby transforms its categorical distrust into a philosophical program dedicated to a modest but secured knowing. Only such a program, according to Sokolowski, can provide the "true philosophical *ataraxia*."

"The Epistemological Significance of Husserl's Theory of Intentionality" is Harrison Hall's contribution to this volume. Hall thinks that Husserl's primary contribution to epistemology is not his theory of evidence but his unique theory of intentionality. What Husserl shows is that the *noema* (or "object" of which consciousness is always conscious) is a meaning and never a fact. In reality we can only refer to facts at all through these *noemata* or meanings. "Meanings and meaning relations" are "independent of or transcendent of that [factual] reality," but they make reference to that reality possible by giving it sense. According to Hall, Husserl argues "that the sole concern of philosophy is with meaning and meaning relationships." In this sense, philosophy does not deny "facts" but it does not concern itself with facts but with meanings or conceptual relationships. For Husserl, confusion can only arise by failing to distinguish sharply questions of fact from questions of meaning. Husserl's epoché, along with

> Husserl's talk of two consciousnesses, one empirical and the other transcendental, two worlds or realms of inquiry, one of fact and one of meaning, and two utterly different kinds of investigation and questioning of our experience, one natural and the other philosophical (phenomenological, transcendental) has a clear purpose—to separate philosophy, its subject matter and method from everything nonphilosophical. This is the key to Husserl's epistemology. The underlying claim is that the unsolvable problems and unanswerable questions in the theory of knowledge are all mixed problems and confused questions—half natural, half philosophical—hence not real problems or questions at all."

According to Hall, this implies that for Husserl skepticism is just such a pseudoproblem. Once we get clear that questions of fact are of a radically different kind from questions of meaning the issue of the relation between facts and meanings can never skeptically imply the nonexistence of facts or the substitution of meanings for facts. Of course, the relation between facts and meanings is a legitimate question for Husserl, but its answer can never take a skeptical form because "it is only our philosophical confusion about the two mutually exclusive realms that makes such questions seem real. . . . It is the elimination of such confusion that is the real epistemological significance of Husserl's theory of intentionality."

Joseph J. Kockelmans's "Association in Husserl's Phenomenology" offers us a concrete look at one aspect of Husserl's phenomenological epistemology, i.e., his doctrine of association. Kockelmans points out that Husserl works on the problem of association as part of his general program of dissociating the valid contributions of empiricism from what Husserl took to be its skeptical consequences. What this requires is an analysis of association that, contrary to the classical empiricists like Locke or Hume, does not confuse "causal types of explanations for phenomena of meaning," but instead seeks to uncover *laws* of association, laws which are transcendental in that they make certain types of experience possible in the first place. "Association has to do with all processes in which meaning becomes constituted according to rules at a level where there is not yet any participation on the part of the active ego." For example, in remembering one instance, another *similar* instance springs to mind, quite apart from the striving of the ego. Here the connecting link, the principle of connection, is similarity. More importantly, memory itself presupposes associations of one sort or another. Without associations based on principles such as similarity we have no link with the past. Because "it is simply impossible to have a human subject if that subject in principle would not be able to have recollections of what has been, it (association) is very important for the phenomenology of consciousness." This connects Husserl's analyses of association with his analyses of time-consciousness and the whole problematic of retention and protention discussed above. Kockelmans has offered us a richly detailed overview of why "association" is so important for Husserl, an account that "lets one see that association is not some mysterious process" that just happens to mark our conscious life, but a rule-bound phenomenon that can be "taken up in critical reflections on the constitution of all meaning by transcendental subjectivity and transcendental intersubjectivity."

It is well known that some of the most influential critiques of Husserl have come from the pen of Jacques Derrida. In his essay "On Derrida's Reading of Husserl," J. N. Mohanty does not focus explicitly on Derrida's critiques but on the reading of Husserl that informs those critiques. Mohanty asks whether Derrida has "*read* Husserl correctly." Mohanty agrees with Derrida's reading of Husserl in part insofar as it assumes no major breaks in Husserl's development. This means, according to Derrida and Mohanty, that there is not an essential difference between the "realist" Husserl of the *Logical Investigations* and the "idealist" Husserl of *Ideas* or the philosopher of the *Lebenswelt* in the *Crisis*. Nevertheless, Mohanty points out that for almost every focal point of Derrida's reading of Husserl there is a corresponding misreading of Husserl's text. With regard to the Husserlian account of the sign, the relation of monologue to dialogue, the "alleged priority of writing over speech," the relation between ideality and repeatability, the privileging of "presence," the freedom of "intentionality from both the subject and the presence of the object," and the misconstrual of Husserl's idea of "genesis," Mohanty points out where Derrida's reading is questionable. Lastly, Mohanty shows that there is trace of irony in Derrida's reading of Husserl's account of history. It turns out, according to Mohanty, that Derrida's reading of Husserl on history is very much in line with other Husserlian readings. With regard to this aspect of his Husserl interpretation, Derrida is about as far from a deconstruction of Husserl as he can be. Whether Derrida's followers see this fact is, of course, another story.

"Many contemporary thinkers have abandoned 'truth' entirely. Viewing it as an outmoded, discredited perhaps even dangerous concept." With this true, all too true, claim, David Detmer turns our attention to "Husserl's Critique of Relativism." Detmer proposes that we consider how three of Husserl's most important arguments against relativism—the self-referential argument, the evidentiary argument, and the eidetic argument—can be applied to a contemporary text. Detmer clearly shows, I think, that the relevance of Husserl's thought for the contemporary intellectual scene needs to be reconsidered. For example, Detmer begins by considering the self-referential argument against the relativist. If the relativist claims that all truth is relative to a specific social setting, is her own claim to be understood as similarly relative? If so, why should we take her seriously? But if the claim to universal relativity is not relative but universally true why should it be the only truth-claim to enjoy universal validity? Detmer considers various rhetorical strategies to escape the self-referential dilemma and shows how each fails by reason of principles Husserl himself employed against the relativists of his day, the same principles, we might add, to which many nonrelativists since Plato have appealed. At the heart of his paper Detmer spends considerable time arguing that "an unwillingness to face up to and take responsibility for that which experience reveals to be inconsistent or improbable is not a purely logical error, but rather a moral, political, and existential failing of the highest order." Detmer argues that a failure to take the law of noncontradiction seriously by applying it consistently across cultural lines does not lead to tolerance and effective intervention on behalf of the oppressed peoples of the world. Rather it leads either to indecisive or inconsistent practical ends. Either way, he argues, "the postmodernist approach to defending tolerance is incoherent, uncritical, and ineffective."

Lester Embree's contribution, "The Constitutional Problematics of Nonrelativity or How to Dump Garbage in Nobody's Backyard" is, like Detmer's work, concerned with some of the practical problems that surround the issue of relativism. Unlike Detmer, however, Embree is not applying Husserlian arguments to a contemporary text but is attempting a Husserlian constitutional analysis that attempts to account for the evolution of a nonrelative moral evaluation. This evolution necessarily begins with an individual, "occasional" evaluation, moves on to a shared, "interindividual" conviction, which can then evolve further into an even more broadly shared "intercollective" judgment that will be seen as holding between different social groups of people. Embree's concrete example is the evolution of political opposition to a proposed garbage dump that will affect several adjacent counties in a state. Far from being just a cognitive development, Embree argues that conative and affective dimensions of the phenomenon are just as important for understanding the emergence of widely shared practical convictions. Embree's intention is not to raise the call for environmental activism against garbage dumps—although he likes them no better than any of us—but to develop a broad phenomenological concern which purports "to show that the problem of nonrelativity holds on practical and evaluative as well as cognitive levels and for intercollective as well as interindividual as well as individual lives."

The broad theme of the "practical" payoff of skepticism continues in Brice Wachterhauser's "The Desire of Reason: A Plea for a 'Practical' Response to Skepticism." Wachterhauser argues that philosophers have often fallen short by simply *refuting* the skeptic and not developing an argument that attempts to *persuade* the skeptic. While persuasion is much more difficult in some respects than refutation, he argues that unless philosophers take up the many-faceted task of persuasion the skeptic will not be dislodged from her place as one of the more prominent cultural influences of our day. To accomplish this task, "logic needs to rejoin forces with rhetoric" to develop an argument that focuses on the practical implications of skepticism and nonskepticism, an argument that will appeal to the intellect as well as the emotions and will. Such an argument cannot be "purely" epistemological because, as Wachterhauser points out, the skeptic is usually not exclusively concerned with epistemology but with the metaphysical and ethical implications of human knowledge-claims. This leads the paper to consider one "metaphysical" and one "ethical" motive for skepticism, motives which are called the "incompleteness of reason" and "human fragility," respectively. Wachterhauser argues that such motives must first be better understood by the nonskeptic before attempting an adequate response to skepticism. If understood correctly, then such motives not only have a much needed tendency to mitigate the nonskeptic's temptation to dogmatically dismiss the skeptic, but also point in positive directions for a broader, more persuasive argument. Wachterhauser contends that such an argument should be significantly like an Aristotelian practical argument in that it would encourage the skeptic to weigh the relative value of skepticism and nonskepticism. Such an argument would put the practical implications of skepticism and the positive practical implications of nonskepticism in the forefront and not insist on complete transparency of its premises. In following this argument the nonskeptic will find herself focusing on the value of logic for communication and reasonably harmonious social relations. In addition, an account of the intrinsic value of the life of reason needs to be developed in what Wachterhauser calls an "erotics" of reason. In addition to the social consequences of reason, the nonskeptic needs to consider how the life of reason is inherently desirable. In Wachterhauser's opinion, this case for reason is best articulated within a metaphysical framework of realism, i.e., an account of knowledge and rationality that sees reason rooted "in the things themselves."

Interesting connections exist between Wachterhauser's concern with the ethical and metaphysical dimensions of skepticism and George Kline's "Meditations of a Russian Neo-Husserlian: Gustav Shpet's 'The

Skeptic and His Soul.' " After an extensive bibliographical and biographical sketch outlining Shpet's relationship to Husserl, Kline launches into a discussion of Shpet's assessment of skepticism. Shpet argues that "skepticism is not a philosophical doctrine or theory." Instead Shpet sees skepticism as "a mood, an attitude, or the state of consciousness that springs from disillusionment with one's projects or with the failed results of demanding labor at a task that has proved to be beyond one's powers." Shpet wants to discredit the skeptic's state of mind by showing that its origin is not based on an apprehension of the truth of skepticism but on resentment or envy of philosophers who can, in fact, discover important truths. "The philosopher, according to Plato, is a man in love," writes Shpet. "The skeptic may be called one who is disappointed in love. Skepticism is the jealous torment of the unsuccessful lover who has been rejected by truth." The result is "a sense of wounded conceit and arrogance" that cannot believe that anyone could possibly have found truth. It is this inability to overcome resentment that shows the skeptic as a moral failure and it is this failure, perhaps, which prevents the skeptic from appreciating the "mystical enthusiasm" that runs through the great "rationalistic" philosophers. Such "mystical overtones" are, Shpet insists, "necessary compliments, which, like a kind of inspiration, accompany the subtlest analyses and most exalted flights of the purest and most perfect work of *reason* alone." If Shpet is right about these mystical overtones, then the connection between eros and reason is clear and the door is open for a reconsideration of this side of reason's appeal.

Errol E. Harris turns our attention to "Skepticism and Dialectic." Harris focuses on Hegel's response to skepticism, particularly ancient skepticism, but not exclusively so. Hegel was well acquainted with the various skepticisms of his day and he knew full well how to distinguish skepticism as such from the movement of the dialectic that employs "negativity" as the motor which drives "the development of truth." But it was Hegel's conviction that the "thought of the ancient skeptics . . . was much more speculative in character, much more aware of the significance of the negative, and gave promise of the understanding to a more adequate grasp of the whole that is the ultimate object of speculative reason." Hence, the core of Harris's paper is the focus on Hegel's response to the ancient skeptics from Cratylus through Sextus. Hegel's analysis of the key skeptical tropes is discussed by Harris to show how Hegel thought of skepticism as an important step in the dialectic which "demonstrates the instability and self-contradictory character integral to the nature of all determinate and finite being." Thus, when the skeptic argues that "whichever of two opposite assertions is maintained, the other can be defended on equally plausible grounds," the skeptic is on to something important about the apprehension of any truth that does not recognize its codependence on other truths. This recognition of logical codependence, however, forces the thinker to make a dialectical move to a higher stage of intellectual development—the stage of the "concept." This is possible because skepticism forces us to attend to the relativity of our grasp of any finite thing. Thus, it prepares the way for the key Hegelian point that "everything is related to everything else." Far from seeing this relativity as inimical to truth, Hegel claims its proper apprehension allows us to see that all relative truths, although they conflict on one level, can nevertheless be reconciled at a higher level of reflection. Harris points out that both Hegel's and Husserl's opposition to skepticism presupposes shared ground with the skeptic, namely, the insistence upon presuppositionless justification. Where they differ from each other is in their understanding of how to achieve presuppositionlessness. For Husserl, like Kant, a program of transcendental analysis supposedly leads to presuppositionless results. But just like Hegel critiqued Kant for wrongly "assuming that a critique of reason could be undertaken without using reason itself," Harris suspects the same flaw in Husserl's method. Only a dialectical method can overcome this shortcoming and Harris holds out the prospect of "rescuing" Husserl's thought by recasting it along dialectical lines. Thus, Husserl's thought is not inherently skeptical according to Harris, but he is not so sanguine about more contemporary forms of thought like those of Foucault and Derrida. The thought of these thinkers succumbs, Harris believes, to a dialectical critique which exposes their thinking as a form of skepticism, which, "like skepticism in general . . . represents the paralysis of thought."

Hegel and Husserl are linked once again in William L. McBride's "The Phenomenological Tradition and the End of History," although Hegel is decidedly in the background in this essay on social and political themes. McBride raises doubts about "the entire conception of history implied by Husserl's choice of focus," i.e., history of ideas or "*Sinnbildung und Sinnsedimentierung.*" History, for Husserl (much like Hegel), is primarily history of ideas and as such it strikes McBride as somewhat removed from the intellectually more recalcitrant and morally more troubling material of social and political reality. But McBride takes Husserl to task on other grounds as well. Husserl's "excessive individualism," or the tendency to see history as "constituted by the individual ego," fails to do justice "to the role played by human collectives such as generations in codetermination in both the goals of individuals and the direction taken by historical developments at any given time." More fundamentally, McBride asks if Husserl's phenomenological reduction, which "brackets" questions about reality in order to isolate questions about essence or meaning, does not ultimately dangerously distort "the *res gestae* of a certain real, finite species that happens to be our species." In contrast, McBride praises Sartre's conception of history with its emphasis on freedom, its insistence upon finite history which cannot be subsumed under any science, and its contention that historical groups, like generations, play an important role in defining meaning in history. This leads McBride to "remain skeptical about the Husserlian—Merleau-Pontyan—Ediean idea of a single history or of a logic of history." Nevertheless, for McBride the very idea of change, perhaps one of the few constants in history, holds out the possibility of a "new hope of liberation" which could follow "a renaissance of the life of the spirit." McBride argues that if this happens, then philosophers like Husserl and Edie will be due some of the credit.

Tom Rockmore also raises doubts about whether the moral and political crises of this century can adequately be described as "crises of reason." In "A Crisis of Reason? Husserl, Heidegger, and National Socialism," Rockmore describes Husserl and Heidegger as exponents, each in their own unique way, of a "canonical view of philosophy," i.e., a view which, among other characteristics, sees philosophy as offering the highest form of knowledge and one which consequently insists that philosophy is indispensable for all social practice. Because of these shared convictions, both Husserl and Heidegger see National Socialism as a "crisis of reason." Rockmore points out that nothing could have been more natural for Husserl because the idea of a crisis of reason, "a crisis in the sciences of man and a crisis in science as such . . . is a red thread running throughout the different phases of his theory." For Heidegger, the crisis is not so much an epistemological crisis, a crisis in the sciences, but an ontological crisis "due to the turn away from the problem of Being posed authentically in early Greek philosophy but later forgotten." It is well known that Heidegger saw the political upheavals of his time as one of the consequences of this "forgetfulness of Being." Consequently, he urges "a political turning to undo the ravages brought by the withdrawal of Being." In Heidegger's mind, the ontological crisis leads to an emphasis on "the need of Germany to act on behalf of itself and the history of the West." This suggests a deep difference between Heidegger and Husserl on the meaning of the Nazi movement. For Husserl, "the rise of National Socialism . . . was a symptom of the crisis of reason, whereas for Heidegger, from a very different perspective, it represented a way to resolve the crisis of reason." "For Husserl, Nazism represents unreason that can be undone in philosophical reason. . . . For Heidegger, although not quite the exemplification of reason, Nazism represents the means to bring it about." Rockmore criticizes Husserl for failing "to grasp the specificity of National Socialism that, from his angle of vision, was merely another, however terrible, form of naturalism." But Heidegger's "misapprehension . . . was certainly deeper than Husserl's" according to Rockmore. Heidegger, Rockmore contends, "failed to perceive a menace at all," but saw Nazism instead "as means to another, better life." Both mistakes, however, raise deeply troubling questions for our understanding of philosophy and, along with it, "the very nature of Western civilization."

Bruce Wilshire ends this volume with a contribution entitled "Edie's Hard-Nosed James and the Retrieval of the Sacred." Wilshire credits Edie with helping to rescue James, the "hard-nosed" philosopher, "from the strange obscurity of his fame." Edie's *William James and Phenomenology* shows James as a protophenomenologist in his concern with the *concrete* conditions of human understanding, a concern, according to Edie, which leads James to recognize the necessary foundations of human practice. On Wilshire's reading, James never loses this artistic sensitivity to the richness of concrete experience. Eventually, James's concern with this richness of human experience even leads to his "attack on reason and his religio-philosophical speculations at the end of his life." Wilshire points out that this development is of a piece with the motivation for James's earlier, protophenomenological work. In fact, "without the background of the *Principles*, which Edie sets forth so well, James's somewhat fragmentary but immensely important last works cannot be understood." Edie's essay "Williams James and Phenomenology of Religious Experience" is credited by Wilshire with being on the right track in understanding James's notions of intentionality as that "of the whole organic being, the whole body-self." This helps us comprehend such important Jamesian concerns as understanding the conditions of mystical experience, the generation of the notion of a "pluralistic universe," the need for a "radical empiricism," and even "James's famous 'attack on reason' at the end of his life." Concern with the full concreteness of experience, "the much at once," leads James to a growing sensitivity for the "fullness of life, this immediate sense of the simplest bits of immediate experience flowing into one another, budding and burgeoning out of one another." But, as Wilshire goes on to point out, if one takes this vision seriously, it raises basic questions about the law of identity. How can everything, as this characterization of experience suggests, be its own other? Without identity, there cannot even be "the contrast requisite for recognition of the prereflective" life, which James finds so fascinating. Nevertheless, this experience leads James to denigrate "conceptualization and 'intellectualist logic.'" This represents for James the intellectual a kind of crisis, a crisis which is left largely unresolved at this death. Nevertheless, Wilshire remains optimistic that James's phenomenological pragmatism could, if rightly worked out, resolve the crisis. I suspect that Wilshire (and James) and Edie would part company here; the pragmatists, Wilshire and James, stressing the mere *pragmatic* validity of the law of identity and Edie, the phenomenologist of universal foundations, insisting on the *apodictic* nature of the same law. Be that as it may, Wilshire's essay demonstrates something of the scope of Edie's scholarship as well the potentially fascinating and difficult range of phenomenology.

Each of the essays in this volume has shown something of that "fascinating and difficult range" of phenomenology. Professor Edie's bibliography, which ends this volume, is sufficient by itself to demonstrate the sweeping and penetrating scope of phenomenology's influence. Of course, there is not unanimous agreement on Husserl's significance or meaning for our day, but there never has been such agreement on the work of any major philosopher. Nevertheless, what these essays show is that far from being an intellectual relic from the past, Husserl's philosophy continues to exercise a profound effect on the contemporary intellectual scene. It is regrettable that the close study of his thought, not to mention the concrete practice of philosophizing according to "the things themselves" has fallen out of favor in so many philosophy departments around the world. Husserl was a philosopher who dug down to the "roots" of our experience, a philosopher who was not afraid of "the most trivial of trivialities" that come forward in such foundational studies. Husserl knew that such "trivialities" as the universal validity of laws of logic are by no means easy to get clear on and adequately defend but he also knew that unless we attained clarity on such fundamental notions our thinking was likely to go astray in larger, more difficult matters. The current predominance of various forms of skepticism in our culture today seems to me evidence for the claim that we have forgotten our "roots." Fortunately it is still possible to reclaim them. What is needed is nothing less than a reconsideration of our rationalistic heritage, of which Husserl is a key part. Of course, such a reconsideration must always be self-critical; it must always be willing to acknowledge reason's failures and limits. After all, reason itself demands nothing less. But such a reconsideration must also develop the courage and conviction that can only come from a proper grasp of reason's indispensable value. Husserl had that courage and conviction and we need to consider again today how it was that his vision grew out of the soil of his confrontation with skepticism. In this confrontation Husserl not only exposed the skeptic's errors but he also made an appeal to reason's enduring value. Husserl calls us back to this testing ground, this fundamental crucible of all responsible philosophical thought. Husserl's emphasis on the value of reason makes many uncomfortable today, but this discomfort is not the discomfort caused by reading someone whose thought has become embarrassingly passé but the discomfort caused by someone who reminds us that we are in danger of forgetting the "one thing necessary." We need to cultivate that discomfort in ourselves and in our students. *Phenomenology and Skepticism* is dedicated to that end.

1

On Confronting Species-Specific Skepticism as We Near the End of the Twentieth Century

James M. Edie

I. The Decentering of the Subject

Ever since Socrates "called philosophy down from heaven to earth" to locate it in the cities and in the lives of individual human beings by exhorting them to turn within to their souls and to the concepts (*logoi*) that dwell therein, to turn to a knowledge of oneself first of all, to examine one's own inner life in its acts of knowing, believing, desiring, willing, evaluating, giving meaning and intelligibility to the chaos of earths, airs, fires, waters and bones, sinews, humors, and joints, which confront us in raw nature, Western philosophy has seen the necessary turn to the foundations of experience and of reality-as-experienced which has come to be called "foundationalism" in philosophy.[1] In their many different ways all of the greatest philosophers of our tradition have been "foundationalists": Plato, Aristotle, Augustine, Aquinas, Descartes, Spinoza, Leibniz, Kant, Hegel, and Husserl, to mention only the "giants," who together and separately constitute the backbone of Western philosophy.

But for many, already in the nineteenth but especially since the middle of the twentieth century, the centrality of human experience has begun to be questioned, the aristo-centric assumption of a necessary, Archimedean basis on which to build a systematic understanding of reality has begun to be denied. This is what is today called the "decentering of the subject," not only in structuralism, but in poststructuralism, deconstructionism, and in all the sociologies of knowledge which are now vying to replace philosophy in the ancient, classical sense. Our topic is but the latest, the philosophic, decentering of the subject, and it fits into a whole series of previous decenterings.

First there was the cosmological decentering which took place, amidst great cultural upheaval, in the sixteenth and seventeenth centuries with the physical astronomy of Copernicus and Galileo. The results of this first major decentering are still just beginning to be understood. Men have not only begun to suspect but already know that the planet earth and the solar system of which it is a part are not at the center of the universe and that it is extremely unlikely that mankind is the final culmination point of the entire creative evolutionary process, nor the only "purpose" of the universe of beings. Our solar system is not even central to our own (Milky Way) galaxy but is, instead, a peripheral tail, perhaps one of many so numerous they are impossible to count. And this galaxy itself is but one local cluster of more than two dozen similar galaxies which are themselves but an infinitesimal part of a universe composed of billions of galaxies. And this universe itself may be but one of many more.

In his unfinished and disorganized final work, *The Visible and the Invisible*, Merleau-Ponty at least three times cites the "inexhaustible question" of the poet Claudel: "Where are we?" and "What time is it?" as the most existentially important philosophical questions for us now.[2] Well, we know not only that we are not at the center of the universe, but also that we literally don't know where we are—except that we are a part of a middling, relatively unimportant, gradually diminishing solar system which will in time exhaust its energy and may well be headed for extinction. We have been thrown into a state of being for which we cannot account, without our advice having been asked, which is unfathomable, and which as a whole, and in each of its parts, including ourselves, may be doomed, as in ancient Greek poetry, to a tragic end. It is *there*, dumb, unwieldy, silent, utterly indifferent to human consciousness and human purposes. There is too much of it; it is the Sartrean "absurd."

But that was not the only displacement, the only decentering. This physical decentering was followed by a biological decentering which can be conveniently dated with the publication of Darwin's *Origin of Species* in 1859, the birthday of "contemporary" philosophy as opposed to "modern" philosophy.[4] Homo sapiens was not created whole and entire in some primeval Garden of Eden but is the result, at the present moment, of an extremely long, hazardous, chancy, almost fortuitous evolution that about fifteen hundred million years ago on this planet brought about the existence of truly living creatures. Of the perhaps four original kingdoms, characterized by having "a well-organized nucleus and chromosomes in each cell,"[3] of the exceedingly large number of organisms (eukaroytes) which developed within these four kingdoms, many of them becoming rapidly extinct, all branching out in myriads of ways in all probable and improbable developments, only the animalian type showed any evolutionary trend toward intelligence, and even that at least fifty different phyla of animals had developed by the Cambrian geological era (many of them becoming rapidly extinct), while the surviving phyla (from about five hundred million years ago) proliferated into multiple classes, orders, families, and lower taxa. "Of the some fifty original phyla of animals, only one, that of the chordates, eventually gave rise to intelligent life."[5] Of all the vertebrates only the anthropoid apes clearly surpassed other mammals in intellectual ability and social organization. Finally less than one-third of a million years ago homo sapiens emerged, due to what many biologists believe to have been "a largely chance event."

However much one admires the intelligence of birds, including the ability to use tools to a certain extent, to learn from past experience, and to pass knowledge on by some form of teaching to their young, or the dolphins, or even the chimpanzees, nobody is going to say that they would be capable of producing the cultures of ancient China, of Sumur, Egypt, Greece, or Rome. Not even the Neanderthals, recognized as homo sapiens, or other forms of early hominid types were capable of civilization and culture in anything but the most rudimentary sense. Whether, given the precarious nature of the development of specifically human intelligence (i.e., "higher intelligence") as we know it in our species of homo sapiens, that such a development could be duplicated or in some way repeated elsewhere in extraterrestrial space, with or without any anatomical similarity to man, is something for which we have no evidence. Clearly, the main lesson of the biological decentering of the human species is to have demonstrated that man is not the necessary culmination point of the system; he may be the *superior* element in the system just now, but he did not *make* the system, he did not dominate it from the start, he certainly *is not* the system; he is but a *part* of the system.

Thirdly, there began already long before Freud the psychological decentering of human consciousness. The discovery of the preconscious and even unconscious drives, instincts, intentionalities, and patterns of behavior, which operate beneath the level of conscious awareness in human behavior has opened up, within about the past seventy-five years, a whole new group of human sciences, i.e., sciences which study specifically human behavior, which can be put under the very general rubric of structuralism. These sciences, while recognized as fully "scientific" and as possessing great explanatory power do not at all employ the hypothetico-deductive methods used in the physical, chemical, and biochemical sciences but rather the descriptive, taxonomic, structuralist model of linguistics and anthropology primarily. Jacques Lacan has said that "the unconscious is structured like language," though nobody to date has been able to give a single example of the application of a recursive rule to unconscious processes that would fully confirm this claim except in the most rudimentary manner. The subject is too difficult to master.

Even in linguistics, where the recursive rules that explain the structures of the phonology, morphology, and syntax of natural languages are beginning to be well developed, there is still but a glimmer of what the rules governing texts, contexts, discourses, and genres of various types would look like. Again, the subject is still too difficult, but at least the question can be posed, whereas some sixty or seventy years ago it could barely have arisen at the level of conscious awareness. Similarly in structural anthropology, sociology, and other disciplines there has been considerable advance in showing how humans operate *according* to quite strict rules of behavior without having any conscious awareness of such rules or any ability to bring them to the level of fully aware, reflective consciousness capable of stating them in language. "The subject" (the ego) has been displaced or decentered even in its own experience of itself and its own behavior.

So much for the scientific decentering of the egological center of traditional philosophy. However, *e contra*, let us not forget the teaching of Hegel, as paraphrased from his *Phenomenology of Mind*: If it is true that man is not at the physical center of the universe, *he is still at the metaphysical center* because he produces its science. The sciences that men have laboriously developed through ages of time are *all* human sciences in the sense that they are at the service of man to explain as best he can to himself his own present experience, whether in terms of past geological ages, his own evolution, the physiological and psychological mechanisms of his own living organism, or the laws of his own use of language and therefore of *thought*. We have no awareness of the circulatory system of our blood stream; Aristotle thought the brain was an organ for cooling the blood; we waited until Harvey to learn the truth. But Aristotle could write brilliantly about the perceptual organization of experience on the basis of a false physiology. We likewise have no conscious awareness of our neurological structures; many even speak as if the brain "knows" things, whereas the fact is that the minds of men have for a very long time been interested in how the brain works, what it does and how it does it, and we have begun to elaborate natural sciences in greater and greater profusion to study the brain. But in all this the brain, as a physiological part of the system, has not the slightest interest in or ability to study the mind.

And as our common ancestor, Socrates, taught us, philosophy is the study of the mind (*nous*) the source of conceptual knowledge (*logoi*), not the study of synapses, neurons, or complex tissues.

II. The Deconstruction of Subjectivity

Here we now face an aporia in the strictest Aristotelian sense of the word. What is the place or the value of philosophy for a decentered man? Indeed, the poststructuralist deconstructionists have added to the list of decenterings given above the most radical decentering possible: they suggest that the logocentricity, the very use of the logic of reason, which enables us to speak and to think, is based on something else.

The first nineteenth-century "skeptics" need hardly detain us. Marx and his followers, who state that at the basis of every philosophical theory there lies a definitely determined state of intellectual knowledge due to social, political, economic, or industrial organization can be readily accommodated in almost any framework, since there is no truth that does not have its "date" (i.e., the time before which it had not been "thought" or "demonstrated" and therefore made available to others to think as well) and its determinate historical situation. All thinkers are time-bound, earth-bound creatures immersed in the irreversible temporal flow of real time and spatial (including social) location. The question is rather whether or not this necessary historicity of experience *causes* thinkers to think in a predetermined manner and, therefore, conditions the rules of rationality by something logically antecedent to and independent of the norms of reason themselves. Is reason essentially dependent on something other than itself?

The kind of evolutionary epistemology espoused by Herbert Spencer, which declared that human intelligence is nothing other than an ad hoc adaptation of a highly developed organism to its hostile and often difficult environment, is no more helpful because, in its vague generality, it explains too much. There is simply nothing that it does not explain. If we can agree that with the various levels of organismic development into more and more complex beings new properties emerge at each stage that were not clearly present in the combining elements or parts of the prior, less developed, organisms, then we will eventually reach the stage at which higher intelligence capable of discovering the eidetic, logical laws that govern true thought and language-using consciousness emerge (because this has already happened). But we do not thereby *explain* the nature of such laws of thought, even though we admit that more primitive creatures could not have envisaged them.

When Husserl undertook at the beginning of the twentieth century to refute what he called "psychologism" in his *Prolegomena to Pure Logic*, he began by saying that the complete skepticism (of the kind Aristotle ascribed to Heraclitus and Cratylus, or that professed by Protagoras, Pyhrro, or Sextus Empiricus) was hardly to be found asserted by anybody anymore. He did not even tarry over the probabilistic skepticism of the kind espoused by the New Academy against which Saint Augustine wrote his first dialogue, *Against the Academics*. What concerned him was the species-specific skepticism of late nineteenth- and early twentieth-century thinkers such as Mill, Bain, Wundt, Sigwart, Erdmann, and Lipps (on the historical background of British Empiricism in general from Ockham to Hume).[6] We will take this up immediately, but the starting point is to ask whether the rules of thought and of reason are essentially dependent on the emergence of *this* human species, homo sapiens, on *this* planet in these determinate historical circumstances or whether the norms of logic are essentially independent of historical, evolutionary circumstances even though they can come into play only in actual, historical acts of thinking performed by individual thinking beings.

By the last decade of the twentieth century we are in a situation in which the many sociological accounts of knowledge, whether based on Heidegger, the Frankfurt School, or Derrida, or Rorty, or some combination thereof, or of other provenance, have for some time proclaimed not only the decentering of the subject (of experience) but the "death" of the subject, the "evanescence"[7] of the subject, the "disappearance" of the subject, and the like. This leads us to the metaphysics of structuralism with which we are quite familiar and which goes far beyond the structuralist methodology which is, in itself, quite innocuous, and, indeed, an inescapable component of any conceptual analysis, of any scientific theory whatsoever.

Let us attempt to pose this question in its contemporary historical perspective. At the beginning of this century philosophers like William James and Edmund Husserl attempted to refute skeptical, relativistic psychologism so as to establish logical thinking and the rules of reasoning on a basis independent of any mentalistic introspectionism or any biological or social causes not derivable from the investigation of meaning as such; now we see, in spite of the triumphs of formal logic in this century, a return at present to an evermore sophisticated form of psychologism in which the influence of the poststructuralist deconstructionism of Jacques

Derrida is, if not all-pervasive, at least taken as one of the most reasonable philosophical stances attainable.

Though Derrida himself based his early philosophical work[8] on the tutelage he had received in phenomenology and the writings of Husserl under Paul Ricoeur and others, he now clearly thinks of Heidegger as his chief philosophical inspiration and most kindred spirit.[9] Heidegger very early on described his program as a *Wiederholung* of the thrust of Western philosophy that would be both pre-Socratic and post-Hegelian, in fact a *destruction* of Western metaphysics since Plato. After his early, more belligerent, period he replaced the word "destruction," with "critique," but there was no need to, since "destruction," like "deconstruction," can have a positive sense: namely, a taking apart, through analysis, of what has already been done, of what has been achieved, to see how it was put together, how it was built up in the first place, to discover the strong points and the flaws in this massive construct that has grown in size and complexity over two thousand years or more.

Central to his program was the study of human consciousness (*Dasein*) which alone structures, gives meaning and value to things (*Seiende*), and alone is concerned with Being (*das Sein des Seiendes*) and sees the ontological difference between Being and beings through its own prereflexive understanding of what it is to be, of Being (*vor-ontologische Seinsverständnis*). Human consciousness is uniquely concerned with this question, that is with "comprehending" beings and "keeping them together," like a "shepherd" of the flocks of beings. But in its relationship to Being, human consciousness is far from the supreme shepherd; it is another, though privileged, being among beings, the locus of the *lumen naturale* of understanding, and the foundation of the comprehension of the Being of beings, but it is not the foundation of the Being of beings, nor of its own being. Man may be the "shepherd" of beings, but Being is not a sheep. Man does not possess Being; he is *had* by Being.

All this is most clearly illustrated by man's relationship to language, "the house of Being." Man does not dominate, much less invent, language, but rather language "has" him. Man, as *zoon logon echon*, speaks, uses language, and therefore is capable of reason, but language was there before him, both in an ontological and logical sense, *Es spricht im Menschen.*[10] Language is thus in some sense the instrument of an impersonal, not-appropriated, anonymous thought.

There would be a perfectly straightforward manner of understanding this conception of man's relationship to language, namely if it were to be taken in the strictly structuralist sense according to which we necessarily speak according to formal rules of phonology, morphology, syntax, and our lexicon without necessarily having the ability on the level of conscious awareness of explaining these subunderstood laws, but Heidegger has something more fundamental in mind. Being is not language, but the ground of language which the philosopher and even more the poet may attempt to "think" but without any sure or clearly guaranteed foundation.

Many of our contemporaries make the best sense out of the obscure writings of Heidegger on this matter by turning to Richard Rorty's analysis of the central meaning of the work of Heidegger, Wittgenstein, and Dewey, "the three most important philosophers of our century."[11] Heidegger especially, he writes, deserves "the credit for working out a way of seeing the search for objective knowledge . . . as [but] one human project among others" through his famous theory of *Lichtungen*[12] (the ways we must think Being in its relations to beings). (Rorty may even think, as Quentin Skinner has asserted, that these three philosophers have brought philosophy to an end[13]—a claim which, in a completely different context, used to be made on behalf of Hegel!)

But we have to be more careful. What have Rorty and Derrida (if we may associate him in this enterprise) actually tried to do? Both of them, in the company of quite a number of continental and analytical philosophers, try to undermine "transcendental philosophy."[14] In fact both of them, but especially Rorty who is the more "historicist" of the two, considers the critique of transcendental thought common to both these traditions to be the one concern that runs through and unifies the whole of contemporary philosophy at the present time. Transcendental philosophy is defined as the search for an ultimate foundation of knowledge that will "block skepticism" by discovering "an overaching permanent neutral matrix" for all inquiry, past and future;[15] it would, indeed, provide a refutation of any possible future skepticism. The destruction (which is at the same time the deconstruction) of transcendental philosophy is accomplished by showing that the historical origin of our conception of foundational knowledge (from Descartes, Locke, and Kant) has come under attack from within (as well as from without) by an increasingly radical questioning of its inner, hidden presuppositions that always involve the privileging of some form of representational consciousness over any other.

When philosophy is relieved of all its "foundations," what remains is a literary and communicating culture *as a conversation* rather than as a structure erected on unchanging foundations, an edifying genuine conversation that does not degenerate into inquiry.[16]

Though Derrida's position is harder to define and much more slippery than Rorty's, it comes to much the same thing. The conversation that we call "speech" is really a form of writing; experience is a text, and *il n'y a pas de hors-texte.* Since all of meaningful language is nothing other than a free play of signifiers, there can be no necessary starting point understanding itself is always a misunderstanding; there has never been any perception.[17] Though Derrida is considerably more colorful than Rorty (logocentrism becomes phallocentrism; within the chain of supplements it is difficult to separate writing from onanism, etc.)[18] his endless process of grafting texts onto texts comes down to something quite similar to Rorty's "conversation of mankind" or "conversation of the West."

Rorty can write very edifying rhetorical prose about the overall holistic, historicist, relativist, conversational project:

> Even if, through some unbelievable stroke of fortune, America survives with its freedoms intact and becomes a rallying point for the nations, the high culture of an unfragmented world need not center around anything specifically American. It may not, indeed, *center* around anything more than anything else; neither poetry, nor social institutions, nor mysticism, nor depth psychology, nor novels, nor philosophy, nor physical science. It may be a culture which is transcendentalist through and through, whose center is everywhere and its circumference nowhere. In such a culture, Jonathan Edwards and Thomas Jefferson, Henry and William James, John Dewey, and Wallace Stevens, Charles Peirce and Thornston Veblen will all be present. No one will be asking which ones are the Americans, or even perhaps, which ones are the philosophers.[19]

To which Alasdair MacIntyre retorted: "If I am doomed to spending the rest of my life talking with literary critics and sociologists and historians and physicists, I am going to have to listen to a great deal of philosophy, most of it inept."[20]

I once had a professor of philosophy who liked to look at the whole history of philosophy as being similar to a seance of the *Academie Française* in which each of the "greats" of the past would have his own fauteuil, each one having earned his place, with not one absent, all engaging in the most penetrating, glorious conversations. But the trouble with the history of philosophy, and with our conversations in general, is that not all those with whom we would wish to talk are present at the same time, or in the same place.

There have been periods such as that between the closing of the pagan schools of Athens by the Emperor Justinian in 529 A.D. and the foundation of the University of Paris in 1200 A.D. when precious little philosophy was done anywhere in the Western world, and, please try to think of all the great philosophers between the death of William of Ockham and the emergence of Descartes. Cardinal Nicholas of Cusa? In the eighteenth century the first great Russian philosopher, Gregory Skovoroda, prayed to God Almighty to let him be a Socrates in Russia;

his prayer was granted and Russia had two extraordinary centuries of philosophical development until it was all stamped out by Bolshevism. But who would say that any of Russian philosophy is anything more than a series of brilliant footnotes to Hegel? And has American culture ever produced a true philosophical giant?

But, in the "conversation of the West" we cannot be concerned only with philosophers but must be concerned with *everybody*. It seems to me that J. N. Mohanty put his finger on the sore spot: "if a history of ideas alone is to be the effective tool for overcoming philosophical mistakes,[21] then we need *a* history of the relevant ideas."[22] If we really take the "conversation of mankind" seriously, we must allow Mohanty to ask his 'preposterous" question: What about including Eastern (particularly Hindu and Buddhist) thinkers as well? This global conversation (still at least taking place solely within the same species of homo sapiens) would be a bewildering *multiversum* of conversations in which it would be impossible for everyone to take part all at once. How large is the given "community" of conversationalists in any one instance? If we are discussing physical theories, it would be the international community of physicists, past and present. If we are doing exobiology, it would be the international community of exobiologists. If we are doing logic and the philosophy of logic, we would have to consider the Sanskrit philosophers' idea of the mental and how it interreacted with the later theory of the realism of universals, the fact that Hindu philosophy never confused consciousness with the mental, whereas in the French Cartesian tradition there always was a tendency to confuse *all* consciousness with thinking (or language-using) consciousness, etc. Are we making progress? Toward what? If we *abstract* from the differences among disparate discourses or subsume them under the most general possible conversation, do we not end up hypostatizing "conversation" and stretching its meaning outwards so as to asymptotically approach a notion of an *ideally* communicating society as a new, though wobbly, transcendental foundation?[23]

III. The Response of Transcendental Philosophy

It is time to sober up, and I propose to do this by examining once again, very briefly, Husserl's conception of eidetic truth and, then, his conception of transcendental consciousness.

But, before we do this, let us inject one, last, empirical fact. We all know that the *Pioneer 10* outer-space probe carries a plaque indicating the planet of its origin (earth) and bearing a picture of the human beings (us), male and female, that created it. We know that we are using our most recent technology and spending billions of dollars on planning extraterrestrial space probes for the future and that we are beaming intelligible signals into outer space on the *explicit assumption* that there *might* be higher intelligence other than our own somewhere in the universe, intelligent beings who might somehow sometime intercept our probes or receive our messages and eventually return them and communicate with us. This explicit assumption, on which we unhesitatingly act in practical ways, though the technology to do so is an extremely recent acquisition of homo sapiens on this lost planet, is a fact of present human behavior.

In spite of the fact that the probability of other intelligent life resembling our own sufficiently to be able to communicate with us is so low as to approach zero, we will nevertheless not rest satisfied until we *know for sure.* This is a practical manifestation of the postulate of reason and science. There is, for instance, the factual existence of the new science of exobiology which studies extraterrestrial life, a very strange "science" in fact since it cannot even demonstrate that its subject matter exists![24] Though we are now quite certain that no other planets capable of sustaining life exist in our solar system, they *may* exist elsewhere in the galaxy and, if we extend our horizons to include more distant galaxies, and extrapolate what has happened on our planet, there may even be hundreds of millions of planets capable of supporting life and, for all we know, intelligent life. We do not know if these extraterrestrial lifeforms or even intellect-forms would be sufficiently like our own to be able to be recognized by us as either living or as intelligent, and, given the distances to be traversed and the absolute character of the speed of light—at least given the present state of our technology—communication of some kind could only be possible over periods of millions of years. The prospect certainly looks bleak, but it is not only science fiction that leads us to investigate the possibility.

We have but one instance[25] before us of the evolution of intelligent life, namely that on earth. But, if it *could* happen once, namely here, it *could*, in principle, happen elsewhere. *De esse ad posse valet illatio.*[26] The hypothesis that there could be, that there may be, intelligent beings elsewhere in the universe will not be discarded by humans for the more resigned, anesthetic, stoical, passive outlook expressed in the opposite hypothesis—namely, that since the probability of ever discovering or coming to know anything at all about such beings is all but zero we might as well give up our practical assumptions and spend our resources more wisely.[27]

This fact illustrates an important characteristic of human intelligence: what James would call the "livelier hypothesis," the more courageous option, the one that gives us something to "press" against, to strive toward, that requires us to go beyond the evident, *that* hypothesis will have the greatest power to stimulate our intellectual and practical abilities. And how would we communicate with other species of intelligent life? Would they, like the Greeks, have discovered the laws of logic and scientific inquiry? Who knows? In attempting to communicate we can only rely on the instruments of our own logical thought.

The ancients, like Aristotle, and the medievals, the Arab and Jewish thinkers no less than the Latins, had no doubt that there was other intelligent life in the universe, though of a nonbodily nature, namely the movers of the spheres, the "separated intelligences," the myriad of angels, each unique in its species, but possessed of intellect and will comparable to ours, though of a much higher potency, with whom limited communication was possible. Well, we have long abandoned this particular folklore in science, but we have not thereby lost at least the teleological hope that there may be intelligent species other than ourselves.[28] This is the practical scientific challenge to species-specific skepticism.

But we do not even have to go to the question of other species who possibly share intelligence similar to our own. It is certainly a practical as well as a theoretical postulate of all anthropological science within our own species of homo sapiens, just on this planet, that however diverse and, on the surface level, "incomprehensible" other cultures we may encounter may be, at the limit, it is always possible for us, ourselves, just as humans, to put ourselves in their place, to experience the world from their perspective, and, at least ideally, to be able to communicate with them. How else could one write "scientific" studies of the Australian aborigines, the Trobiand Islanders, the Indian tribes of the Amazon valley in Brazil, or the multifarious tribes of New Guinea and even North America? We describe their languages, we describe their social structures, we in fact communicate with them and they with us, and each can come to see the common world of experience through the eyes of the other.[29] The objectivity, universality, and the validity required of "scientific" (and therefore of "rational") laws *requires* that all human experience is, ideally, interchangeable, that we can *always* put ourselves at the point of view of another and experience the world as the other does. And in fact this is accomplished, perhaps not totally—given the ineffability of individual differences—but sufficiently for scientifically rational discourse to continue to take place.

A. The Eidetic

This espousal of a postulate of rationality is something for which Husserl has been both praised and blamed. It is almost an embarrassment to have to repeat now some of the truths we have learned from Husserl. It is certainly a defect in a thinker to be able to do nothing but repeat the lessons from the past that he has been taught by his teachers, but it may be an equally and even more serious defect to have remembered nothing. Is it really necessary now to recall to Western philosophers what has for long been called the "the Greek miracle"?—namely, the discovery of just what it is that distinguishes philosophy from nonphilosophy, the discovery of the necessary, universally valid and absolutely coercive laws of thought which we call formal logic and which enable us to establish scientific knowledge, particularly in the eidetic, a priori sense which leads to apodictic insight into the formal structures of reason itself. The levels of formal logic which give us proof-forms can be conceived so "purely" as to be freed from all content and all reference to any concrete domain of knowledge. Without such proof-forms unrelated to any particular or individual case, there would be no "science" at all, because they establish the ideal conditions of the possibility of science in general, the pure theory of any possible science whatsoever. What is distinctive of philosophy is not some higher, inherent "dignity" which places it above other types of investigations or realms of discourse, but rather the simple fact that only philosophers study the norms of logic, the a priori, *ex professo.* Philosophy, among other things, *is* the study of the structures of thinking (language-using consciousness) which are so fundamental that all persons and all scientists always already take them for granted.[30]

In this Husserl was very Greek and had learned the lesson of Socrates, as taught in the *Phaedo,* very well: it is the peculiar task of the philosopher to distinguish and separate out in experience conceptual a prioris. It is for this reason that philosophers can know that no physicist, no physiologist, no historian, no sociologist, or any other scientist can violate a single law of formal logic without his statements and arguments becoming subject to incoherence, contradiction, and error. No other branch of investigation studies logic or the philosophy of logic as such, nor does it need to. It is, in fact, not easy to violate a law of formal logic because we almost always think *according to* these stringent and universal conditions of thought without bringing them at each instance to the level of fully conscious, reflexive awareness. In fact the Egyptians, the Babylonians, the Cro-Magnons all thought *according to* the laws of formal logic long before the early Greek thinkers began to make them the subject of a special investigation and brought them to light as the necessary basis of all *theorein.*

It is not necessary here to repeat in any great detail how all this involves Husserl in the refutation of psychologism.[31] Against the species-specific "psychologism" of his contemporaries who held that logical laws, the rules of thought, were nothing other than the natural laws governing psychological processes in human minds, who made out logic to be "the physics" of thought, Husserl argued that since psychology is a natural science, its laws can never be exact or apodictic, never a priori or evident to insight, but must always be vague generalizations based on statistical probabilities. The mistake of the "psychologists" of his time was to confuse the *contents of judgments* with *acts of judging.* Acts of judging are real, datable events, real occurrences which have causes and effects in the living, thinking organism; but the contents of judgments are ideal entities, concepts. We must not confuse the ideal with the real. No real event, no act of consciousness is ever repeatable or identically the same (*idem numero actus*) as any other; but the *same* content can occur again and again, at different times, in different consciousnesses, under different conditions.[32] Whenever a truth is discovered for the first time, and established as true, we experience "the retroactive effect of the true" (to use Merleau-Ponty's happy expression) so that we see with the evidence of immediate insight that it had been true all along, even though nobody had discovered it or brought out into the full light of reflexive consciousness until that date and in those circumstances. Or take our calculators: they are built using the means of industrial mechanics and engineering; but they operate according to a binary, either-or, yes-no, logic based on the same ancient principles of identity, noncontradiction, and the excluded middle that the ancients, Aristotle and Aquinas, called "the first principles of demonstration" which are immediately evident as soon as any thinking subject grasps the idea of anything whatsoever (being, *ens,* something, *res*).

We are not coerced by the law of noncontradiction because, as Mill said, we are psychologically incapable of believing two contradictories to be true, or because only acts of belief can be called true or false. Our greater novelists and other thinkers, like Dostoevsky, Kierkegaard, and Nietzsche, have always known that human beings not only can, but almost always do, hold and act on contradictory impulses and beliefs. What Husserl says is not that we cannot *believe* two contradictories to be true at the same time and in the same respect, but that they cannot both *be* true.

The whole error of species-specific skepticism comes down to our concept of truth, of the meaning-analysis of what it is to entertain a true proposition in the mind. Husserl believed that "species" skepticism, or relativism, or "anthropologism" was easily refutable. There is no need to *persuade* the skeptic that he is wrong; this, as we can see about us, is probably psychologically impossible anyway; our only task is to *refute* him.

We will make a long story short: if species-specific skepticism were true, we would have to conclude that what could be true for one species of thinking being could be false for another. But whenever the words "true" and "false" are used *in their proper meanings*, this possibility is ruled out a priori. The constitution of *this* species of homo sapiens is a matter of fact, but no a priori truth is an empirical or factual matter. Truths are ideal, conceptual, nontemporal contents of judgments; they are not empirical acts of judging, The fact that I judge 2 times 2 to be 4 is a causally determined event, but the truth that 2 times 2 equals 4 is not. What Husserl calls "the kingdom of truth" in the *Logical Investigations* is much the same as what the platonist Augustine called the "eternal truths," except that for "eternal" Husserl substitutes: "omnitemporal," "at all times," and "omnispatial," in all places (*für Jederman*). Augustine argued that the truth cannot perish or be altered, because if, *per impossible*, the truth should perish, it would still remain true that the truth had perished, *ergo*, the truth cannot perish.[33] To say that there is no truth, or that all men are liars, or that it is impossible to know the truth, or that all truth is relative, is the same as to say that it true that there is no truth, etc.

However, Husserl by no means considered his task finished when he established the eidetic and ideal character of the most fundamental structures of logic and experienced reality. He may be a "logical absolutist" in one sense of the word, a platonist with a small "p" (and therefore never a "nominalist" of the kind found especially in British Empiricism), but he did want to recognize the rights, if not of "psychologism," at least of "the psychological." It is a fact that the laws of logic, though independent of any actual acts of thinking, are nevertheless present only to and for thinking subjects; there is a transcendental relationship between the laws of thinking and the acts of thinking which they govern; we must learn not only to distinguish the ideal from the real but to see how the ideal can live in the real, in the psychic lives of individual, experiencing egos.[34] Truth is, in fact, experienced; something ideal can be discovered by and in a real act of experiencing. That is the puzzle and challenge which motivated Husserl's search for an eidetic phenomenology of the whole of lifeworld experience.

B. The Transcendental

Transcendental consciousness, the transcendental ego in the final analysis, is the real experiencing ego; the transcendental and the empirical egos are not two separate realities, but two "attitudes." The real, mundane, experiencing ego can (but is not always required to) take a transcendental attitude toward its own experience and, when it does, it discovers eidetic laws applicable to its own experience (and to any experience as such) which it is the task of phenomenology (as an eidetic science) to uncover. There are eidetic laws discoverable not only in the *mathesis universalis* of formal ontology (i.e., formal logic plus the laws of objectivity in general) but also in the various other "regions" of experience. Husserl even accepts the Platonic analysis that brightness is related to, and is "founded in" color, as color is "founded in" spatial figures, and so on, as an eidetic discovery, even though the notion of brightness cannot be deduced from or found to be contained in the idea of color, nor the idea of color be deduced from the notion of surface.[35]

But there is a much more important example to be found in human experience and the several phenomenologies it inspires: namely, there is no intrinsic reason deducible from the essence of consciousness that it should perceive, imagine, remember, think, be affected by emotions, and otherwise exercise just the ways of "having objects" that it does. Phenomenology is necessarily a descriptive science, while remaining at the same time an eidetic science. There is no reason why consciousness should perceive, but, given the fact of a perceiving consciousness, we can (through the method of free variation) discover the laws of any possible perceiving consciousness and come to see that these a priori structures "found" other structures of imagining, remembering, and even thinking, without the higher structures ever being "reducible" to the founding stratum of perception, but nevertheless being always "founded" on it in such wise that the "founded" eidetic laws of thinking can be seen to be prefigured in the prepredicative structures of perception.[36] This is what is meant by a phenomenology of perception.

The laws of transcendental consciousness, thus eidetically established, do not give us a mental or a mundane thing, but make the constitution of the mundane, the mental (or "psychic") empirical ego susceptible of objectification. Again, *the transcendental ego* is not another ego distinct from the empirical ego, but a possibility of any actually existing ego and, *just as transcendental*, does not presuppose any preferred set of categories (as does Kant's "transcendental psychologism"), any preferred world-picture, or scientifically explanatory theory of how it came about. It is beyond body-mind dualism, physicalism, and mentalism.[37] It is capable of constituting the *sense* of all these alternatives and more.

Husserl calls himself a "Cartesian," but in the sense of one who has emptied Cartesianism of all its doctrinal content. When Descartes discovered the *cogito* (or consciousness) as the indubitable point of departure, he identified it with human reality; his "ego sum" is a man, of the species homo sapiens, a little "tag end" of the real world. Husserl's consciousness is "transcendental," meaning that it is structured according to the minimal conditions necessary and sufficient to describe *any* consciousness capable of intelligent life or reason. That Husserl's "foundationalism" is not what his critics have mistakenly taken it to be is clear: it is "foundational" but not in a species-specific sense.

Conclusion

In conclusion we must return to the original topic of this essay: On Confronting Species-Specific Skepticism as We Near the End of the Twentieth Century. One might have hoped that James and Husserl, Frege and Russell, had bequeathed to the twentieth century the possibility of a future philosophy without either dogmatism or skepticism; we see, at the end of the century, that this is far from being the case. I will conclude by giving what I think would be Husserl's answer to those who think of texts as nothing other than the free play of signifiers, or discourse as nothing other than the chance conversations of everyday life and common sense, in this or any other possible universe of thought.

Those who focus their attention on the "textuality" of the text or the discourses of the "conversation of mankind" should give some thought to what is meant by a text.[38] There is the empirical fact of intelligible communication among those speaking different languages, but one cannot blithely make that fact the bedrock, the unexamined basis of all intelligibility without asking *just how* it is possible. A text is, first of all, a string of meaningful sentences, laid out in time if spoken, put down from left to right (or in some conventional notational system) if written. The first requirement of the sentences so constructed into a text is that its fundamental units make sense. There are dependent or incomplete meanings such as words, and then there are words grammatically formed into complete and independent units of meaning which we call sentences.

The first level of formal logic, pure logical grammar, will guarantee the meaningfulness of sentences. But a string of meaningful sentences cannot just follow one another in random order. There is a higher order of formal logic which governs the rules of coherence and implication. The sentences in a given string (or perhaps in a paragraph) cannot contradict one another (at a minimum) but, more stringently, must belong in some way together, must pertain to the same realm of discourse, must follow from one another in such wise that the later sentences are implied by the earlier and flow from them, or build on them in some structured and necessary way.

But even this is not yet sufficient to constitute a text. It is the third, and highest level of formal logic (which brings us into the realm of semantics and extratextual verification) which establishes the rules of the testability of a text as to its truth or falsity. Now these rules will of course be very different for scientific texts than they will be for literary, or historical, or theological, or other kinds of texts, and it would be too much to go into all of the theories of truth that would have to be considered in this connection, but *the essential matter* is that every text belongs to a context of utterance and refers beyond itself to something outside of itself which it will clarify. Now all of these rules of textuality are, in the first instance, a priori or conceptual constraints. They are not matters of sociology, historical circumstances, the genetic endowment of the race, or necessarily species-specific.

As Husserl wrote in the "Fourth Logical Investigation":

> If we inquire into the reason why certain combinations are permitted and certain others prohibited in our language, we shall be, in a very great measure, referred to accidental linguistic habits, and, in general, to facts of linguistic development that are different in different linguistic communities. But, in another part, we meet with the essential distinction between independent and dependent meanings, as also with the apriori laws—essentially connected with that distinction—of combinations of meanings and meaning modifications, laws that must more or less clearly exhibit themselves in the theory of grammatical forms in a corresponding class of grammatical incompatibilities in every developed language.[39]

We could go on to a description of the categories of meanings, categories of the composition of meanings, categories of the modification of meanings, and so on, but this is sufficient to indicate that, on purely conceptual grounds, there is a solid reason for distinguishing what happens on the level of the surface string, of ordinary conversation, from the logical and a priori constraints on meaningfulness, noncontradiction, and possible truth, on the level of the depth grammar (or what Husserl called "pure logical grammar") necessary to the structure of any possible natural language, discourse, or text.

Both Russell and Wittgenstein saw the need for this distinction but provided no clear theory for it. The fourteenth-century Franciscan *modistae* and the seventeenth-century Cartesians had also seen the need for such a distinction and laid down *some* (very few) laws governing what is now called depth (or logical) grammar. Husserl approached the question purely as a logician; Chomsky and his school approach it as empirical scientists. But all these approaches give us solid reasons for not abandoning what is now called "foundationalism" as it has here been defined.[40] Merleau-Ponty, speaking again as a disciple of Husserl, perhaps puts it best:

> The idea of a single history or of a logic of history is, in a sense, implied in the least human exchange, in the least social perception. For example, anthropology supposes that civilizations very different from ours are comprehensible to us, that they can be situated in relation to ours and vice-versa, that all civilizations belong to the same universe of thought, since *the least use of language implies an idea of truth*. . . . Our life is essentially universal.[41]

2

Thoughts on Phenomenology and Skepticism

Robert Sokolowski

Husserl's relationship to skepticism is more complicated than it might appear at first sight. Certainly he argues against skepticism; the first move in his *Logical Investigations* is an extended criticism of psychologism, which he sees as closely related to relativism.[1] He not only criticizes the attempt to melt logical and conceptual ideality down into natural psychological states; he also takes the ideality of truth, logic, and science as the main topic for his analysis in the rest of the *Investigations*, and thus supplements his negative critique with a positive exploration of the truth that the skeptic would refrain from affirming. Husserl does not only show that skepticism is untenable; he also shows how truth is possible. Furthermore, psychologism and relativism remain throughout his writings as permanent opponents, the constant alternatives against which he develops his own philosophy. In *Formal and Transcendental Logic*, for example, the entire first chapter of part 2 is devoted to a refutation of *das Schreckbild des Psychologismus*.[2] Husserl even considers the phenomenon of skepticism as a kind of stimulus that calls forth true philosophy. In *Erste Philosophie* he looks back to the sophists as the original proponents of relativistic skepticism and sees them as provoking the response of Socrates and Plato, the first step in the career of philosophy.[3] Just as skepticism and relativism served to call philosophy into being, so their modern version in psychologism serves throughout Husserl's writings as a foil and provocation for his own philosophical work. Thus, it is clear that Husserl stands opposed to the skeptical position.

On the other hand, Husserl did take over a word used by the Greek skeptics, the term *epoché*, to name a move and an attitude that are necessary as a preparation for his own philosophy. Furthermore, in Sextus Empiricus we find phrases that sound very much like Husserl's own. Sextus says that the skeptic, the Pyrrhonian philosopher, "assents to none of the things that are nonevident," a formulation that resembles Husserl's principle of all principles, the manifesto that his philosophy will appeal only to what is actually given in intuitive experience.[4] In the passage we have just quoted from Sextus, the Greek term for the nonevident is *ta adéla*, the things that are not manifested. In Sextus, furthermore, the term *epoché* denotes a "restfulness [*stasis*] of the mind through which we neither deny nor affirm anything," and this description is not unlike the mental condition that Husserl tries to bring about when he recommends the epoché to us: when we enter the phenomenological attitude, we put out of action all the "positings," whether affirmative, negative, or of any other modality, that are present in the natural attitude.[5] For Sextus, the epoché will lead us to a state of quietude, *ataraxia*, in which we are no longer buffeted by conflicting dogmatic opinions.[6] This state is not unlike that of the phenomenological or transcendental attitude, in which we do not engage in the controversies being carried on in the natural attitude, but instead contemplate the formal structures that make such controversies possible. Thus, there are similarities and analogies between Husserl and the skepticism of Sextus Empiricus.

Despite these similarities, there are many differences between the two thinkers, most of them rooted in the different understandings that they have of appearance. Husserl has a much wider sense of appearence. For him, it is not only the views and profiles of things that are valid appearances; the *identity* of things also appears to us in a categorial presentation, and so do many other higher-level objects that Sextus would consider as moving beyond appearance into the domain of opinion or belief. For Sextus, appearance (*to phainomenon*) means almost exclusively simple perceptual experience (*phantasia*). He says, "When we question whether the underlying object [*to hypokeimenon*] is as it appears, we grant that it appears, and we question not about the appearance but about that which is said about the appearance."[7] Thus, it is in regard to "that which is said," the categorial articulation, that the skeptical reservations come into play. The immediate appearance is indubitable, but whatever transcends the immediate appearance is subject to reservation. Even the sameness of a thing, the identity that a thing can present in many appearances, seems to be philosophically overlooked by Sextus; he observes, taking his cue from the more ancient skeptics, that the same tower looks round when we look at it from close up and square when seen from a distance;

the same porch seems symmetrical when seen from a point at its center but angular when seen from one of its corners.[8] In such examples, the identity of the thing, the tower's being recognized as the same tower in its various profiles, the porch's being manifested as one and the same porch, is either overlooked and taken for granted by Sextus or considered by him to be one of the *adēla*, while for Husserl it is a phenomenon of a newer, higher level, different from what is given at the level of sensibility.

Husserl's understanding of appearance is so flexible and wide-ranging that it can even encompass the absent. Whereas for Sextus it is only the actually appearing features that are accepted as indubitable, for Husserl anything that actually appears is always surrounded by a halo of potential appearances that are cogiven. They are the correlates to the empty intentions that accompany every filled intention. The absent sides are given to us precisely as absent; hence, one of the things that appears to us is the absence of these absent sides. Other forms of absence appear as played off against other kinds of presence: the temporal absence of the past, which is analogous to but different from spatial absence, is given to us in our experience of time; the absence of something forgotten is given when we try to remember a word or a name or an idea; a special absence of the meaning of words is given when we hear someone speak a language we do not understand; the absence to us of the inner life of another person is given to us when we try but fail to share in someone else's feeling. Somewhat paradoxically, in all these ways the absent as such becomes a *dēlon*, one of the things that is manifested to us. Furthermore, the identity of various sorts of objects is given to us precisely in the appropriate mixtures of empty and filled intentions, which are correlated to appropriate mixtures of absences and presences on the objective side.

We have described the categorial domain and the domain of the absent as two types of manifestation that Husserl acknowledges but that would be considered as *adēla* by Sextus Empiricus. There is one more domain that we should mention. Husserl claims that something new comes into view for us when we move from the natural to the phenomenological attitude. When we perform the epoché and, instead of remaining engaged in our natural intentions, make these intentions the target of our reflection, then the various intendings and their mixtures become present to us. They had been marginally present to us before we made the turn, but now they become explicitly our theme. As the intendings become present to us in this new, explicit manner, so do their objective correlates, the things and categorial formations that the intendings achieve, disclose, and intend. Both the noetic and the noematic are the special concern of the transcendental attitude. Within this attitude, we carry out the descriptive analyses of the various forms of intending and the various forms of objects and presences and absences that are achieved through them.[9] In doing this, we do not enter into something totally new and unheard-of in the natural attitude; the ideas of an intention and an object were obviously familiar to us before we undertook philosophical tasks, but they were vaguely and inappropriately known to us. Their true sense is reached only from the detached viewpoint given by philosophical reflection.

Furthermore, the philosophical sense of truth is also given from this detached viewpoint. Truth is what skepticism is skeptical about. Skepticism wishes to avoid dogmatism, the hasty conviction that goes beyond what can legitimately be asserted. But truth is the achievement of recognitions and differentiations within the natural attitude, and phenomenology is the description of how such achievements, such evidences, take place. One of the factors that gives phenomenology resources against skepticism is that it is especially sensitive to the limitations of evidences. Phenomenology is concerned not only with the actual presence of identities, but also with the fringes of absence, of possible misinterpretation, of unclarity and ambiguity, of mediate as opposed to immediate givenness. Everything that can be recognized and confirmed can also be taken erroneously, according to a manner appropriate to the kind of thing in question. We are mistaken in different ways about things we perceive, things we articulate, memories we try to recall, persons we try to evaluate. Everyone knows that Husserl's principle of all principles demands that we are to turn only toward what is originally given to us in intuition as a validation for our claims, but the phrase that Husserl adds to this demand is often overlooked: we are to accept what intuition gives, "but also only within the limits in which it is presented there."[10] That is, we are to be aware philosophically of the limits and restrictions on what is presented; we are to be aware of what is not present. Thus, the skeptical reservations are built into the phenomenological proposal, but they are there in a systematic and reflective way. Precisely by taking note of limitations, phenomenology protects itself against the dogmatism that skepticism fears and thus inoculates itself against skepticism. And by accounting for such limitations, phenomenology can avoid the desperation of skepticism, which is so impressed by the possibility of error and confusion that it refrains even from judicious assertions. Phenomenology possesses a rational fear of that which skepticism fears irrationally.

But does not Husserl make some claims about phenomenological evidences that seem to justify the qualms of skepticism? He goes beyond claiming that a new field of study is opened up by the transcendental reduction; he says further that the philosophical judgments he makes in describing what is found in this field enjoy apodictic certainty.[11] Is this not a point at which he becomes vulnerable to skeptical attack? One might be willing to concede that there are things given to us in our phenomenological reflection, but one might think that it is excessive to claim that such presences can warrant apodictic certainty, the assurance that the things we see there could not be other than they are. In making such a claim, it might appear, Husserl goes beyond a proper reserve into an unwarranted projection. The Cartesian flavor of his argument, moreover, the strongly introspective character of his justification of these claims to apodicticity, seem to make him look even more dogmatic.

But if we look more closely at what he tells us are apodictic philosophical truths, we find that the claims are less excessive than they might appear at first. To say that a bodily object, a cube, is perceptually given to us as an identity in presences and absences, that it is recognized as one through a mixture of filled and empty intentions, does have something apodictic about it. We do sense that an object could not perceptually be given to us in any other way. There is something necessary about this: not because we can derive its necessity from some prior premise or axiom, but simply because we see that it could not be otherwise. Similarly, the various relationships that can be registered between picturing and perception, or between memory and perception, or between perception and categorial articulation, are all necessary and recognized as such when we succeed in teasing out the parts and wholes that are appropriate to such intentional forms. We can have a kind of certainty about these things that we cannot have about the things that we experience in the natural attitude, and we can have that certainty precisely because of the abstention, the epoché, we practice toward our worldly judgments. Even skeptics claim apodictic assurance for the legitimacy of their skepticism, which is based on how the forms of presentation have to be. It would not be questionable for Sextus Empiricus that there are *adēla* as well as *dēla*, the nonmanifest as well as the manifest. We might also add that we can be mistaken in regard to a given instance of phenomenological articulation, but then we are mistaken precisely about an apodictic evidence; we thought we had one when we did not. Error can occur in regard to the apodictic, but it follows its own proper style in that domain.[12]

But the skeptic might answer that the statements Husserl makes in his phenomenology (concerning, say, the mixtures of presence and absence in which a thing is perceived) are so obvious and trivial that no one would bother to question them; but that is precisely the point. Only when we get to what Husserl somewhere calls "the most trivial of trivialities" do we reach apodictic evidence. Well then, the skeptic would respond, why should such trivialities be stated at all? If everyone knows them already and no one could deny them once they are stated, why bother to formulate them? Why do they even need to be expressed? The answer is: first, because it is not easy to state the obvious; second, because it is good, rewarding, and illuminating to know such things; and third, because many perplexities arise because of confusions regarding issues that are self-evident when they are brought to clarity. In the natural attitude we are usually engaged in trying to find out what is new. What must be taken for granted as we look for the new seems old and trivial, but if we have a taste for philosophy, it is precisely the old and trivial, that which must have always been taken for granted, that interests us. Such a restraint in judging, a restriction to what is obviously and always so, is part of the shift from the natural attitude to the phenomenological and philosophical attitude. If philosophy were to try to tell us something that is not recognized as what we must have known all along, then it is probably veering from philosophy to science or news or information. If phenomenology seems to be telling us new facts about ourselves, it is probably becoming psychologistic. Satisfaction with the obvious and acceptance of its necessity are the source of the true philosophical *ataraxia.*

But why should philosophical statements be so difficult to formulate, if what whey say is so self-evidently true? The problem is that it is not easy to bring the obvious and the simple to words and to bring the virtual to the actual. We have all had the experience of reading papers in philosophy—whether students' essays or journal articles and books—that just seem to say too much. They keep making a lot of claims, but never get to the single, decisive point that clarifies the issue: that remembering involves presenting the past as past, that something depicted is present in a picture and is not merely symbolized by it, that the economic is not as such the political. Very little needs to be said, but it is hard to say that little. The reason it is so hard to say it is that we have only a vague possession of the phenomenon in question. It is there for us, but it is there only vaguely: perception, remembering, picturing, and measuring, or the political, the economic, the familial, and the moral, are all mixed up for us, even though we have a rough and ready appreciation for what each of these things is. It is not easy, for example, to say how words and pictures are related, even though what we say is obvious and "trivial" once we have succeeded in saying it.

There is another important difference between Husserl and the ancient skeptic Sextus Empiricus. Sextus, after reviewing the various reasons why we should be reserved in our judgments, describes the state or act of "nonassertion," of *aphasia* that we should adopt.[13] At first blush, this state of nonassertion might appear to be like the suspension of judgment that Husserl says we practice when we enter into the phenomenological attitude. The two, however, are different. In Husserlian terms, Sextus's *aphasia* is still an action performed by the ego in the natural attitude. In the chapters preceding his treatment of *aphasia*, Sextus reviews all the things that can make our judgments fallible: the differences among animals, the differences among various social groups, the differences among our senses, and the like. Because of such perturbing factors, we must, he says, always forego any judgments that go beyond those that register our immediate impressions or *phantasiai*. But such a suspension is a modal transformation within the natural attitude. We do not affirm or deny, we merely abstain from affirming or denying, but this is not done because we have begun to reflect on our intentions. It is done merely because we do not want to be rash and dogmatic in our judgments. We remain engaged with the world and its things and events, and indeed, according to Sextus, we continue to affirm what our immediate impressions force us to affirm.[14] It is not the case that we suspend all judgments, even the world-belief that underlies them all, and that we bracket the world and everything in it. In Sextus the spell of the natural attitude has not been broken and the move into a contemplative philosophy has not begun.

For Husserl, in contrast, the suspension of belief brought about by the epoché is carried out by the phenomenologically reflecting ego only; all natural beliefs are kept alive by the naturally engaged ego that is now the object of the reflecting ego's study. Thus, for Husserl a split arises within the ego; there is a divergence of the ego into the natural carrier of intendings and the phenomenological reflector on these intendings. The ego of the natural attitude grows or develops explicitly into a new dimension; a new bubble is grown that encompasses the original worldly life, and yet it is always one and the same ego, one and the same self that is capable of both enjoying the natural attitude and growing into the philosophical. The ego must carry out some fancy footwork in keeping both domains distinct, because there is always the danger that the philosophical dimension will collapse back into the natural, and that philosophical speeches, with their special reflective focus and apodicticity, will be taken as speeches uttered in the natural attitude. Then philosophy will begin to sound like psychology.

There is one widespread modern opinion that reinforces the skepticism that Husserl has to overcome but that Sextus and the ancient skeptics did not have as a resource. It is the understanding that sees consciousness as an enclosed whole cut off from the so-called "outside" world. According to this image, inside and outside are radically separated, and we are supposed to have a kind of immediate familiarity with the inside, but must perform inferences to reach things in the outside. Samuel Beckett gives us a literary expression of this Cartesian self-understanding in his novel *Murphy*.[15] About a third of the way through the novel, Beckett interrupts his story to undertake "a justification of the expression 'Murphy's mind.' " He says, "Murphy's mind pictured itself as a large hollow sphere, hermetically closed to the universe without." Everything in the outside universe is represented in this sphere, where ideas and forms move from virtual to actual and back again to virtual. "The mind felt its actual part to be above and bright, its virtual beneath and fading into dark. . . ." Murphy feels himself "split in two, a body and a mind. . . . But he felt his mind to be bodytight" and he could not understand how there could be commerce between the body and the mind.

This ironic description catches something of the general opinion that people have of the mind, the picture that captivates us when we start talking about thinking and truth. Beckett's chapter is not a philosophical treatise, but it may be all the more effective for that, because it captures the feeling that is common: somehow the whole outside world is ruled by the laws of nature, but "inside" there is consciousness, and in this "large hollow sphere" we have the world of consciousness and thought. How we get from the inside to the outside is the great epistemological problem. The prevalence of this picture in our culture means that we have to start philosophy with skepticism in place, daring us to try to dislodge it: we do not begin with things taken simply as they are. Moreover, the picture means that our skepticism will be something of a psychologism, because it rests on the supposed immediate awareness we have of everything "inside" as opposed to the "outside." Husserl did as much as anyone to overcome this picture, but even much of his writing seems to have the picture floating behind it; the point of the *Prolegomena*, for example, is to show that truth, logic, and science cannot be reduced to the activities that are inside the hollow sphere. There is no trace of such a self-understanding in Sextus Empiricus. The tropes and modes he gives to support his skepticism are not based on introspection but on worldly, matter-of-fact observations about animals, men, society, and the senses. The "large hollow sphere" is something we have inherited from the Renaissance and the intellectual currents, scientific, philosophical, and theological, that began at that time. This intensely introspective picture, when assumed at the beginning of philosophy, strongly reinforces the skeptical and psychologistic position. Husserl's teaching on intentionality is meant to shatter the picture, but it shows the effects of having started with it. Thus, Husserl begins his description of intentionality in the "Fifth Logical Investigation" by insisting strongly that the experiences we have within the "large hollow sphere" are truly about something outside; they are intentional and by their nature are directed toward targets beyond. One of the best strategies Husserl uses in overcoming the picture is to begin the "First Logical Investigation" not with a study of consciousness but with an analysis of signs and words, with distinctions between expressions and indications. These are public facts and get us out of the "large hollow sphere" at the start. Another successful strategy that Husserl uses in his later work is to turn our attention not toward the domain of consciousness simply, but to the correlation between the world and our consciousness of it, thus avoiding getting trapped in Murphy's sphere.[16]

Skepticism will always be part of the cultural scene, struggling against dogmatism. The two extremes, undershooting and overshooting the evidence of things, will always be played off one against the other, and each bespeaks a naiveté grounded in the natural attitude.[17] Neither position attains the moderation of philosophy, which acknowledges, contemplates, and describes the evidences that things give to us, but only within the limits that are proper to them.

3

The Epistemological Significance of Husserl's Theory of Intentionality

Harrison Hall

It is tempting to look for Husserl's contributions to epistemology in his numerous discussions of evidence and certainty (adequacy, apodicticity). These discussions occupy a significant place in his writings from the *Logical Investigations* through the *Crisis*, and there is no doubt whatsoever that Husserl attached great importance to them. But if one looks here for a solution to any of the skeptical problems that are the epistemological legacy of the modern period, one is likely to be very disappointed. The claims to certainty that Husserl makes in *Ideas*, *Cartesian Meditations*, and the *Crisis* look either naive or preposterous. And the discussions of the various kinds of evidence we have for various belief- and knowledge-claims seem to beg all the interesting philosophical questions.

Nonetheless, it is no accident that Husserl placed himself in the Cartesian tradition, and no accident that he found interesting affinities with Hume's doubts about empirical knowledge and Hume's skeptical "solution" to them. In fact, it is Husserl's taking these problems of knowledge very seriously and his belief that he could, for the first time in the history of philosophy, unravel them, that help to explain his otherwise mysterious lack of sympathy for Kant. The more generous reading of Husserl's relation to Kant is that Kant's supposed transcendental solution to these problems covered up the need for a real transcendental solution, namely Husserl's, and hence was less helpful in pointing the way to the needed radical philosophical breakthrough than were the problems alone. The less generous reading is that Kant had already stolen some of Husserl's thunder.

Be that as it may, one of the keys to making sense of Husserl's epistemological claims is an appreciation of the full extent of the beliefs he shares with Descartes and Hume. Husserl shares Descartes's analysis of his current philosophical milieu, the lack of clear and lasting achievements, and the need for radical change. One cannot help but think of Descartes's seventeenth-century lament when one reads Husserl's words:

> The splintering of present-day philosophy, with its perplexed activity, sets us thinking. . . . Instead of a unitary living philosophy, we have a philosophical literature growing beyond all bounds and almost without coherence. Instead of a serious discussion among conflicting theories that, in their very conflict, demonstrate the intimacy with which they belong together, the commonness of their underlying convictions, and an unswerving belief in a true philosophy, we have a pseudo-reporting and a pseudo-criticizing, a mere semblance of philosophizing seriously with and for one another. . . . To be sure, we still have philosophical congresses. The philosophers meet but, unfortunately, not the philosophies.[1]

And he shares Descartes's conviction that the solution to these difficulties lies in finding the correct philosophical method and, with that in hand, starting the task of philosophy from the very beginning, with nothing taken for granted. Add to this a demand for absolute certainty, the belief that what the philosophical thinker can know has a foundational structure and, hence, a natural order in which it can be known, the belief that the first steps toward such knowledge and certainty involve a turning away from the reality we think our experience reaches and a turning inward toward the thinking consciousness and its contents, and the path is indeed a familiar one.

Husserl believes, like Hume, that the way to understand an idea or concept is to retrace the steps that give rise to or "constitute" it from its origins in our experience. And he even acknowledges the analogy between his transcendental principles according to which consciousness constitutes meaning and Hume's laws of mental association. Add to this an "in the (philosophical) study"/"out of the (philosophical) study" dichotomy which is probably the most radical in the history of philosophy, and the debt to Hume begins to look as great as it was in the case of Descartes.

But Husserl's debt to certain of his predecessors is only part of the story that needs to be told in order to assess the significance of his theory of intentionality. Equally important is a break with the philosophical tradition which Husserl describes as a "total revolution . . . for the idea and method of philosophy over and against the total tradition."[2] This radical break consists, of course, of Husserl's "phenomenological reduction," which he takes to be the answer to Descartes's inward search for philosophical certainty and the nonskeptical solution to Hume's problems. The reduction is discovered in connection with Husserl's attempt to explain how it is that states of consciousness can be of or about entities and states of affairs in the real world—that is, the reduction is part of Husserl's theory of the intentionality of consciousness.

Husserl had learned from Brentano and Meinong of the difficulties encountered when one takes the "contents" of consciousness that account for its directedness beyond itself to be concrete entities of any kind. Brentano could not give an adequate account of various failures of conscious acts to reach their intended objectives, and Meinong was forced by such failures of reference to multiply entities almost indefinitely. Husserl opted for a Frege-like view of the entities that mediate the relation between conscious acts and their real objectives. These entities he took to be abstract intensional structures like Frege's meanings (*Sinne*), which are to be sharply distinguished from both ends of the intentional relation between consciousness and the world which they somehow mediate. Husserl devoted most of his philosophical life to investigating the details of that "somehow" across the full range of conscious acts and the various "regions" of objects at which such acts are aimed. In the process of that investigation, Husserl believed that he discovered the true scope and method of the philosophical enterprise and, with that discovery, the key to the solution of virtually every serious problem in epistemology. What I will try to do in what follows is to paint a clear enough picture of that discovery to make sense of Husserl's beliefs about its epistemological payoff.

There is, unfortunately, no obvious place to start in presenting the essential features of Husserl's theory of intentionality. Each piece of the theory seems to need the rest in order to make sense of it. One of the ingredients is a view of consciousness as consisting essentially of acts, not just in the sense of containing isolable or identifiable episodes, but in the sense of being literally active. For Husserl, following Meinong, conscious experience is never to be understood as the passive registering and mechanical associating of meaningless data, but is always to be construed as involving an active or interpretive function. Consciousness organizes or structures some less organized or relatively unstructured material, literally "makes sense" of things in the process of experiencing them. So the mediating entities that Husserl appeals to in his theory of intentionality must explain this organization or structuring in addition to accounting for the simple fact of the relatedness of consciousness to experienced objects.

Husserl refers to the abstract intensional structures that mediate the relation of consciousness to its objects as meanings and to conscious acts as meaning-giving or meaning-constituting to designate their active or interpretive nature. To avoid confusion with other uses of the term "meaning" he frequently uses the technical term *noema* (pl. *noemata*) or *noetic act* for the conscious acts directed "through" them. Brentano's (and his student Meinong's) problematic thesis that every conscious act has an object is thus transformed into the claim that every conscious act has a noema. This noema accounts for the act's directedness or intentionality whether or not it successfully reaches its intended objective. Noemata have elaborate structures according to Husserl, not all of the details of which are relevant here. In the case of perceptual consciousness, they seem to fill something like the role of a perceptual gestalt, accounting for perceptual reference, misidentification, correction, etc. There is a component of the noema which is associated with bare reference (Husserl's "X," which seems to carry the demonstrative sense of a "this thing here" or "that thing there"), components corresponding to the various predicate senses that are apparently true of the object, and components which refer beyond what is fully perceived in a single perceptual act (Husserl's "horizons"). It is not at all clear that Husserl believed that these meaning-components of perceptual acts alone determined the referents of the acts, although his view has been interpreted in this way.[3] What is perfectly clear, however, is that these meanings or noemata mediate the reference of any perceptual act, determining what sort of thing can be its successful referent. The activity of perception consists of the matching of these meanings to the relatively unstructured matter which experience offers through the senses. Successful perception involves a fit between meaning and referent that holds over time across a succession of acts aimed at the same object.

Husserl's account of how these meanings or noemata function to distinguish successful from unsuccessful perceptual reference and his analysis of the nature and limits of perceptual evidence do play a role in his epistemology. As I tried to indicate in an introductory way, however, none of these occupies center stage and none of these solves any serious epistemological problem when taken out of the context in which Husserl presents them. That context is created by the (in)famous phenomenological reduction, the crucial ingredient in a methodology that Husserl took to radically distinguish his philosophy from that of any of his predecessors. Husserl seems to have realized that many of his readers either might not understand or might not fully appreciate the consequences of this methodological move. In many of his published works from *Ideas* onward, he spends more time describing and talking about the reduction and what it can do for philosophy than he does actually doing anything with it.[4] Synonyms for the reduction are readily available—bracketing, epoché. The full formal title is transcendental phenomenological reduction. None of the names is of much help and each of them seems to have occasioned some sort of misreading of Husserl's intent.

Husserl's phenomenological reduction suspends or puts out of play our natural involvement in the real world of facts and things. When naturally involved in the world, we attend to things by virtue of the meanings or noemata that mediate our experience of them. These meanings themselves are not the objects of our attention. Phenomenological reduction changes that, focusing attention on these meanings and making it possible for us to see the ways in which they enable the conscious intending of objects and states of affairs. Husserl also refers to this as bracketing—since the reality of the world of facts and things is neither doubted nor denied, but "placed in brackets" or set aside, so as not to interfere with the study of the world *as meant*, that is, with the noemata through which the world is experienced. This represents an epoché, a break from or pause in our natural experience of things so as to substitute an unnatural attention to their meanings. Husserl refers to the reduction as "phenomenological" because the relation between meaning and thing is at least akin to the relation of phenomena to noumena in Kant, and because these noemata *are* the phenomena of philosophical experience. "Transcendental" is appropriate because noemata make possible the experience of objects and also because noemata are, in an important sense, transcendent to ordinary or natural experience. Husserl had learned a lesson in antipsychologism which he never forgot from Frege's critical review of his *Philosophy of Arithmetic*. That lesson was that the truths of logic and mathematics are not to be accounted for in terms of the natural laws governing psychological states and their causal relations to the rest of reality. The meanings and meaning relations that make such truths true are, in important ways, independent of or transcendent to that reality. Husserl dubs the consciousness that attends to such transcendent meanings and relations "transcendental," and this has occasioned a great deal of unnecessary discussion of Husserl's two consciousnesses and the mysterious relation that holds between them, when what is really at issue here are two perspectives on the whole of our experience.

In *Logical Investigations* Husserl treats the shift of attention from the things of ordinary experience to which our words refer to the meanings which mediate such linguistic reference as a relatively easy one—and in the context of investigations into logic (in Husserl's broad sense of that term) it probably is. What he came to see is that the total shift from thing to meaning across the entire range of conscious experience, that is, the total shift in attitude from the natural to the philosophical, was extraordinarily difficult to accomplish but absolutely essential to the success of the philosophical enterprise. Husserl characterizes the natural attitude or standpoint in terms of a general thesis or positing of the existence of the real world of facts and things. This world may be other than we think at numerous points, but the "it exists and actually is" remains always in place as the background of all of our natural lives.

Husserl has an impressive historical mandate for his belief that the sole concern of philosophy is with meaning and meaning relationships. From the questions that drive Plato's dialogues to the analyses of twentieth-century linguistic philosophy, meanings seem to be the focal point of philosophical discourse, in spite of disagreements about what those meanings are of (ideas, concepts, words, practices, institutions) or how and where to look for them (dialectic, meditation, critical analysis, ordinary language, practical activity). Husserl's view is that meaning is coextensive with intentionality and, hence, there to be found in virtually all of the places philosophers have ever sought it. One might think that Husserl wants to say, however, that such meaning will be found only if one looks for it in the right way, namely, through phenomenological reduction. Actually Husserl thinks that meanings are fairly easy to grasp. What his special philosophical method guarantees is that one doesn't misunderstand just what one has gotten hold of. Husserl's typical gloss on his predecessors, for example, is not that they have failed to reach the meaning contents of experience, but rather that they have misunderstood such meanings as part of natural reality. What is special about philosophy is that it is completely unnatural, and Husserl's phenomenology keeps us from losing sight of this fact.

Husserl's talk about two consciousnesses, one empirical and the other transcendental, two worlds or realms of inquiry, one of fact and one of meaning, and two utterly different kinds of investigation and questioning of our experience, one natural and the other philosophical (phenomenological, transcendental), has a clear purpose—to separate philosophy, its subject matter and method, from everything nonphilosophical. This is the key to Husserl's epistemology. The underlying claim is that the unsolvable problems and unanswerable questions in the theory of knowledge are all mixed problems and confused questions—

half natural, half philosophical—hence, not real problems or questions at all. Husserl's phenomenology clears up this confusion by making it impossible to keep one foot on each side of the dividing line between the philosophical and the nonphilosophical, that is (in Husserl's words), by making it impossible even to attempt to cross, philosophically, the "unbridgeable gulf between ideal and real."[5]

Consider the traditional questions associated with our knowledge of the external world, of the existence of things outside our minds to which our mental representations accurately correspond: "Do we know . . . ?" and "How do we know of the existence of such a world of objects?" What Husserl wants to say is that there are two very different sorts of inquiry hidden within these traditional questions. It's easier to see what he means if we work with more specific questions and then return to the one about the world of objects in general. Is there a table in the next classroom? Are there such things as neutrinos? Understood as natural questions there is nothing terribly exciting about them. If we don't already know the answer to the first question, we can go to the next classroom and find out. In typical circumstances opening the door and looking in would be sufficient. If the classroom were designed for holographic image projecting in the area where a table appeared to be, we might have to look a little closer. In no case would we have to deal with the philosophical skeptic. The natural context of such ordinary experience keeps any radical skeptical questioning of such claims from being appropriate or needing to be taken seriously. This is what G. E. Moore was constantly bringing to our attention.[6] Construed naturally, questions about whether and how we know that certain tables exist are to be answered, and those answers in turn to be questioned, if at all, in the ordinary ways with which we are all familiar. And none of that process is capable of loosening our grip on the real world of facts and things that forms the background of all of our natural experience.

The question about neutrinos looks much more interesting because of the remoteness of its subject matter from most of our daily lives. But it isn't really of any special philosophical interest from Husserl's point of view. As a natural question asked of the physicist, it calls for no more than the application of familiar scientific procedures for determining the presence of particles with the appropriate mass and charge characteristics.

When we shift to the philosophical questions about the table and neutrinos, everything changes. The existence of the things of natural (both everyday and empirical scientific) experience has now dropped out as irrelevant, "placed in brackets" until we return to the natural attitude. What is at issue philosophically, according to Husserl, are the meanings (noemata) which make it possible for tables and neutrinos to be part of our sense of things, to be part of our natural experience. It is to this perspective on our experience that the legitimate questions of epistemology belong. They are questions about the kinds of evidence appropriate to the various "regions" of objects, questions about the existence of things, and questions about what is involved in the discovery and correction of various sorts of mistakes in our beliefs—from perceptual errors to inadequate scientific theories. But none of these questions is a question *of fact*. They are all questions about the meaning contents of natural experience and how they enable us to make sense of things so as to give rise to the various sorts of natural knowledge-claims.

Husserl pursued these questions relentlessly. For ordinary perceptual experience of the sort that gives rise to beliefs about tables, he came up with the following analysis. The components of perceptual noemata which correspond to the actual or real existence of things are those associated with a set of structured anticipations and associations (Husserl's "internal" and "external horizons"). It is the nature of perceptual noemata to be of whole objects, but of perceptual experience to provide sensuous "filling" for only certain aspects of intended objects, namely those that could interact with the senses. The rest of the object is "also meant" (Husserl's "internal horizon"), "co-present" as "co-intended," but the intending of it is sensuously "empty." The sense or meaning "actually exists" corresponds to the overlapping and interlocking of filled and unfilled meaning components in our ongoing experiencing of the same object. Since most ordinary objects typically occur in groups with some common practical function, tables with chairs and other things, for example, there is also a set of very loose associations between the intended object and other related objects (Husserl's "external horizon"), which explains our anticipation of or surprise at certain contents of further experience. And these, in turn make some small contribution to our sense of perceived things as actually existing.

Husserl is quick to acknowledge that the evidence appropriate to objects of perception is of a radically different kind from that appropriate to mathematical or abstract objects. The relevant criterion in the latter case is apodicticity, the intuition of necessary truth which accompanies the conscious grasping of the meanings and meaning-relations involved (Hume's "relations of ideas" and, for Husserl, quite a bit more). In the case of perception, not only is apodicticity beyond our reach, but so is evidential adequacy. By adequacy of evidence Husserl means having all of the evidence in a single conscious grasp, the kind of intuitive self-evidence possessed by claims that could not be affected by further experience. But perception never gives us that kind of grasp of either individual objects or the perceived world. Both are inexhaustible in principle as far as sensuous presence is concerned, the experience of them spread out indefinitely over time, never completed. For Husserl all of this describes the nature of perceptual evidence, the kind of evidence appropriate to perceptual claims. None of this could have the implication that perceptual evidence is insufficient for perceptual knowledge. Philosophy can contribute to an understanding of factual knowledge-claims. It cannot possibly overthrow them. Philosophical reflection can reveal how the epistemic criteria that function tacitly in our natural experience of the world can help us to understand our empirical knowledge of that world. It could never show us that we don't have any.

Husserl sometimes treats skeptical doubts such as Descartes's almost sympathetically. But this should not mislead us. What is right about skeptical doubt is that it tends to destroy the natural context of experience and to catapult us from the world of fact to the realm of meaning. What is wrong is that it does not do so self-consciously. It is at the level of meaning, with our natural belief in the existence of the world suspended, that we can see what it is for us to intend things as actually existing, understand what it means for something in our experience to count as part of that world. What we can't do from the level of meaning is make factual claims about real existence or our natural knowledge of it. So Descartes becomes, on Husserl's view, the "father of transcendental realism, an absurd position,"[7] when he tries to prove that we have apodictic certainty of the actual existence of various things. The "absurdity" is twofold—trying to establish factual claims via philosophical inquiry, that is, from the level of meaning, and using the criterion of evidence appropriate to meaning-claims for factual claims about actual existence.

Ultimately, for Husserl, at the level of meaning we know that there is a table in the next classroom because of the consistency of the contents of our experiences of it and its surroundings with the systems of noemata that enable us to intend things as tables. Husserl wanted to tell an analogous story about the objects of "mathematical natural science," as he called them, by showing how such science was rooted in our natural experience of the world. The beginnings of such a story can be found in the *Crisis*,[8] but Husserl does not come close to giving the details that would be required to connect claims about neutrinos with the meaning contents of the natural experience of the physicist. Nonetheless, there must be such a story as long as the natural experience of empirical scientists is consistently "of neutrinos"—since the meaning contents of that experience have to be what makes possible the intending of anything *as neutrinos*. The details may be interesting and important, but they are still no more than details. The methodological move and assumptions do all the real work. If the division between the natural and the philosophical can be drawn as sharply as and along the lines that Husserl believes it can, then the meaning contents of experience cannot help but contain all the resources needed to account for everything experienced *as it is experienced*, including its actual existence or reality.

The most detailed account of how our experience coincides with the meaning "actually existing others"—thus providing a philosophical *understanding of* our belief in such things—is Husserl's treatment of "others" in the "Fifth Cartesian Meditation." Those who look here for an answer to skepticism about other minds are inevitably disappointed. Husserl has no way to prove that our "apparent" experience of others is actually caused by and/or accurately represents actually existing other subjects of experience. Husserl doesn't try to provide any such proof, nor does he believe that any legitimate request for such proof can be made. What Husserl does in the "Fifth Meditation" is show how our ongoing experience of others progressively satisfies the requirements contained in our noemata for "actually existing others" and offer an account of how our stock of noemata could have come to include the relevant meanings.[9] And his point isn't just that that's the best we can do in this case. His point is that that's all we can ever be asked to do in any case. And it's the natural/philosophical dichotomy which makes that so. Natural questions about the reality, existence, perceivability, truth of claims about . . . tables, neutrinos, other minds, or whatever, leave untouched our implicit background faith in the reality of the natural world and the possibility of successful access to it. In fact it is that background faith which makes possible any such questioning of our natural or ordinary knowledge-claims in the first place. Without such faith beyond the reach of our natural questioning, the questions themselves lose all their epistemic force if not their meaningful content.[10] With such faith the questions have natural and obvious answers of the sort that Austin and Moore were fond of providing. In fact Moore, the seemingly incurable plain (or natural, in Husserl's vocabulary) man was able to hear even the most general questions about the real world and our knowledge of it as natural questions to be answered by holding up one's hands and making some philosophically uninteresting claims about their nature and number rather than mounting a philosophical defense against the skeptic.

What Husserl tried to get very clear about, and his claim to be first may well have been correct on this point, is the way in which philosophical questioning "changes the subject" completely. According to Husserl that is from fact to meaning. The only questions of fact about the existence or our knowledge of material objects, other minds, etc., are the ones which Moore and Austin typically answered. Raising verbally similar questions without natural motivation produces a radical shift in attitude or standpoint. These are truly philosophical questions, perfectly legitimate in their own right, and with respect to which Austin's and Moore's sorts of answers are completely irrelevant. But the answers to these questions will not tell us whether the things in question in fact exist or whether we know or fail to know anything about them. The relevant answers to the philosophical questions about the world and our knowledge of it will tell us what it means for things to exist and what kind of evidence experience must provide in order for them to count as real and our beliefs about them to count as knowledge. Given Husserl's very rich conception of meaning, these philosophical answers turn out to be quite complex. The work of finding all of these and explaining their interconnection and implication for the nature of conscious experience and its relation to the rest of reality constitute the whole of metaphysics ("regional ontology") and epistemology (theory of *Evidenz*) for Husserl. But they do not constitute an answer to skepticism in any of its forms. There are no answers to skepticism because there are no legitimate questions for which skepticism would represent the extreme negative answer. There is no space in between the natural and the philosophical from which to raise unnatural questions of fact about reality, and it is only our philosophical confusion about the two mutually exclusive realms which makes such questions seem real and any answers seem inadequate. It is the elimination of such confusion that is the real epistemological significance of Husserl's theory of intentionality.

4

Association in Husserl's Phenomenology

Joseph J. Kockelmans

For more than forty years Husserl was engaged in a battle with psychologism and skepticism. His criticism of these views led him to an effort to overcome classical empiricism, with which he had become familiar in the lectures of Brentano. The expression "overcoming classical empiricism" does not mean here to suggest a radical refutation and rejection of empiricism, but to place it on a solid, transcendental foundation. This effort implies that whatever is important and illuminating in classical empiricism is to be maintained, but now in a form that can be fully justified methodically in such a manner that there is no longer any place for psychologism or skepticism.

In this paper I have decided not to focus on the basic issue in its universality, but rather to take a concrete case and show how Husserl tried to place an empiricist doctrine on a proper foundation. The case in point is the empiricist conception of association. Husserl was convinced, as was Brentano, that the doctrine of the "association of ideas" is important and to be maintained in any acceptable form of thought. Yet the doctrine is to be provided with a solid basis and to be explained with the help of the proper methods. The concrete issue therefore is: What can transcendental phenomenology contribute to the classical doctrine of association?

I. Some Historical Observations

The doctrine known as "the association of ideas" has a venerable history.[1] Although the term itself is of recent origin (the English word, derived from the French, appeared for the first time in the sixteenth century), the doctrine to which it refers seems to have been proposed for the first time by Aristotle in the second chapter of his brief treatise "On Memory and Reminiscence." Aristotle's conception of reminiscence was later interpreted by Greek, Arabic, and Latin commentators, notably by Themistius, Averroes, and Aquinas. It was mainly through the interpretation of Aquinas that the doctrine became known in the Aristotelian tradition of the centuries to follow. In that form it was known by Locke and Hume. It seems that Hume's library contained a copy of Aquinas's commentary on Aristotle's treatise on memory, and that some of the examples given by Aristotle and Aquinas were later used by Hume.

Yet, as is well known, in Locke and Hume the doctrine of the "association of ideas" received a substantially different meaning than that which it had had up until the seventeenth century; and in this new form it deeply influenced both Kant and the psychologists of the nineteenth century. In the nineteenth century several treatises on association had been written and the most important of them were known to Brentano. Brentano was also familiar with the much older conception of association, found in Aristotle and the subsequent Aristotelian tradition. Brentano himself used the doctrine of association, which he interpreted in his own way, to clarify his conception of the consciousness of time.

I do not know how far Husserl himself was acquainted with the history of the doctrine of association.[2] We do know that he was familiar with the conception of Kant, who had given association an important place in the subjective deduction of the categories where he introduces the transcendental, figurative synthesis of the imagination. On a few occasions Husserl refers to Kant's view and then indicates how a phenomenological theory of association can deal with the problems Kant had to leave unresolved. Husserl also had a manuscript of a lecture course on time in which Brentano explains the part association has to play in the consciousness of time. Husserl discusses Brentano's views in his "Lectures on Inner Time-Consciousness," and explains there why Brentano's own view is not completely acceptable from a phenomenological point of view. From the manner in which Husserl speaks about association and its laws it is clear that we may assume that he was familiar with both the empiricist and the psychological treatises on association.

Since some of the themes with which Husserl is concerned here were also discussed by Gestalt psychology and psychoanalysis, albeit from a completely different point of view, it is necessary to say a few words about Husserl's relation to Gestalt psychology and psychoanalysis.

Husserl explicitly claims that his so-called "*figurale Momente*" were discovered independently of von Ehrenfels's essay "Über Gestaltqualitäten," even though Husserl's book on the concept of number was published one year later than von Ehrenfels's first publication in 1890. By the way, there are reasons to believe that the first one who discussed these ideas may have been Stumpf in his *Verschmelzungslehre*.[3]

Between 1925 and 1930 Husserl criticized Gestalt psychology, which by then had established itself in the works of Wertheimer, Kohler, Koffka, and Lewin, among others. Husserl accused these authors of maintaining a form of naturalism, of being stuck in the categories of classical sensualism, of unphenomenologically using causal types of explanations for phenomena of meaning, of presenting wholes as stable and completed objects without ever realizing the genetic constitution of these wholes in processes of syntheses, etc.[4]

Husserl was more or less familiar with the ideas of von Ehrenfels, Meinong, and Cornelius. He knew rather little about the work of Wertheimer, Kohler, Koffka, and Lewin who constituted the so-called Berlin school; he even knew nothing at all about the members of the Leipzig school, but became later quite familiar with the work of Buhler of the Vienna school. Husserl also was somewhat familiar with what Cassirer, Linke, and Scheler had written on the subject. Yet according to Holenstein one may assume that Husserl developed his own ideas independently of the work of these authors, as it were "from the things themselves," in rigorous, genetic analyses of the various configurations involved.[5]

Husserl's influence on Gestalt psychology was minimal, at least if we limit ourselves to the leading Gestalt psychologists who wrote before 1938. Later Gurwitsch made an effort to relate phenomenology and Gestalt psychology in a manner that is both critical and systematic. Finally, many ideas that have come up in the debate about Gestalt psychology have also been raised in the French literature on phenomenology. We find in the work of Merleau-Ponty in particular a very successful effort to integrate Gestalt psychology into a phenomenology of perception.[6]

The relationship between Husserl and psychoanalysis is marginal. Husserl was not really influenced by ideas of Freud, about which he knew little. He was somewhat more familiar with the ideas of Jung. It is true that Husserl did know about the psychoanalytic theory of the unconscious, suppression, etc. Yet what Husserl himself says about both these issues was not inspired by Freud or Jung, but rather again derived from "the things themselves." However, it is not impossible that Husserl selected the relevant terms because he had become familiar with them through his knowledge of psychoanalysis.[7]

In the pages to come I am mainly interested in describing the context in which Husserl speaks about association and to give the reader a clear idea of the radically new conception of association that phenomenology was able to develop. I also want to indicate very briefly the importance of the investigations for a better understanding of Merleau-Ponty's *Phenomenology of Perception*, and notably of his doctrine concerning the "body-subject," on the one hand, and for a possible foundation and explanation of the notion of the "unconscious," on the other. In view of the fact that there is virtually no literature on the subject in English, I must refer the reader for all issues not mentioned here to the excellent study by Holenstein just cited. But let us return to Husserl himself.

Husserl dealt with issues that pertain to association from the very beginning of his career.[8] Yet a systematic study of association dates from the twenties. At that time he raised the issue of association in the context of reflections on "passive synthesis" in which a phenomenologically reinterpreted conception of association is to play an essential part. For Husserl association has to do with all processes in which meaning becomes constituted according to rules at a level where there is not yet any participation on the part of the active ego. The objects that are constituted in these processes are all pregiven to the conscious ego, and this is the case already at the lowest level of constitution.

Even though association does not function exclusively in the domain of the original constitution of inner time, the time analyses are nonetheless a privileged domain in which the issue of association is to be raised first. It is also in that very realm, notably in the context of reflections on retention and protention, that Husserl encountered the concept of association in a lecture course on time given by Brentano.[9]

Yet association plays an important part in all constitutive analyses. Such analyses belong to the domain of genetic phenomenology, which Husserl opposes to static phenomenology. The distinction between static and genetic phenomenology became important for Husserl's conception of phenomenology only after 1917. Both forms of phenomenology are concerned with constitutional problems, i.e., with problems concerning the manner in which objects become present to consciousness. Static phenomenology is concerned with static constitution; it takes its point of departure from stable and complete kinds of objects, from real natural things, or from ideal mathematical entities and relations, etc., and then examines in a noetic and noematic manner those contexts of lived experiences in which the objects of the relevant kind are made present to consciousness. The noetic-noematic analysis of the perception of a house would be a good example of static phenomenological analysis. In these analyses the relevant objects are taken "in phenomenological reduction" as the pure, objective correlates of consciousness. The aim of the subsequent analysis is to bring the meaning of those objects to light and explain them by means of noetic and noematic analyses and descriptions. Genetic phenomenology, on the other hand, is not concerned with the analysis of stable and complete objects and systems of correlation, but rather with the genesis of such objects and systems of correlation; in other words, it is concerned with the *genesis of the constitution* itself as well as of the objects constituted therein, particularly insofar as this also pertains to the mundane and transcendental egos.

Genetic phenomenology itself is again divided into active and passive genesis. Analyses of active genesis are concerned with the achievements of the ego in which cultural objects, artworks, mathematical objects, and logical entities become constituted and brought to light. Passive genesis, on the other hand, is concerned with constitution of meaning in which the ego is not actively involved.

The basic and universal principle of passive genesis is association. The term is here to be taken not in the sense of the tradition, but in a typically phenomenological sense. Thus, it merely means the set of processes in which any given object is able to bring to mind certain other objects. Husserl distinguishes here between association as the principle of the formation of unity through synthesis, and association as the principle of the apperception of objects as objects of a determinate sense on the basis of an associative awakening of earlier experiences, and of the analogizing transfer of meaning as an associative induction or an inductive association.[10]

II. Association

We have seen that for a phenomenologist the term "association" refers to processes of consciousness in which meaning becomes constituted passively and yet in conformity with rules that pertain to passive genesis.[11] For example, in the domain of pure consciousness that is now present we find first of all the flowing, present consciousness itself and in it one or more actual objects which in each case are constituted perceptually and are now bodily present. We find there also concrete perceptions together with their retentional components. And all of this is given in the form of a retentional flowing away, as disappearing in the distant horizon of retention. Finally, we can encounter there also genuine recollections.

Between the noematic components of what is present and of what is recollected there is a characteristic form of interaction. Phenomenologically one can describe this by saying that what is present brings what is recollected to mind. Sometimes we find a recollection which in the same manner brings a second recollection to mind. In that case our perceptual and originarily constituting consciousness can be characterized as an awakening consciousness that evokes a reproductive consciousness. And the latter can again function in the same manner in regard to an earlier representation.

It should be noted here at once that associations of this kind often occur unnoticed. Yet in reflection one can always go back to them. But even then several aspects will still remain unnoticed at first. Speaking generally, one could say that the one awareness often awakens another because there is some relation between them, i.e., between the awakening and the awakened awareness. In such cases the association may rest for instance on similarity. For the transition from the awakening awareness or its intentional correlate to the awakened one presupposes some link. In the case under discussion similarity is this link. Since similarity may vary from one case to the next, it is necessary to submit these cases to careful analysis in order to explain how in each case the particular awakening comes to pass. For only in this manner can the problem be resolved of how the pure ego can gain consciousness of the fact that it has behind itself an endless field of past, lived experiences as its own experiences that time and again can be awakened through recollections. Since it is simply impossible to have a human subject if that subject in principle would not be able to have recollections of what has been, it is clear that the doctrine of association is very important for the phenomenology of consciousness (*APS*, 117–24).

It is not difficult to see that every form of association presupposes the synthesis which continuously comes about in original time-consciousness. In every actual, concretely full, flowing and living present we find in a unified form present, past, and future in a certain mode of givenness. But the manner in which the subject becomes conscious of its past and future life in the present is always incomplete. Also, past and future would be meaningless for the ego if nothing could awake or provoke them. Then, both the retentions and the protentions together with their indiscriminate horizons taken as such are still empty and purely formal. And yet without this beginning there would be no possibility of further development and progress. In the realm of the constitution of all objects of which one can become conscious, including the constitution of the ego itself, the synthesis of original time-consciousness is fundamental. We find here a universal synthetically constituted formal frame, in which all other possible syntheses must take part.

There are manifestly many other forms of synthesis which are transcendental in the sense that they are apodictically necessary for the genesis of the subject; for the subject can be thought of only as in genesis. These latter forms of synthesis take their courses together with the time-form just mentioned. Kant has seen this clearly in the transcendental deduction of the first edition of the first Critique, even though Kant was unable to develop this issue in all of its implications in a methodical manner.

Be this as it may, it should be noted here first that what has been said about the present, retention and protention also holds for the present that I actually live. It, too, receives its unity from a synthesis that encompasses it. Furthermore, while my life flows from life moment to life moment new, higher-level syntheses are accomplished. The totality of all objects, which through these syntheses become constituted, can be presented under the general title: the coexistence and succession of all immanent objects in relation to each other. In each moment of our lives we have constituted some time-object or another. Each has its own momentary horizon of retentional having-been-ness (*Gewesenheit*) and its momentary structure is continually flowing, and synthetically forms a unity, and as such it constitutes its time-object, say an enduring tone. Yet in the same moment of my concrete life and its flowing away into the past, other temporal objects can be constituted, say another tone or a color. Herewith simultaneity is necessarily constituted, also. Yet it is not the case that each temporal object has its own temporality. A now becomes constituted that at the same time is the now for the one temporal object as well as for the other. This now brings the now of the one object and that of the other to a unity of identity. And the same holds true for the entire form-structure of the subjective modi of time.

Thus, to every now there corresponds a universal synthesis by which a universal, concrete present is constituted and in which all unities that can be distinguished are arranged. Furthermore, in the flowing away of the now there is a second universal synthesis to be found in our lives that becomes constituted, by means of which the different presents that flow away are made conscious as a unity of succession. In other words, what is experienced as simultaneous and successive is constituted as simultaneous and successive from an originally synthetic unity.

This is the first and most universal synthesis which necessarily connects all particular objects which, originally in passive synthesis, become conscious in whatever way their content may be constituted as a unity.

In pointing this out, Husserl says, we focused mainly on that which gives temporal unity to different temporal objects in regard to one another. Yet one should note that the synthesis of time-consciousness contains the presuppositions for those syntheses in which any object whatsoever becomes constituted as a unity, as identically one and the same, and as enduring. Time-consciousness is thus the original domain and abode (*Urstatte*) for the constitution of the unity of identity as well as for the coexistence and succession of all objects of which we can become conscious. Yet it is merely a universal form and thus to some degree still an abstraction. This is the reason why we must now turn to other analyses (*APS*, 125–28).

Husserl next discusses a second form of synthesis in which association plays an important part. He calls the next phase in the analysis the analysis of the synthesis of homogeneity. Homogeneity is not just similarity; it is similarity in a certain respect, in quantity, in shape or quality, etc. To explain these forms of synthesis Husserl uses very simple examples. Let us assume that a number of immanent objects already have been constituted. We assume thus that we already have individual objects as well as certain groups of objects. In addition, we also have wholes articulated into parts. In order to explain the function of association in this case, we must ask: What are the fundamental and primordial phenomena? The only things we actually have at this level are the immanent objects mentioned. The most universal connection determined by content between separate objects manifestly is similarity or dissimilarity, equality or inequality; speaking generally one can say that we have connections of homogeneity or heterogeneity. Note that in the domain of consciousness connection really always means achievement through synthesis by consciousness. Thus, we have here a new form of synthesis, namely synthesis of homogeneity.

When in the natural attitude we speak about two things of the real world and say that they are similar we usually do not imply that there is a real relation or connection between them. In the case of immanent data this is quite different. If such objects indeed are similar, then they form a unity in a manner that is peculiar to consciousness, i.e., a unity of relatedness (*Verwandtschaft*). If for instance in our visual field we find constituted data of different colors, then the ones that are similar in color are connected in a special way. The same holds good for other such cases. The most perfect form of connection or similarity is manifestly identity, or perhaps better, equality. The data of consciousness that are equal form a unity, a special group; it is a plurality given as a unity, it is a "whole" which connects the individual data by somehow relating them to each other. We have the same in the case of similarity; but then the unity is less strong and obvious.

We have just seen how in a static description of the coexistence of two or more objects related in content, their unity comes about because of homogeneity. By considering several of such cases one can make a distinction between different degrees of the intimacy of the connection. The deeper nature of this connection reveals itself in a kinetic description where one can compare the related objects and see the one going over into the other. The latter appears in this transition as the "repetition" of the former. It is as if the one consciousness slides over the other, and the first immanent object begins to coincide with the other; in case the two objects are perfectly equal, there even is congruence. If the two objects are merely similar to each other, we find both coincidence and conflict. The latter implies that something is being "suppressed"; suppression here merely means that one object in part conceals the other, whereas the latter strives toward revealment.

We can also observe that in the case in which coincidence is without conflict, there no longer is a twofold or duality as far as content is concerned; there is no more separation or division. We then observe a blending and fusion of the contents. When two things overlap that are merely similar without being perfectly equal, there, too, we find some form of fusion, but this leads to a unity that leaves room for hiding and concealing, for suppression, and later possible emergence. We can therefore say that what we *statically* encounter as connections based on perfect equality or mere similarity between separate contents is itself already a mode of synthesis of coincidence. One could speak here of a coincidence at a distance. To this a certain tendency belongs. For what has been set apart by itself begins to function in an affective way; it invites the ego to restore a connection. And a connection of objects set apart on the basis of homogeneity exercises even a more intense, affective force on the ego. The ego lets this affective force in turn come to fulfillment by turning to the relevant, immanent objects thereby bringing about the kinetic form typical of the transition from one member to the next. But all of this takes place at a level that still precedes the level of the higher activities of the ego where one knowingly establishes relationships.

It is also important to observe that any time we find something set apart we also find what was set apart in contrast with what was not set apart in this way. We can distinguish various degrees of contrast. The stronger the fusion of the members of a group is, the clearer is the contrast between the group and the rest. In cases in which one has a plurality of homogeneous groups one always has both fusion and contrast.

Husserl next turns to cases in which there is similarity in one respect and dissimilarity in another. Take two similar triangles, one painted red, the other blue. We then say that as triangles they are equal or similar, but as colored objects they are dissimilar. Furthermore, a red triangle can form a group of similarity with other red objects; in that case the similarity is in color and the dissimilarity in shape or figure. We can then distinguish those objects that are equal in shape and those that are equal in color. If two objects similar in a certain respect appear together in the flowing present, then they appear as a pair: a pair of triangles. If we have two such pairs, one similar in color, the other pair similar in shape, we have another pair of pairs. The two pairs have now entered a synthesis of homogeneity. Husserl mentions other cases and gives additional examples. They all are to show that what in our actual conscious life we can describe and explain as forms of synthesis, already was prepared in passivity at a much lower level on the basis of the "laws" of association (*APS*, 128–33).

We must now turn, Husserl says, to the problems connected with unity based on *order*. We must again begin by asking the question: What are in this case primal phenomena? In the preceding we focused on the following primal phenomena: an isolated immanent object, a plurality of such objects in coexistence or succession, objects related to each other because of homogeneity. One of the latter phenomena is that of order and lack of order. One primal phenomenon of disorder is a group of spots on a plain surface. It is not impossible that even in this case purely passively some order comes to the fore; that, too, would then be a primal phenomenon. One can have a set of colored dots gradually progressing from dark red to dark blue; a series of triangles of the same shape but gradually increasing in magnitude. One can also take a series of objects which in time follow one another in some order in some respect. In this case there is not just the formation of pairs and groups on the basis of similarity; the principle of order is here the gradual increase or decrease.

We must now ask the question: What is it that brings the concatenation and joining of the elements about, and how do these concatenations in opposition to pure multiplicities come about in mere passivity? Husserl mentions first the primal phenomenon of succession, which is a primal ordering achievement of time-constituting consciousness. Whatever from present to present has been set apart as an individual object and constitutes itself in the train of present moments as something, as an enduring unity of identity, is temporally concatenated. Once this primal ordering has been brought about between data, then the increases that are determined by content (such as increases in color intensity, or in magnitude) can in temporal sequence begin to concatenate themselves, and in this way form serial unities of consistent increases (in intensity, magnitude, etc.). In the latter case the gradual succession increases the strength of the unity among the elements of the series (*APS*, 135).

Husserl also discusses the case in which concatenations come about in the realm of coexistence, where the order is not determined by the order of the succession of the elements. Even if one disregards content for a moment, and merely focuses on the field itself that is given, take the visual field, one will find that there, too, order is present in the form of possible lines or directions. Succession provides us always with one, linear order, whereas in the visual field usually various forms of order can manifest themselves, different series of possible concatenations. We can always distinguish various places which are now filled by this content and later by another. In the visual field there is thus one privileged form of order, the local order (*APS*, 133–42).

What in the field of the present is concretely simultaneous has its identical temporal duration; it has its identical "place" in time. The distinction between temporal equality and temporal identity is fundamental. For example, several tones which follow each other can all endure equally long. Yet the equality of the duration is merely the equality of the temporal form, not the identity of the stretch of time. Here we encounter the problem of individuation, i.e., the most original individuation in internal time-consciousness. To clarify this let us take a melody played on a violin. Were one to repeat the melody after its completion, the temporal form (its duration or length) would be completely equal to the first; yet individually seen, a new temporal object has become constituted, even though one completely equal to the first. When we repeat a melody in the same manner we played it before, we have something that is completely equal, not only in content but also in duration or length. To each temporal point of the first melody there belongs a similar temporal point in the second. Yet the temporal stretches themselves within the unitary ordering of time, are irreducibly different from one another and, as such, they cannot be repeated in principle. The temporal objects taken as a whole take part in the irrepeatability of the temporal points and stretches (*APS*, 142–43). Similar explanations can be given of spatial locality. It is spatial locality which orders the coexisting elements of each homogeneous domain and individualizes within it what is simultaneously completely equal (*APS*, 143–44).

That which becomes constituted in consciousness as an object in an original manner becomes constituted with essential necessity in original time-consciousness as something that is continually identical and permanently identifiable as such. The ever new, continual, synthetic identification of the changing content maintains itself necessarily in an unmixed form in the progressing constitution of what is immanent. The uniqueness of an object's *temporal place* is therefore nothing else but the correlate of the *form* of the identification which in each case is enacted, taken in its unique connectedness of our constituting life in which this object becomes constituted as such and only can be identified by the fact that consciousness can always go back to its original constituting act, can awake it again, and can find it as the object that at each time can be recognized as such. On the other hand, each object constituted in consciousness has its own individuality. Yet at the same time it also has its typical *eidos* on the basis of which the logical predication is made possible. In other words, each object has not only a number of characteristics, its specific essence according to which it can be connected with other such objects conceptually according to genus and species, but it also has even as a presupposition for this common essence, its individuality, its thisness, i.e., it has already become constituted as this individual object which can be recognized continually as this object and which, as such, belongs to the determined connection of the originally constituting life.

From here on one would have to proceed to a systematic phenomenology of the universal temporal field and the different fields of the various senses. In these areas, too, one can show the passive constitution of meaning on the basis of principles of association (*APS*, 146–48). Since all of this lies far beyond the scope of this essay, we shall turn instead to the phenomenon of affection mentioned above.

III. The Phenomenon of Affection

Husserl next turns his attention more extensively to the large domain of affections which, in a more direct way, will lead us to important questions concerning association. By "affection" Husserl means the pull that an object exerts on the ego. In the perceptual order an object may affect the ego, upon which the ego may or may not begin to pay attention to the object; eventually the ego may go over to an act of perception. The pull relaxes when the ego turns toward the object, and even more when the ego begins to strive toward a perception in which the object becomes given in a manner that is progressively revealing. The rays of affection can originate in objects that already have become constituted as such and have already been separated and set apart, but they can originate also from parts or moments of these objects. There are other things in the realm of consciousness that do not yet really affect the ego, even though they, too, have the tendency toward affection. Finally, there are the mere sense data, which also send out rays of affection toward the ego, but which are too weak to really affect the ego.

Genuine affection presupposes that the object has already become separated and set apart and this implies, on the one hand, fusion of the content and, on the other, contrast. To some degree affection is a function of contrast. There can be gradation in contrast and this brings about gradation in affection. Extreme contrasts usually dominate all other contrasts. One could take as an example someone who is exposed to three different kinds of noises: the passing of a truck, the sounding of a melody, and the sound of an explosion. The sound of the explosion will dominate over the other two, whereas the melody usually will dominate over the sound of the truck. A person who is affected by a smell and a melody will usually turn to the melody, except in special cases, such as imminent danger.

If we leave these extreme cases aside for the moment and focus on cases in which several objects already have been set apart, then the ego will be affected by one of these objects, but not by all, and at first it is not clear which one eventually will begin to affect the ego. Yet as a general rule one can say that the originating affection is functionally codependent on the relative size of the contrast and on the strength of the feeling that a given object, that has already been set apart, evokes.

One should note that in our present reflection we have limited ourselves to cases that occur at the lowest level of analysis. Thus, we did as if the world of the ego was given only in the present in actual impressions; furthermore, we also excluded all apperception and paid no attention to the knowledge that the ego has already acquired in its life in the world; we also excluded all aesthetic and practical interests, etc. Thus, all of this would have to be examined in much greater detail (*APS*, 148–51). Yet instead of pursuing these themes here further, we must now focus our attention on another important issue.

Let us assume that the ego has already become affected by a certain object constituted in consciousness. The question then is one of whether or not there are rules that govern the propagation of these first affections. One of the rules holding here is the one that stipulates that in the associative transfer of the awakening toward *new* data one is bound by homogeneity. For the domain of hyletic data this means that the original association comes about only and exclusively within the field of one given sense, say the visual field.

Now each of these fields, taken as a whole and with respect to certain objects already set apart and also with respect to various groups of such objects, is a unity that is becoming temporally: it comes to be and passes away. And herewith relatively enduring coexistences of groups of objects become constituted to which eventually new members may be added or from which old ones can be eliminated. In this process of becoming, for each field of sense, connected unities of temporal and homogeneous elements as well as connected sequences, such as successions of colors, melodies, etc., become constituted. The question now is: Precisely when is that which we consider to be becoming through concrescence and contrast truly and genuinely present to us affectively? As far as succession is concerned, the answer seems to be simple: only when a melody or a series has sufficiently become constituted. This happens only when the affection has propagated itself as genuine affection by proceeding from one or more of its points or elements. Once the first members have been awakened the rest will be awakened also. Obviously, it is possible that the awakening becomes more and more weak. In that case the series, the melody, etc., may just disappear. Yet it is important to note here that sometimes it will set itself through anyway.

Husserl discusses in this context a number of similar or related phenomena. In the course of his investigation he observes at a certain moment that the phenomena he is discussing here and the reflections made in their regard can also be presented under the "famous" title of *the "unconscious."* For the issue here is about a phenomenology of what is *unconscious,* a phenomenology which tries to show how certain objects of which the ego is not or not fully conscious find their way into the conscious life of the ego by means of processes in which the ego itself is not actively engaged (passive synthesis). Assume that from a hill at night you are looking down into a valley. Let us assume also that in the valley there begins to appear a series of white lights all going in the same direction. These lights immediately become set apart affectively as a unity that "demands" attention. Yet the attraction affectively generated by the series of lights need not necessarily lead me to turn to it attentively. To take another example: sometimes it happens that a symphony sounds, even though it does not become affectively present to the ego, because the ego is preoccupied with something else to the degree that the symphony does not at all come to the fore as such, and thus does not yet actually affect the ego either. Assume now that suddenly an oboe plays a particularly beautiful melody. Already the first tones can set the entire work apart, even though a few minutes before the symphony was completely unrecognized and paid no attention to. Here again there is question of passive synthesis in which association plays the fundamental part (*APS,* 151–58).

In the preceding, Husserl continues, we have spoken about various forms or ways in which the ego can be affected in such a manner that certain forms of unification will then be brought about because of it. But in so doing we assumed that the objective structure of the field of the living present was already given and, thus, that in this field already certain objects, taken as unities of meaning, were given as actually present. And in this way we appealed only to affection and association to explain the passive genesis of higher-order objects that constitute unities. Now the question must be asked of whether affection is presupposed in every form of the constitution of unities of meaning. The answer is manifestly "no." For there are many unities that become constituted without any affection being involved. Husserl mentions here the constitution of the time-form and the form of the local field. The flowing of time in immanence cannot be the result of an achievement of affection. The fusion of its various phases into a unity is an original continuous one that takes place without any affection being involved. Each field of vision, furthermore, becomes also constituted without any affection being implied, even though in the formation of groups of related objects, affection may already begin to play a part.

Husserl admits that perhaps one could interpret the data differently than he has done. Yet he himself was convinced that the achievements of passive genesis at the lowest level do not yet involve affection. As we said, this is so for the time-form, the organization of the hyletic data, as well as for a number of simple objects. But objects are present to consciousness such that consciousness is conscious of them; in that case affectivity must have been somehow involved. Once the field and certain objects in it are given, it is possible that one or more of these objects present there may begin to exert an attraction on the ego such that the ego is led to respond to the attraction, but first grasping and ultimately understanding the objects unified in the process. Affective unities must become constituted in order that a world of objects can become constituted in the ego (*APS*, 159–66).

We must now turn, Husserl continues, to the graduality of the affection. Let us first focus on the living present and let us begin with a simple example. Take a noise that constantly becomes more intensive. When the noise increases, its affectivity and its presence in consciousness begins to increase as well. This implies that the noise begins to attract the ego more and more. Finally the ego turns to the noise. On closer inspection it appears that already before the actual turn toward the noise there is a change in the affection; when the noise increases, at a certain moment it really begins to touch the ego so that the ego begins to notice it; the noise has then as it were entered the anteroom of the ego's consciousness. The ego hears the noise already, but it does not yet focus on it. This hearing it and singling it out from among other noises implies that in the ego there is already a tendency to turn to the noise; it has become "interested" in it. At a certain moment this switches over, in turn, into an explicit turning to the noise so that the original tendency now comes to be fulfilled. We see thus that a modal change has taken place from one in which the noise merely affects the ego to one in which the ego explicitly responds to it.

Next we must consider the case of retention. We know that every datum of the sphere of the living present sinks away into the phenomenal past, and is subject to retentional changes. And in so doing it necessarily ends up ultimately in the affective zero-domain. In this domain, it, too, is not nothing because it always can be called back if need be (*APS*, 163). If we now turn our attention to this affective zero-domain, we can characterize the living present from that point of view with the expression "affective relief." With this expression Husserl tries to describe the living present as a whole. There are high points in it, but also ridges and lower points; these reflect the intensity of the affections and the responses. This analogy also indicates that there are centers where there is more lively action than elsewhere in the same field. Finally, one should realize also that this affective relief manifests itself on the basis of a background of affective inactivity (affective zero). Within the domain of affective activity there are ever new affective awakenings and transfers of affective activity.

The aboriginal source of affection, as taken in this context, lies in the primal impressions, each of which has its greater or smaller affective force. Retention is connected with the primal impressions insofar as retention is the necessary consequence of the ever-changing primal impressions. Whatever at one time was given in original intuition in bodily selfhood, modally changed into something that is evermore past. The constitutive process involved in this case, as in all modifications of consciousness, is a continuous synthesis of identification. In this case one is always conscious of the same thing, but of the thing as sinking back deeper and deeper (*APS*, 168). When an object, given in and through primal impressions, sinks away in the past ever deeper, it gradually loses part of its affective force. At the same time it loses its separateness and identity (*APS*, 166–72).

IV. The Achievement of Affective Awakening and Reproductive Association

Husserl next turns to the opposite of what was shown to be the case in the preceding section. Let us assume that what is given at one time in primal impression has sunk away in the past such that it is no longer distinguishable and is without affective force. The question then is one of how such an object can affectively be awakened and what the function is of the reproductive association that plays a role in the various forms of "recollection."

The process called "awakening" plays an essential part in the living present. Awakening can refer to something conscious as well as to something that has become concealed. Each living present offers ever new, original constitutions of objects, ever new data of perception in ever new extensive arrangements, ultimately in the form of some ordered world. In this process there are thus ever new affective forces which exert their influence by overflowing into the retentionally constituted unities of meaning as well as into the contexts one encounters as coexisting, and so make possible syntheses of fusion, connection, and contrast. Wherever there is a real connection, a genuine formation of unity, there affective force and affective difference are necessarily presupposed.

What is more important, affective achievement can also awaken something that is hidden, something concealed in some implicit intentionality. If an affective force were to be added to it, a force which itself obviously ultimately originates in the impressional sphere, a retention which has very little affective content can become able to give back what now is completely hidden as far as its content of meaning is concerned. Retentions cannot be analyzed; they cannot be unfolded as stable entities. One cannot stop the process: what sinks away in the past will eventually become "unconscious." Yet if in the present there is a content with a strong affective force the process can be held up for quite some time. It is even possible to recall the thing back in an affective act of recollection; yet usually such an object is only held on to affectively in the empty form of representation.

Let us now assume for a moment that a given object has become concealed and that from an explicit it has become an implicit object. If in this case we speak later of awakening, then we thus must imply that what first was implicit can again be made explicit. This process must take the course in which the empty retention in which almost nothing is affective as far as the objective meaning is concerned changes over into another *almost* empty retention in which something that is already more affective is to be found, to a retention in which the objective meaning can be observed and grasped (*APS*, 172–74).

In an effort to clarify how all of this precisely comes about, Husserl first points out that this process in principle is analogous to what takes place in the synthesis of identification that rests on coexistence, even though in this case we speak about elements that are not coexisting, but really succeeding each other. What he has in mind is then explained with examples of a ringing bell or a melody. Let us assume it is noon, and a clock chimes twelve times. When the fifth sound is heard the first is gone, has disappeared in a retentional empty presentation. Yet it is the ever new sound that calls the earlier ones back and fills them with affective force. The whole series appears to take part in the affective force of the actually sounding one. Another example given is that of a melody in which the earlier tones must somehow be present in order for us to be able to understand the actually sounding tone as part of a melody (*APS*, 174, 174–77).

In the preceding section Husserl was concerned mainly with contents that have already sunk *in the domain of the unconscious*, but are still very close to what actual primal impressions offer; thus those contents belong to the *near-sphere.* But what happens when such contents are in the unconscious sphere and have no longer anything at all to do with primal impressions of the present moment? Originally Husserl had assumed that what is actually given flows back into the past in the serial order in which it once actually occurred; primal impression, retention, retention of retention, etc., such that the first element of the chain is still connected with the last one. In 1926 he no longer believed this to be necessary. Whatever has been actual eventually ends up in an empty horizon. He calls it the lasting reservoir. *We are not consciously aware of them;* yet they are all still there. The question of how all of this can again become constitutively actual is again one of association. What will again come to conscious presence is determined by what actually takes place in consciousness. Thus, the motives that are needed to awaken a certain content must be found in the living present. And these motives can be described by the term "interest," but then taken in the broadest sense; some of these motives may very well belong to our emotional life, instincts, emotional impulses, etc.

The most important thing to notice here is that there is a marked and clear distinction to be made between those contents that belong to the near-sphere and those that belong to the far-sphere. In the latter case the awakening is possible insofar as the constituted meaning really is in an implicit manner in our background consciousness, even though in a not-living form and at first without affective force. *The constituted meaning is said to be in the unconscious (Unbewusstein)*. The awakening must in this case, too, be the production (*Herstellung*) of an affective communication and thus the production of an actual synthesis, a content-like connection in the form of an object. What at one time is constituted as an object can enter into a connection with any other object that has been constituted (*APS*, 179). In this case two sets of conditions must be fulfilled: the first condition has to do with the compatibility or contrast of the content; the other is connected with conditions that are related to the consciousness of the contents involved. For in consciousness only those things can be connected which are consciously present in consciousness and can exert an affection.

The awakening of something that belongs to the far-domain is at first still an empty awakening. It is made possible by the fact that in consciousness a certain content is explicitly present which in some sense is similar to the content in the far-domain. The sound of an oboe can awaken the sound of an oboe heard a long time ago. Similarity and contrast are here, too, the important factors. It should be noted that in this passive genesis no object proper becomes constituted. This can take place only in actual recollection. Association and awakening of certain contents of the past constitute only the fundamental part of the act of recollection.

In an effort to explain the achievements of association we spoke first about the primal association between contents that actually already are in consciousness; on this level we were concerned with the original syntheses of unification of manifolds. The second level is formed by the domain of contents that have come about by awakening of empty presentations. We focused here particularly on the awakening of empty presentations, on the awakening of representations of the "zero-sphere." At the third level we find the transition from awakened empty representations to reproductive intuitions, i.e., to recollections.

Husserl states here first that recollections can originate only through awakening of empty presentations. Husserl then shows that an object or content that is actually present in consciousness can awaken an empty presentation from the zero-domain; this preconstituted meaning is the condition for the constitution of the meaning experienced in the past *as if* it were a constitution of a meaning that is now actually present. Husserl mentions here that there are several factors (motives) that may facilitate the actual awakening and the following recollecting. I assume that there also may be factors (such as fear, etc.) that make the awakening and recollection difficult if not simply impossible (*APS*, 182).

V. The Phenomenon of Expectation

Husserl next turns to a new direction in his study of the lawful character of association. It must have come to your attention, Husserl says, that until now I have not yet said one word about protention and expectation, which are such important characteristics of every original experience that takes place in the living present. The reason why expectation was not mentioned earlier is due to the fact that association rests on similarity, equality, and contrast between constituted forms of meaning and objects, and thus is bound to the present and the past. Protention and expectation do not constitute objects but presuppose them.

Yet if we look more carefully, it will become clear that even here protention and expectation have an important part to play, namely everywhere one finds a number of things being coexistent and forming some series or other, but where one element appears to be missing that was nonetheless expected. This same phenomenon occurs wherever in a series of succession one can turn to these phenomena only on the basis of what already has been said about the primal impressions, primordial experience, and recollection. This suggests that with expectation one enters genetically the most original source of the modalization.

Even if we limit ourselves to elementary phenomena it is clear that perception and retention always have to precede protention and expectation. Once a melody has been observed in part, the actually heard notes and the ones that have gone before, but are still present in retention, make us expect certain other notes to follow. We expect that the process that has been going on will continue in a certain way. And what in each case is expected is either a continuation of what has been, or a change in regard to what has been. What motivates us to expect either this or that is manifestly contained in what is and has been; both somehow predelineate what is expected. And what is expected is not the same as what actually is, or is retained in retention, and yet what has been and actually is, is the archetype for what is expected (*APS*, 186).

Husserl now explains in greater detail how whatever happened in the past and is still happening in the actual present always projects ahead expectations of what will appear to consciousness, regardless of whether what has been the case rested on coexistence or succession. If we have observed that upon p a certain q always follows, then given the appearance of p' in the present we expect q' to appear in the future. By developing this more systematically, we can show that in this expectation the root of what we call induction is to be found. One can see in the motivational causality of the process a necessity. If I did experience in the past that r follows q and q follows o, then if in the present I see p' and q' appear, I do with necessity expect r' (*APS*, 188).

It is obvious that my belief built upon expectation can have different degrees and that this belief increases with the number of the instances that occurred *under similar circumstances.* It is clear also that the belief will decrease in degree if there are gaps or irregularities in what appears according to expectation. Husserl explains this first with a series of occurrences which follow each other in succession under certain circumstances. If under circumstance C, I have often experienced the successive sequence a, b, s then under a similar circumstance C', once I see a' appear I expect b' and s'. Should I have seen both a' and b' appear, my belief to expect s' is then obviously doubled. Husserl then explains the same with configurations. Take for example the case of a visual field of the present in which a number of objects is given which appear to me in a certain configuration. If at a later time I perceive a similar field and I see some of the elements of the field suggest a certain configuration, then my belief in the appearance of the same configuration is motivated, because I expect that what formerly appeared to belong together will now, too, belong together (*APS*, 191).

Conclusion

If we compare what Husserl has to say about association with the "classical" treatises on association of either Aristotle or Hume, or even with that of Kant to whose views Husserl's own ideas in one respect come quite close, then it is evident that Husserl has made a very important contribution to our understanding of the genuine meaning and function of association. This is due not so much because of the new categories, concepts, or ideas Husserl has introduced, nor because he proposed in the process new principles and "laws" or rules, even though in both areas Husserl did indeed make a significant contribution also, but most of all because he approached the complex issue from a much broader perspective than any other author of the past had ever done. Husserl researched the issue with a completely new, phenomenological method that lets one see that association is not some mysterious process, but rather a whole set of processes, each of which develops according to its own rules that can be brought to light and understood.

Hume's doctrine of the association of ideas is an essential part of his doctrine of man's understanding, and the latter is intrinsically skeptical. Hume, himself, was aware of this and explicitly admits it.[12] Kant thought that the root of this skepticism, which in his view was to be overcome by transcendental philosophy, is to be found in the impossibility of any effort to solve basic philosophical (metaphysical) issues with the help of a "certain physiology" of the human understanding.[13] Later Husserl would make a similar claim and state that the root of Hume's skepticism is to be found in his psychologism. Yet, at the same time Husserl praises Hume for having shaken the dogmatic objectivism of Descartes and his rationalist successors to its foundations.[14] Although Husserl himself gives the doctrine of association an important place in his transcendental phenomenology, it is obvious that in his case there is not the slightest danger of skepticism in view of the fact that the reflections on passive genesis in genetic phenomenology are to be taken up in critical reflections on the constitution of all meaning by transcendental subjectivity and transcendental intersubjectivity.

On several occasions Husserl stated that he was fully aware of the limitations of his research in this area. At the end of his reflections on association he admits that much work is still to be done here. On other occasions he speaks of having considered something that is really no more than an abstraction. In many cases many important aspects and details are completely passed by in order to keep the analyses within manageable proportions. And these limitations may even have been much more severe than Husserl himself may have realized. Husserl was in his analyses of passive synthesis predominantly concerned with perceptual problems and more generally with cognitive problems in which perception still plays an important part. It seems to me that these analyses could very well become even much more important if they could be expanded so as to include forms of association that go far beyond the "association of ideas." When I am in a state of excitement, it is possible that a similar excitement may come to mind; the same is true for all emotions and feelings. It is also possible to include in the field of research much more complex phenomena. Assume that in playing a piano concerto you make an error; it is possible that this error brings another similar error to mind with all the embarrassment it brought with it; it is even possible that the earlier event was somehow "causally" related to the error you just made. In these and numerous other cases one phenomenon brings another phenomenon to mind in ways in which the conscious ego is not actively involved. They, too, are instances of association.

Gurwitsch has shown that many of Husserl's ideas about perceptual phenomena can be related to new insights brought to light first by Gestalt psychology, and then developed further from a phenomenological point of view. Merleau-Ponty has employed some of Husserl's insights in *Phenomenology of Perception* where he discusses issues first raised by Gestalt psychology. Inspired by the ideas of the Gestaltists, Merleau-Ponty developed his theory concerning the human body as subject of meaning and showed how the body can be a legitimate source of meaning at a level at which the conscious ego is not yet actively involved. To give just one example: when Merleau-Ponty critically discusses claims made by Gestalt psychologists he often speaks about processes that imply forms of association in which the "coming to mind" really is the result of the actions of a subject, but a subject that is not yet conscious and free. When I see in an ambiguous drawing a vase because of its similarity with a vase I have once seen before then I consciously see the vase; yet the subject that made it possible for me to see the vase and captured it before I could consciously see it is the body which with its eyes "incidentally" hit upon these lines in the drawing. At any rate, here is another large domain in which one encounters forms of association, even though one cannot speak of "association of ideas."

Finally, when Husserl introduces the notion of the "unconscious," not by postulating it, but by showing how it arises in concrete analyses, then the unconscious is in these cases no more than the domain of ideas and representations which now have become part of my past and of which at this moment I am not consciously aware. It is clear that if the field of research were to be enlarged in the manner indicated above, it would be possible to come to a conception of the unconscious that would be much richer. It may then perhaps be possible to explain the influence of the "unconscious" on conscious phenomena in a way in which every claim made can indeed be brought back to phenomena we all know and can analyze. But even if one were to follow this route, it would still be necessary to transcend Husserl's entire framework of meaning and engage in reflection of the kind Merleau-Ponty has indicated in his research about the body as subject as well as Heidegger's investigations concerning the human body as well as some neuroses.[15] Yet this is an issue for another essay.[16]

5

On Derrida's Reading of Husserl

J. N. Mohanty

Derrida is a master reader, and has heightened our critical awareness of reading a text. He has also been seriously concerned with Husserl's philosophy, and has produced some fine readings as well as interpretive commentaries (and deep critiques) of Husserl's texts. But has he *read* Husserl correctly? Some of his criticisms of Husserl, as is unavoidable, presuppose the validity of his reading. It is therefore imperative that we look carefully at the latter. Such a project may require that one also keeps in mind any general theory of reading that Derrida may have. But I will not, for the purposes of this lecture, undertake to expound and critique that theory, and will prefer to go directly to Derrida in relation to Husserl's texts. I will not also be directly concerned with Derrida's various criticisms and his deconstruction of Husserl; however, to the extent such criticisms and deconstruction rest on his understanding of Husserl, they would unavoidably be affected by our evaluation of that understanding. Although Derrida originally develops some of his own philosophical concepts in the context of his reading and critique of Husserl, they are not dependent on that reading and that critique—so that even if Derrida's understanding of Husserl is found to be seriously flawed, it would by no means follow that his own philosophy must therefore be rejected. But if his deconstruction of Husserl fails, then one may be led to suspect whether or not all such deconstructions rest upon a reading (deliberately or not) made to suit those deconstructive projects. But if deconstruction is a mode of reading that suspicion may be unfounded, and if deconstruction seems to rest upon a reading made to serve that purpose, that is precisely as it should be. For in that case, there would not be two things—a reading and then deconstruction—but one move: namely, a deconstructive reading, which may then be *judged* as a reading. All these questions will be untouched in this essay.

Let me recall, however, that Derrida often speaks of, in his context of reading Husserl, a "reading that can be neither simple commentary nor simple interpretation."[1] As we all know, that is more often than not the case with *all* reading, so that the fact that one is always staking a middle ground need not bother us, for we just cannot do anything else.

I

Before Derrida came on the scene, there had already developed a distinctive line of Husserl interpretation in Belgium and France by men such as G. Berger, J. P. Sartre, M. Merleau-Ponty, A. DeWaehlens, E. Levinas, and P. Ricoeur. In all these, leaving Berger aside (who wrote the first major essay on Husserl in French, and who was more inclined toward a Cartesian than an existential reading), the influence of Heidegger was decisive in the formation of the picture, in varying degrees and forms, of an existential Husserl. Consequently, certain general features allow themselves to stand out: a rejection of "transcendental reduction," an underplaying of Husserl's *Logical Investigations,* an injection of the hermeneutic standpoint into the reading and critique of Husserl, critique of Husserl's so-called "theoretical" prejudice, (Merleau-Ponty's) priority of "operative" intentionalities over the so-called act-intentionalities; Levinas's critique of Husserl's prejudice in favor of the theoretical; Ricoeur's prioritization of the will and reading of intentionality as being basically voluntaristic, and recognition of the centrality of history (à la Hegel and Marx) and historicity (à la Heidegger) to the Husserlian doctrine of constitution. In this reading and critique of Husserl, Hegel and Marx, as seen through Heidegger, and as expounded by Kojève and Hyppolite, played a dominant role. Nevertheless, i.e., despite these mediations, the ideas of subjectivity, intentionality, meaning-constitution, and "lived time" retained their unquestionably Husserlian ancestry. The result became what may be called an "anthropological reading" of Husserl.

This peculiar French reading stood in sharp contrast to the two schools of German Husserlians: the earlier "realist" phenomenologists who, inspired by Husserl's Göttingen program of eidetic research, retain the essentialism and correlative intuitionism of Husserl's so-called "realistic" period: and the transcendentalists, who took the alleged "idealistic turn" of Husserl, according to which all meanings, including the meaning of the world and of others are constituted within the life of the transcendental ego.

There is also a common point of view, taken over unquestioningly by a successive generation of Husserl scholars, which divides Husserl's thinking career into several well demarcated phases marked by radical breaks and conversions (allegedly in response to external challenges). Briefly put, the account runs like this: as a student of Brentano, Husserl began as a "psychologistic" philosopher of mathematics; Frege's highly critical review of his first published work, *Philosophie der Arithmetik*, led Husserl to abandon that psychologism in favor of an objectivistic and Platonist theory of essences and meanings (and a concept of "pure logic"); the Neo-Kantian influences of Paul Natorp led to a "reversal" of this realistic position into an idealism (a return to the earlier psychologism with the addendum that now he was speaking of transcendental subjectivity, not the maligned psychological) of a sort (now called transcendental-phenomenological idealism); and, finally (again, allegedly, as a response to the challenge of the growing influence of Heidegger's thought), this transcendental idealism was abandoned in favor of a return to the thesis of the primacy of the *Lebenswelt*, the lived intersubjective world.

I do not wish to give reasons, in this essay, why I consider this account of the development of Husserl's thought—this story about ruptures and reversals—mistaken.

But it is against the background of this varied tradition of Husserl scholarship—to which may be added the linguistic and analytic Husserl interpretation pursued in this country by such philosophers as Føllesdal and his students, Jakko Hintikka, and this author—that I want to place Derrida's reading of Husserl, so that we can appreciate the novelty as well as the frailty of that attempt.

II

Derrida's reading of Husserl, when considered in the light of the above summary account of the traditions of Husserl scholarship, is remarkably daring. Insisting as he does, and rightly in my view, on the continuity of Husserl's thought (and so, by implication rejecting the above-sketched story of the development of Husserl's thought), Derrida begins by focusing first on Husserl's last major essay ("The Origin of Geometry") and on the opening sections of his first *Logical Investigations* (separated by a period of thirty six years). By taking the *Logical Investigations* seriously, as being central to Husserl's thought, such that the *Ideas* not only does not contradict the *Investigations* but "continuously clarifies it,"[2] Derrida stands apart from the tradition of Husserl scholarship formed in France. (In this judgment, I will make an exception in the case of Ricoeur who, in developing his account of the relation between phenomenology and hermeneutics, always returns to the "First Logical Investigation.") Neither is Derrida, unlike his French predecessors, a critic of Husserl's transcendental move. On the contrary, in an important sense, he carried Husserl's transcendental reduction to its *supposedly* logical consequence.[3] Furthermore, his interest in the *Logical Investigations* is not confined to the theory of meaning; he takes Husserl's idea of a "pure logical grammar" most seriously, and claims to free it from the constraints Husserl supposedly placed on it.[4]

Since he believes in the continuity of Husserl's thought, he may be said to read—as Barry Smith, a dear friend, complained of me—the earlier work of Husserl in the light of the later. In other words, he reads the very opening paragraphs of the "First Investigation" as containing a phenomenological reduction (whereas not until 1905 did Husserl on his own account discover the reduction recorded in the so-called Seefelder manuscripts).

Convinced though he was of the inseparability of Husserl's early philosophy of meaning from the transcendental problematic,[5] and though he may be regarded in one way as having radicalized Husserl's reductions, he was not yet quite free from the influence of Merleau-Ponty's thesis that a complete reduction is not possible. Derrida writes: "As soon as it is admitted that autoaffection is the condition for self-presence, no pure transcendental reduction is possible," and adds: "But it was necessary to pass through the transcendental reduction in order to grasp [this]."[6]

But just as the thesis of continuity in Husserl's case saves us from the dangers of positing imagined ruptures (neglecting the lessons to be drawn from the mass of manuscripts left behind and now being made available), that thesis should be correctly understood, for otherwise in finding the latter thesis in the earlier works one misses the point that continuity does not mean absence of any new discoveries and certainly not the possibility of *deepening* of the problems and solutions as are to be found in the earlier works.[7]

In another respect, Derrida remains within the tradition by modifying the primacy of the theoretical, and construes—not unlike Ricoeur—intentionality as being in essence voluntaristic,[8] Husserl's *Bedeutung* as "wanting to say" (*vouloir-dire*),[9] and transcendental phenomenology as "transcendental voluntarism."[10]

However, what is most important is that Derrida unequivocally rejects the anthropological reading of Husserl (as also of the other two: Hegel and Heidegger, espoused by Kojève). Wasn't the critique of anthropologism one of the initial motives of Husserl's thinking?[11] This critique concerns not only empirical anthropologism, but also transcendental anthropologism. The transcendental subjectivity of Husserl is not what the French existential phenomenologists called "human reality." Derrida rejects a similar anthropological reading, in postwar France, of Heidegger's analytic of *Dasein.* Neither Husserl nor Heidegger was an anthropologistic thinker, although Husserl, on Derrida's view, "precipitously interpreted *Sein und Zeit* as an anthropologistic deviation from transcendental phenomenology."[12] Since I am not, in this lecture, concerned with Derrida's reading of Heidegger, I will not comment on this last issue. But I will suggest that one good place we should look at, in order to think if Heidegger's thinking in *Sein and Zeit* was not a sort of anthropologism as Husserl had complained, is the "correspondence" between the two in connection with Husserl's article on phenomenology for the *Encyclopedia Britannica.*[13]

III

After these general remarks, I will focus, in this essay, on Derrida's interpretations of some of the fundamental Husserlian concepts. These are: intentionality, ideality, expression and meaning, and time.

First, as to intentionality: Husserl's position regarding intentionality, as developed in the *Investigations* and the *Ideas* amounts to the following structure: Ego → hyle + noetic act → noema → object. For Derrida's general remarks on intentionality, I will depend on his *Limited Inc* as well as on *Speech and Phenomena.* It is not true that Derrida rejects intentionality; what he rejects is the priority, the universal legislative power, of intentionality. This last claim is what he questions, always drawing upon Husserlian resources. Doesn't Husserl say that the intentional directedness of an act does not logically entail that the object toward which it is directed must be a real entity? "It makes no difference whether the object exists or is fictitious or even impossible."[14] At the same time, the telos of intentionality—construed voluntaristically—is total "fulfillment, realization and actualization." But such total fulfillment is, in no case, possible—as Husserl himself well recognizes. Thus, by its very nature, intentionality is doomed to failure, and so strives in vain to actualize itself. There is necessarily a *presumption* that the intention will be fulfilled, but this is no more than a presumption. Even the very possibility of frustration, of no fulfillment—to take a weaker claim—belongs *structurally* to the essence of intentionality. Derrida calls it "possibility qua necessity."[15] Thus, starting with Husserl, Derrida argues, one can see that Husserl both recognizes this presumptive character of the claim to fulfillment, and yet is still committed to the possibility of fulfillment. And yet, just as Merleau-Ponty had said that "the absolute positing of a single object is the death of consciousness,"[16] so Derrida asks: Isn't the pure realization of self-presence, the presence of a fulfilled and completely actualized intention, itself also death?[17]

The other aspect of intentionality is the noema or the ideal meaning, which is an ideal object. A large part of Derrida's thinking about Husserl concerns the constitution of an ideal object. Ideality, so says Derrida, drawing upon Husserl, is "the correlate of a possibility of indefinite repetition."[18] But, again, at this point Husserl's texts exhibit a paradoxical feature. On the one hand, ideality is constituted by pure repetition, and yet, on the other, the ideal object is present, is intuited, is given, in the living present.[19] Infinite repeatability implies endless postponement, deferral. Constitution of meaning, of ideality, is never complete. Note that Derrida is not saying that constitution of new meanings is always going on, he is rather saying that no ideality ever gets constituted, for that would involve an endless process of repetition. So much is a part of his reading of Husserl, but Derrida himself goes beyond this, and argues that iteration, repetition involves difference (besides identity), *the same* is identified in and through differences, so that each constituted identity is split from within by differences.

Let us proceed further. Husserl's intentional act, belonging to an ego, perishes, but the meaning, the ideal noema, remains. Thus, both the subject and the object may be absent without affecting the ideality of the meaning (and also of the text, i.e., the linguistic ideality). If that is so, then like the possible absence of the object, also the possible death of the subject, "structurally" and necessarily, belongs to the nature of the ideal object. To quote Derrida, "the purportedly ideal structure must necessarily be such that his corruption will be 'always possible.' "[20]

There is another aspect of the Husserlian theory of intentionality which Derrida takes most seriously: this is the thesis that every intentionality has a horizonal character, which means that all intending is in a given context. The horizon consists of determinate features and further determinable features, anticipated in generalities more or less emptily, to be filled in as one progresses in one's explorations. But the context, once recognized (as it was by Husserl), cannot be kept within limits. It is never exhaustively determinable, it "is always, and always has been, a work *within* the plan and not only around it."[21] It is also always "tranformative-tranformable, exportative-exportable."[22] As a matter of fact, Derrida says that one of the definitions of "deconstruction" is the "effort to take the limitless context into account; and thus to an incessant movement of recontextualization."[23] Given such possibilities of "recontextualization," such "limitlessness" of context, identity, identification, and total idealization are not possible: an "essential non-totalization" holds good.

This leads me back to Derrida's early concern with Husserl's concept of sign.

Husserl's "First Logical Investigation" begins with a distinction between two kinds of signs: signs which are merely indications, and those which are expressions of meaning. Every sign however is a sign for something: this is its generic feature which, Derrida complains, Husserl never gives. Every sign—no matter if it is an indicator or an expression—is a sign for something: that indeed is its generic feature. A generic feature is always to be found along with specific features. Being a sign for something can be either in the mode of an indication (in which case, in the first place, there is a lack of insight into the relation between the sign and the signified, the relation being one of "motivation" bred by association, and, in the second place, the sign as an *existent* entity motivates belief in the *existence* of the signified) or in the mode of an expression (in which case what is *expressed* is a *sense*, or a thought). After drawing this distinction, Husserl distinguishes between *not* two kinds of expressions, but two roles that expressions may play—or rather two contexts in which they may function—i.e., in monologue and in dialogue. This change of function has nothing to do with whatever makes an expression an expression. What Husserl does is a kind of eidetic variation, in order to bring out what is invariant in both contexts. What is invariant is expression of a *sense*—which constitutes the essence of an expression qua expression. Another function which an expression performs when uttered by a speaker in a communicative situation is what Husserl calls "intimation" (*Kundgebung*). The speaker's utterance intimates to the hearer what mental experiences the speaker is having (believing, doubting, questioning, ordering, etc.). Clearly, in monologue, the speaker and the hearer being the same, this intimation is redundant. Moreover, while in communication an actual production of the physical word (in speech or in writing) is needed, in monologue the words are merely imagined and not perceived as existent. What we have is an "imaginative production of the word." But that the word does not actually exist, but is only imagined (not perceived), does not interest us. Hence, the monologue is a case of pure expression, for the function of expression is not here mixed up, contaminated, polluted by the other function of intimation.

Derrida finds here several decisive steps—and these findings are intertwined with a way of reading Husserl. Note that the question is not whether Husserl's emphasis on monologue or soliloquy in order to let the essence of expressions show itself is a step in the right direction or not. The question rather is: Why did Husserl take this step, to what purpose and how does this questionable step hang together with his later moves, such as epoché and transcendental phenomenology?

The thesis of the priority of writing over speaking is extended by Derrida to his work on Husserl's 1936 essay on the origin of geometry.[24] Note that Husserl already speaks of "the origin of geometry" in *Philosophie der Arithmetik* (p. 241 fn). Geometry as an ideal structure is constituted not alone by the inner acts of thinking by the geometrician, by his creative mental activities, but by language, through which—as Husserl writes—"it receives, so to speak, its linguistic living body [*Sprachleib*]."[25] For what Husserl there calls "the *persisting existence*" of the "ideal objects," what is needed is *written documentation* which makes communication possible "without immediate or mediate personal address."[26] "[W]riting-down effects a transformation of the original mode of being of the meaning-structure."[27] Derrida finds here a confirmation of his thesis that the constitution of idealities needs—contrary to the claim of transcendental phenomenology—"written texts," "documentation," i.e., recording in sensible, empirical, material signs. At the same time, Husserl recognizes the importance of history—of a new sort of history—for phenomenology: the history of the constitution of ideal objects, of meanings, which constitute a tradition. Derrida sees in this new concept of history a departure from the "historicist empiricism" of Dilthey (does he understand Dilthey correctly at this point?), and understands Husserl as avoiding "the philosophical nonsense of . . . empiricism." But, as in the case of "sign" (where he asks: what is the meaning of "sign in general"?), so also here he asks: What is the "*unitary ground*" which makes the distinction between factual history and intentional history possible? (as he will also ask later: What is the *unitary meaning* of "life" which makes the distinction between empirical life and transcendental life possible?). Thus, as always, Derrida sees Husserl's phenomenology "stretched between the finitizing consciousness of its principle (i.e., evidence as the immediate presence of the thing itself 'in person' and *now*) and the *infinitizing* consciousness of its final *institution*, the goal being indefinitely postponed, deferred in its content but always evident in its regulative value."[28]

Some Critical Remarks

Who is here the metaphysician? Husserl or Derrida? Without answering this question, let me make a series of remarks touching upon the points

Derrida raises in course of his reading of Husserl. Again, let me repeat: Derrida may be right in his criticisms of Husserl's views, but for me the question is: Does he rightly interpret Husserl?

1. First, as to sign in general: "indication" (or indicating, *Anzeichen*) is *not*, for Husserl, genus of "expression."[29] Nor is indication a coordinate species (along with "expression") coming under the genus "sign": for, if it were so, then an expression could not also function as an indication (in communicative speech). The unity of "sign" (as comprehending indications and expressions) is not a generic unity. The unitary meaning of "sign" is "to stand for something." But the sense in which an indicative sign stands for something and the sense in which an expressive sign stands for something are radically different senses of "standing for." The common notion of "standing for" is rather an analogical notion, not a generic one. To say, as Derrida does, that Husserl does not tell us what sign in general is, is to *presuppose* mistakenly that, on Husserl's view, "sign in general" is a generic notion.

2. Husserl's consideration of monologue, before determining the essence of expressions, is *misleading* inasmuch as expressions are expressions insofar as they express publicly sharable ideas—but *not private* meanings. It is *not* the case that monological expressions alone are *pure* expressions and that expressions functioning in dialogue are impure. The case of monologue only serves to bring into operation an eidetic variation, bringing to light the eidetic fact that expressions, to be expressions, must *express* meanings—no matter whether they also serve as indications or not. If triangles, in order to be triangles, need not be right angled, or be of any specific dimension, that does not entail that any specific triangle, for example, a right-angled triangle is not a pure triangle. It is also not true, as Derrida supposes, that with the transition to monological speech Husserl reduces empirical worldly existence,[30] that we have Husserl's transcendental reduction already in operation, that the existence of the world is not implied or that the imagined world is a noema. All of these are based on a misreading of Husserl's text. The only function that drops—on Husserl's view—out of operation is *Kundgebung* or intimation of the speaker's mental states to the auditor. The function of referring to the world remains, as does also the mundaneity of the act of inner speaking or imagining (which just because it is not publicly heard or seen does not become transcendental). The ideal meaning, on Husserl's theory, is the correlate also of the empirical consciousness, not only of the transcendentally reduced one.

3. What then about the alleged priority of writing over speech? On Husserl's own view, the production of ideal meanings does not require inscriptions, but the constitution of a science *as a tradition* to be inherited by

succeeding generations requires the production of written texts. Derrida need not have found this recognition in as late a text as "The Origin of Geometry." Already, in the early *Philosophie der Arithmetik*, Husserl writes:

> Das es eine wichtige Aufgabe der Wissenschaft wäre, sich mit scheinbar so untergeordneten Dinge zu beschäftigen, als es die Wahl sinnlicher Zeichen ist, dürfte im ersten Augenblicke Bedenken erregen; . . . wir werden sogleich sehen, wie der Unterschied zwischen Wort und Schrift-Zeichen für die Arithmetik so wesentlich ist, dass eine notwendige Beschränkung auf die ersteren eine erheblichere Entwicklung der Arithmetik zur Unmöglichkeit gemacht hätte.[31]

Husserl continues to say that it is even important whether one writes with pen and ink on paper or on a dusty tablet with a stick—which can influence the progress of arithmetical method. Then he asks, should not this be a part of the logical method?

I will not here ask if in holding this view Husserl as well as Derrida is right, but Derrida, to my mind, confirms Husserl's own early view, and not one against him.

4. One of Derrida's more powerful, and often repeated, criticisms of Husserl, which makes use of certain reading of the texts, concerns the relation between ideality (of meanings, noemata, and of essences) and repeatability. Husserl certainly held that the ideal entity is repeatable, it is not a unique occurrence—which would make it real (and, so, temporal). However, Derrida misleadingly reads Husserl's position to be that ideality is *constituted* by repeatability, by the "and so on endlessly" ("*immer weiter*") of the process of repetition. From this reading, it becomes for him an easy step to argue that this endless repetition both (1) endlessly postpones (defers) the constitution of idealities and (2) introduces a difference into the texture of an ideal entity's very being (for every repetition is different from every other). I must point out that Husserl's view regarding the constitution of idealities is, however, quite different. In order to bring that out briefly, I must distinguish between constitution of physical objects and constitution of idealities. A physical object—more accurately, the sense "physical object"—is constituted by the possibility of perceiving (visual and tactual, at the least) the same object from different perspectives. This possibility is never exhausted, as for Husserl the sense "physical object" has a presumptive character about it. Derrida, unfortunately, reads Husserl's texts about ideality in the same manner. However, an ideality is constituted not by an endless series of actual and possible repetitions, but by and in the very act in which it is grasped by itself. If the ideality is a meaning, it is constituted by the act of intending/grasping

it; if it is an essence, it is constituted by this act of eidetic intuition resulting from the process of eidetic variation. An ideal entity is repeatable. Repeatability is a mark of ideality, not what makes it ideal. And what is more important—and Derrida misses the point altogether—is that we should *not* construe "repeatability" *nominalistically* or extensionally as a never-ending succession of particular acts of reiteration,[32] but *eidetically* as *essential possibility* of iteration. The nominalistically construed series cannot be brought to an end, but the *essential possibility* of iteration is grasped in one single act of iteration *of the same*. It is a nominalistically conceived idea of repeatability as an endless succession of particular acts of repetition which sustains Derrida's thesis that constitution is bound to be perpetually "deferred." For Husserl, there is then no such deferral.

If, however, "repeatability" is construed as "imaginability of repetition," then Derrida's argument seems to rely upon the fact that imagination refers to perception. Thus he writes: "[Imagination] retains a primary reference to a primordial presentation, that is, to a perception and positing of existence, to a belief in general."[33] This argument again is misleading, and certainly does not prove what it is meant to.

5. These above remarks lead to two of Derrida's most powerful interpretation-cum-critiques of Husserl. One concerns Husserl's privileging of "presence," the other frees intentionality from both the subject and the presence of the object. In each case, it is difficult to separate Derrida's reading of Husserl from his critique of Husserl. Taken as a reading, the first one is more correct, the second simply is off the mark. It is undoubtedly true that in spite of his "opening up" the present, the now, to the just elapsed past (by retention) and the just-about-to-come future (by protention) the *now* remains the center of the retention-protention structure, so that even if no object is merely now, my awareness, my flowing experience, is always passing through, and at any point of time, is a now phase. If Heidegger's analysis of time privileged the future, Husserl's privileged the present—even if the present is a "spacious present." Privileging the present, however, need not imply either adequacy or apodicticity of what is given. Thus, even if Husserl considerably modified his earlier claims to adequate and apodictic cognition, the primacy of the present (although surrounded by a horizon of absences, even of an absence, the just past, that is present to retention) remains. *In this sense,* he is logocentric, but whether logocentrism is a disease, a failure, an illusion to be gotten rid of or a philosophical strength, a virtue, an insight to be preserved, has to be decided on other independent grounds. My own preference is for the latter alternative.

6. The misconstrual of "repeatability" that I have pointed out has its counterpart in a misconstrual of Husserl's ideal of "genesis." Derrida

rightly emphasized, even in his first work (on Husserl) only now published, that the idea of "genesis" is central to Husserl's thinking. But Husserl's own understanding of *genesis* must be read *together with* his structuralist-essentialist position, and not in opposition to it. Derrida recognizes that even in his structuralist phase, Husserl does not reject all genesis but only that which is causal and naturalistic.[34] Distinguishing between three directions Husserl's later genetic phenomenology takes—the logical (in *Experience and Judgement* and *Formal and Transcendental Logic*), the egological (in *Cartesian Meditations*), and the historical-teleological (in the *Crisis*)—Derrida follows the last of these as leading to a metaphysics of history, so that he could conclude that the result of phenomenology is metaphysics. In view of this *critique*—but not refutation—of Husserl, I will, briefly though for this essay, take a look at Husserl's conceptions of history and genetic phenomenology.

Although Husserl did sometimes speak about factual history or the history of the historians, and *always* rejected historicism (insofar as "historicism" is understood in terms of factual history), what he develops in the *Crisis* is not a theory of *that* history, nor does he ever come to accept the historicism he had earlier rejected, notably in the *Logos* essay.[35] The history he now begins to make room for is (1) intentional history understood as sedimentation of meanings; (2) this genesis can be retrieved not in terms of factual historical research,[36] but rather within the reflecting ego's own "reduced" mental life (as Husserl does in the case of the genesis of modern physics); (3) this history requires, not a Heracleitean conception of flux, but a theory of identity of meanings so that the constitut*ed* meanings are again and again available; (4) it is also inseparable from the inner time-consciousness of the ego in communion with other egos, so that the intentional history is the history of a community. Husserl's history then is not even a mundane history of ideas; it is rather a transcendental history of subjectivity, insofar as this subjectivity is already communal. As Husserl writes in the *Crisis*, it is "nichts anderes als die lebendige Bewegung des Miteinander und Ineinander von ursprünglicher Sinnbildung und Sinnsedimentierung."[37] This historical process is teleologically directed toward rationality, toward *Vernunft*. (The "inner history," Husserl writes, "necessarily leads further to the already explained highest question regarding a universal teleology of reason."[38]) It is this last thesis which is so much likely to be misunderstood. We cannot correctly interpret Husserl at this point unless and until we correctly understand what he means by "reason," and what sort of "teleology" he wants to maintain.

Husserl's idea of *Vernunft*, despite his use of words such as "absolute," has *nothing* to do with a metaphysical idea of *Vernunft* as an absolute reality which stands behind, and expresses itself in and through history and nature. For Husserl, the idea of *Vernunft* is connected with (1) absolutely grounded truth-in-itself; (2) the idea of the thing that is presented as being self-given in adequate and apodictic evidence appropriate to the sense of that thing; and (3) the idea of reason as belonging to the essence of a human person. From (2) it follows that *Vernunft*, for Husserl, should not be identified with intellect; a thing may be self-given in sensory experience, through bodily kinaesthetic experiences and through passive synthesis. In any case, the idea of adequate and apodictic self-giveness remains an infinite idea. It is such rational knowledge, and the consequent rational ethical self-responsibility which is the telos of "intentional history."

Derrida rightly emphasizes that Husserl is concerned not with the external history of facts, but with the *inner* history,[39] that he reduces empirical history to this "pure" history,[40] that all historicism, according to Husserl, remains at the level of factual history, that the universal a priori of history is the "inner historicity" of the ego in its intersubjectivity,[41] and that this historicity—which is the same as the universal and essential structure of transcendental subjectivity—is itself *Vernunft* or reason, so that "reason" should not be construed as a human faculty.[42]

To show the nature of Derrida's interpretation of Husserl's understanding of "history" and "historicity," let me recall another, more recent, commentator's interpretation of the same. Elisabeth Ströker insists[43] that the question of transcendental-phenomenological genesis is not a genuinely historical question, that Husserl's concern is not *when* the constitutive achievement in question came about, but *how*, that Husserl had not found a point of access to genuine history, that Husserl's sense-history was history so-to-speak, which explains why Husserl speaks of "history" always in quotation marks, and that although Husserl carried out much of his investigation pertaining to history in close connection with the analysis of time, he never attended to the specific structure of historical time.[44] Husserl inquired into depth-problems quite unknown to ordinary history[45]—working back through the manifold *layers* of sense formations.[46] This inner history, according to Ströker, is "in principle nothing but intentional analysis pursued to the point of complete exhaustion of its methodological possibilities as intentional history."[47]

In this last quotation, Ströker points to the limits of phenomenology. Not unlike her, Derrida also sees in Husserl's late thinking an attempt to radicalize phenomenology up to a point where phenomenology encounters its own limit. This happens when eidetic phenomenology returns to come to terms with a transcendental *fact* (as distinguished from the transcendent, constitut*ed* fact),[48] where the distinction between outer and inner is obliterated, where the finiteness of phenomenological evidence yields room to the infinity of a Kantian Idea, i.e., the idea of endless determinability of Being. These are all perfectly sound readings of Husserl, and have been noted by many writers on Husserl not particularly interested in Derridean deconstruction.

If Husserl's late writings exhibit metaphysical pronouncements, that is not because phenomenology turns—by an internal negation—into metaphysics. It is because Husserl always recognized that phenomenology was not coextensive with philosophy and that phenomenology left room for metaphysics, by which he meant not a concern with "naive and inconsistent ideas of things in themselves," but all concern with contingencies of the facticity of life and death and questions about the "meaning" of history.[49] It has been mistakenly maintained that Husserl's constitutional analysis looks for an apodictic grounding of the world. On the contrary, the constituting transcendental subjectivity is not apodictic in any meaningful sense. The *fact* of constituting subjectivity, the absolute Being, the *Urfaktum*, is possibly a metaphysical concept, but marks a point where the metaphysics is transcendental-phenomenological.

Concluding Remarks

Derrida's understanding of Husserl, as we find it in his Introduction to "The Origin of Geometry" is in my view as "Husserlian" as that of any other. One does not expect all interpreters of a philosopher—especially of a philosopher as complex as Husserl—to agree in their interpretations. Derrida's is a viable interpretation, faithful to the texts, aware of the enormous complexities of Husserl's thinking, and willing to understand rather than to refute. However, as the "deconstructive" project grows and takes over, and clichés such as "logocentrism" and "metaphysics of presence" dominate the critique, the remarks on Husserl tend to lose that original faithfulness. In no case, however, should Derrida be read as having attempted a refutation of Husserl. For American Derrideans who have unthinkingly taken over those clichés, and have too hastily taken Derrida to be refuting (or, better still "deconstructing") Husserl, a text from Derrida, dating from 1985, is worth quoting. The text occurs in the context of a commentary on Apel. Derrida refers to his own work as "ein wirkungsvolles und vielleicht unbeendbares Hindurchgehen durch die transzendentale Phänomenologie Husserls."[50] Rejecting the charge that he is a relativist or historicist, Derrida continues: "Was mich betrift, so habe ich zu sehr meine Muttermilch an der Brust der transzendentalen

Phänomenologie eingesogen, die zunächst eine rigorose Kritik des Relativismus, des Psychologismus, des Empirismus, des Skeptizismus und des Historisismus war, um gegen diese Quasi-Dämonen nicht gefreit zu sein." He goes on to say that his deconstruction of Husserl "ist von mir immer nicht der Ermahnung versehen worden, die transzendentale Dimension eines Denkens der Spur zu berücksichtigen."[51]

6

Husserl's Critique of Relativism

David Detmer

Many contemporary thinkers have abandoned "truth" entirely, viewing it as an outmoded, discredited, perhaps even dangerous concept. Others, while retaining the notion of truth, have insisted upon understanding it in a radically subjectivist or relativist sense, far removed from the robust sense of truth as something "hard" and objective.[1]

In this respect, at least, our *fin de siècle* "postmodern" condition bears a remarkable similarity to the intellectual climate confronting Husserl at the dawn of this century, when he published his *Logical Investigations.* For Husserl evidently found that climate to be so pervaded by various forms of relativism, subjectivism, and skepticism as to warrant his decision to precede the presentation of his many constructive and original findings in the area of logic with a lengthy "Prolegomena," largely devoted to the refutation of such deflationary epistemologies—epistemologies the widespread acceptance of which would tend to preclude at the outset a serious appreciation of the fruits of his enormous labors.[2]

While a glance at the current intellectual scene would tend to suggest that Husserl's arguments against relativism have failed to find favor, it does not follow, needless to say, that they deserve such a fate. In fact, it may very well be that many contemporary thinkers, indeed, even amongst the ranks of philosophers, are unfamiliar with Husserl's arguments. For one thing, while the cultural split between the predominantly English speaking "analytical" philosophers, on the one hand, and those more at home in the European "continental" tradition, on the other, is nowhere near as severe as it was just a few decades ago, it remains true that a good many members of the former camp have no substantial acquaintance with the details of Husserl's thought. Furthermore, it seems to be the case even within the continental tradition that its more recent recruits tend to see no need to consult Husserl firsthand, taking it for granted that he is a hopelessly old-fashioned "logocentric" rationalist who has been decisively refuted, or better, "deconstructed," by Derrida.[3] Indeed, my sense is that such a perspective on continental philosophy is also widely, and uncritically, adopted by nonspecialists in that tradition, with the result that, even when they conscientiously endeavor to keep up with currents within that field, they tend to focus almost exclusively upon Nietzsche and Heidegger and their many followers, including the (variously classified) poststructuralists, deconstructionists, and (other) postmodernists. Finally, while it must of course be acknowledged, in spite of what the preceding remarks might suggest, that Husserl has exerted, and clearly continues to exert, a wide, deep, and multifarious influence on contemporary philosophy,[4] nonetheless his arguments against relativism, perhaps because they are preliminary to, rather than central and essential to, his greatest and most singular contribution to philosophy, namely, his project of phenomenology, have suffered comparative, and possibly undeserved, neglect.[5] Thus, in light of their obvious relevance to our contemporary situation, it seems worthwhile to attempt to relieve that neglect somewhat, and to look again at Husserl's arguments against relativism, to see what they might yet have to teach us as the twentieth century comes to a close.

In order to keep the discussion to manageable length, however, I shall focus on just three of Husserl's many arguments, and only one in great detail, though in my own defense I might point out both that these are clearly central arguments, as evidenced by the fact that Husserl repeatedly presents them in his many different treatments of relativism and skepticism, and that I shall also be touching on several additional arguments, if only in passing, during the course of my own discussion.

As a final preliminary to that discussion, I think it will prove worthwhile to examine a substantial quoted passage representing (and, indeed, confidently summarizing and defending) the "postmodern" position against which I am eager to press Husserl's arguments. I do this in part to ward off the criticism that I am enlisting the aid of Husserl merely for the purposes of attacking a "straw man." Of course, one might always argue that I have chosen an unrepresentative example, but I am confident that students of the contemporary intellectual scene will recognize the rhetoric and position taken in the quoted passage, by Tom Bridges, as quite similar to what they have heard and read over and over again in recent years. Bridges's statement is atypical, in my judgment at least, only in its clarity and succinctness, and also, though perhaps less so, in its pugnacious tone. Bridges writes:

> [T]he failure of the Enlightenment project is by now simply a fact. . . . Of course, there are still many in our midst who out of misunderstanding, habit and resistance to intellectual change routinely make claims to objective knowledge of history and nature. The trouble is that such people cannot give us a credible account of how such knowledge is possible. Since the publication of Kuhn's *The Structure of Scientific Revolutions* in 1962, a vast arsenal of arguments has been stockpiled—arguments drawn from Dewey, Wittgenstein, Heidegger, Gadamer, Foucault, Derrida and Rorty, to name just a few—arguments entirely sufficient to persuade anyone paying attention that human knowledge is historically conditioned, that there is no privileged standpoint outside of history from which human beings can contemplate things or events as they really are in themselves. Do . . . any of the defenders of objective truth have any response to these arguments? Can they show precisely how it is that a particular human being, conditioned by gender, historical and spatial location, class, ethnicity, nationality and religion, can somehow assume the purely universal and timeless standpoint of a pure knower? Just how is this miracle possible? How do we manage to jump out of our historical skins to rub up against the cold steely surfaces of objective fact? . . . Progressive today is not a return to the foundationalist conceptions of truth and knowledge that served us in the past, but rather the new postmodernist rhetorical conceptions of discourse that alone are capable of giving pluralistic, multivocal and multifaceted critical political discourses the central place they must have in any free society.[6]

I. The Self-Referential Inconsistency Argument

One of the most persistent criticisms of postmodern forms of relativism or skepticism, and one which Husserl repeatedly pressed against earlier versions,[7] concerns their failure to deal adequately with straightforward questions concerning their self-referentiality. To illustrate, consider the popular position which is sometimes called "cultural relativism": the doctrine that all "truth" is socially constructed, and thus must be understood as obtaining only within a particular culture, which it can in no way transcend. The present objection to such a position is brought out by considering such questions as: If all "truth" is merely relative to a particular culture, then is not *this* truth merely relative to the culture in which it is asserted? If so, then how is the claim to be understood, since it appears to be a universal, transcultural claim? On the other hand, if this truth is an exception to the general rule that all truths are merely relative to a particular culture, then why cannot there be other exceptions? Similarly, if one claims that all truth is socially constructed, what is the status of *this* claim? Is it, too, simply the product of a particular culture, and thus devoid of valid application outside of and beyond it? And if there is no truth, what is the nature and status of the *claim* that there is no truth?

Let us now apply all of this to our representative specimen of postmodernist thinking. Recall Bridges's assertion that we cannot "rub up against the cold steely surfaces of objective fact," since "human knowledge is historically conditioned," and also "conditioned by gender . . . , class, ethnicity, nationality," and so forth. Notice that, on Bridges's own terms, his statements must be taken, not as capturing the way things really are—not as objective truths—but rather as expressions of his own peculiar perspective, which is through-and-through conditioned by his gender, ethnicity, nationality, and so on, and which, therefore, cannot be assumed to be otherwise, let alone universally or uniquely, valid. The way is left fully clear for others, with different perspectives, perhaps, as Bridges would have it, because of the different kinds of conditioning they have undergone, to deny everything he says. What seems needed, then, is a standpoint external to these opposed standpoints, from which their opposition might be adjudicated. But Bridges, of course, denies that this is possible, as when, in connection, specifically, with historical conditioning, he remarks: "there is no privileged standpoint outside of history from which human beings can contemplate things or events as they really are in themselves." So Bridges is stuck.

Part of his problem, it would seem, is that his argument depends upon, and his rhetoric also suggests, the idea that his claims are really true, or at least better than their denials, and this in turn entails, at the very least, that something more can be said for his claims than that his conditioning has *led* him to believe them and to issue them. For, with regard to his rhetoric, it is perhaps sufficient to note that he calls it "simply a fact" that the Enlightenment project has failed, only to ridicule, a scant three sentences later, those who are foolish enough to "make claims to objective knowledge of history." As for his arguments, it is not only that his conclusion seems to undermine itself (e.g., "all knowledge claims are historically conditioned, and do not necessarily reflect how things really are" clearly implies that "the *claim* that all knowledge claims are historically conditioned is *itself* historically conditioned, and does not necessarily reflect how things really are"); his conclusion also seems to undermine its own premises and the pattern of its logical reasoning. For Bridges's rhetoric surely suggests—and here I will not quote again, but rather ask readers to go back, so as to verify it for themselves—that he regards the claims supporting his conclusion as true, or at least better than their denials, and holds that these claims do indeed lend support to his conclusion. And if he is not right about this there is no need to take his argument seriously, for why should we lend our credence to a conclusion which is based upon premises that are no better than their denials, or which is not supported by its premises? Sadly, however, if Bridges's conclusion is accepted, then he is not right in his implicit claims about his premises and reasoning. He has fallen into the trap Husserl diagnosed years ago: "All genuine skepticism of whatever kind and persuasion is indicated by the essentially necessary countersense that, in its argumentations, it implicitly presupposes as conditions of the possibility of its validity precisely what it denies in its theses."[8]

How might Bridges, and other postmodernists, escape or overcome this objection? I will discuss three common strategies. One is to give up the claim that one's claims are really "true," or "warranted," or what have you, and instead frankly admit that they have only relative, or subjective, or rhetorical merit.[9] As Husserl puts it, such a person "will not bow to the ordinary objection that in setting up his theory he is making a claim to be convincing to others, a claim presupposing that very objectivity of truth which his thesis denies. He will naturally reply: My theory expresses my standpoint, what is true for me, and need be true for no one else."[10] I will only point out, by way of reply, that such a stance relieves anyone not initially tempted to adopt the thesis in question of any obligation to refute it.

A second strategy, favored especially by Heidegger, Derrida, and some of their followers, is to claim that such incoherence is at present unavoidable since, while we are able to see that the "logocentric" Western metaphysical tradition, with its characteristic understanding of, and emphasis on, truth, objectivity, reason, and kindred concepts, is thoroughly exhausted, untenable, and in need of replacement, we are not yet able to see how to think, write, and speak in the radically new way that is required, so we are forced, reluctantly, to make use of the very concepts and ways of thinking, writing, and speaking, that we are simultaneously attempting to overthrow. The incoherence of this approach can be somewhat mitigated by the use of irony, and, in general, a highly literary, rather than expository and argumentative, style of presentation, together with the use of lines to cross out some of the problematical words, so that the words are both used (because written down) and not used (because crossed out).

Derrida's term for this technique, which he takes over from Heidegger but develops in his own way, is writing "under erasure."

Without wishing to assert that such a technique is in principle unscrupulous, or that it cannot be used to produce intriguing literary effects, surely there is no gainsaying James Edie's quite restrained remark that "we must still ask ourselves common-sensically from time to time what it means to use a vocabulary 'under erasure,' and what it all eventually comes to."[11] I think it is fair to add, however, and without wishing to advance a philistine position on the matter, or to deny in general the benefit which can accrue from avant-garde experimentation in the uses of language, that there is considerable danger that this technique can be abused so that it functions simply as an immunizing device. After all, one cannot show that a claim is mistaken if one does not know what it means.

A final response, and perhaps the most common one, which defenders of postmodern claims issue in reply to the charge that such claims are self-referentially inconsistent is to reply that those who press such claims are nitpickers who are hung up on the strictures of logic, and who are either unable or unwilling to embrace a more expansive, albeit more uncertain, way of looking at things. Thus, G. B. Madison states, approvingly, that "postmodern philosophical discourse . . . often deliberately ignores the requirements of logic (e.g., the principle of noncontradiction), because what it wishes to say necessarily cannot be said in logic (in the eyes of many postmodernists it is no objection to an utterance that it be 'inconsistent' or 'improbable')."[12]

By way of reply, it is necessary to point out, once again, how readily such a position can function, whether intentionally or not, as an immunizing device. For, as Patrick Colm Hogan points out, "those who deny the Principle of Non-Contradiction quite literally allow no contradiction. There simply is no way of disputing their claim[s]."[13]

I will refrain, however, from further pursuing this line of argument here, so as to point out instead, I think very much in the spirit of Husserl,[14] that an unwillingness to face up to, and to take responsibility for, that which experience reveals to be inconsistent or improbable, is not a purely logical error, but rather a moral, political, and existential failing of the highest order, as is the refusal to eliminate flat contradictions from one's thinking. Moreover, the fact that postmodernists tend to renounce a robust sense of logic and of truth in their more reflective, theoretical moments, only to appeal to it implicitly when they are doing so (e.g., it is true that there is no truth) and explicitly at unguarded moments in their lives (e.g. "I did *not* do that, and that is the absolute truth!—look, here is the evidence to prove it!"), strongly suggests that such a robust sense of truth (and a similar point could easily be made about their sense of evidence, of consistency, and of probability) is deeply present to them in their own experience. Thus, the fault that I think Husserl, and even more so his "existentialist" followers, such as Sartre,[15] would find in many contemporary postmodernists is not merely that they fail to subject their beliefs to abstract, artificial, purely formal and logical tests, but that they fail to notice that they cannot live by those beliefs. A desire to live according to their theorizing and to theorize according to their living (experience)[16] would thus lead the defenders of postmodernism to reject from their thinking those relativistic or skeptical notions by which they cannot live—for who knows how to put into practice a self-contradictory idea?—or, better still, to work hard on reconciling what still seems valid in these notions with that in their experience which seems to render them untenable.

Moreover, since the more expansive stance from which logic is often rejected as overly constricting is typically a moral and political one, and since, in general, postmodern claims are frequently defended on moral and political grounds, I will close this discussion of the self-referential inconsistency objection with a brief consideration of it in precisely such a context. The point I wish to make here is that it is far from clear that any relativizing or subjectivizing of truth, or any reduction of it to multiple opinions or perspectives (recall the concluding sentence from the passage quoted from Bridges above), entails greater tolerance for diverse voices, let alone increased respect for them. For the claim that such a move does provide a rationale or justification for tolerance yields, once again, the familiar self-referential paradoxes. If the claim that we should be tolerant is to be upheld as a universal truth, how can this be squared with the idea that all truths are relative, perspectival, and thoroughly conditioned? If this claim is an exception to the general rule, what are the grounds for this, and why can there not be other universal (transcultural, transperspectival) truths? If, on the other hand, the idea that we should be tolerant is to be considered as just one perspective among others, then such relativism is inimical to the claim that everyone, irrespective of the peculiarities of their own cultural perspective and conditioning, is truly obliged to be tolerant, and leaves us powerless in the face of those whose perspective is one of the opposition to tolerance. And how can such perspectivalism yield respect for the other, when, on the epistemology in question, we always know beforehand that the other's perspective is just different from ours, and not inferior (as relativists are quick to insist) or superior (as they are not) to it? Thus, relativism removes one of our most powerful motives to study the views of the other—the idea that the other might be right and we might be wrong.

Here is one real-life example which illustrates some of these points, showing in particular that self-referential confusions and paradoxes should not be dismissed as of merely academic or narrowly intellectual concern (the sort of thing about which logical nitpickers are obsessed), because in fact they bring forth significant, and often unfortunate, consequences in the social and political realm.

At an antiwar meeting held in Chicago during the recent Gulf War, several opponents of the war advocated the circulation of a petition documenting the rampant sexism of the policies of the government of Kuwait, and condemning this sexism. A sizable group of self-proclaimed "postmodernists" opposed this, on the grounds that it would be arrogant and intolerant for "us" to make such a judgment, and to impose "our" standards on the people of Kuwait. Notice: (1) the paradox of invoking the value of tolerance to justify refusing to oppose intolerance in the form of sexism; (2) the futile attempt to be neutral—"Who are we to judge them?" was a common refrain—resulting, in effect, in the taking of sides; (3) that the side taken is the repressive, intolerant one, in that the side supported, if only by means of opposing criticism of it, is that of the sexists of Kuwait, with the side opposed being those who would criticize them; (4) that the postmodernists' argument implies, though I feel certain this is unintentional, the racist assumption that all of the people of Kuwait think alike—"Who are we to judge them?"—as if there were not feminists in Kuwait who would endorse the petition; and (5) that the argument depends on the denial of the eidetic dimension of experience (to be discussed in the final section of this paper), in that it assumes that we, not being members of the culture in question, cannot possibly be in a position to understand and judge the sexism in Kuwait, overlooking, or else denying, that the essential structure of sexism might be such that we can at least partially understand sexism in Kuwait on analogy to sexism in the United States, with this admittedly partial and fallible level of understanding of this sexism being sufficient to render us competent to judge it as wrong, and to entail that we are not acting irresponsibly in condemning it.[17]

What this example suggests, I think, is that the postmodernists' approach to defending tolerance is incoherent, uncritical, and ineffective. What is more, this is true in large part because of the self-referential inconsistencies which pervade it, and which might otherwise, though mistakenly, be dismissed as matters solely of formal and logical concern, far removed from all social and political import.

II. The Evidentiary Argument

Let us next take up one of Husserl's principal arguments against "psychologism"—the thesis that logical truths are, in fact, empirical truths about the ways in which human beings happen to think.[18] According to psychologism, the argument "either A or B; not A; therefore B," reduces to something like: "all people are so constituted psychologically that if they believe that either A or B is true, and if they further believe that A is not true, then they cannot help but believe that B is true."[19]

I will not pursue the obvious objection that, as everyone who has ever taught logic knows all too well, it simply is not the case that "all people are so constituted psychologically that if they believe that either A or B is true, and if they further believe that A is not true, then they cannot help but believe that B is true."[20] I also will not linger over the point that reasoning in psychology—for example, the drawing of inferences concerning how people in fact tend to think, on the basis of empirical data of some kind—depends on principles of logic, as does all reasoning, so that the reduction of logic to psychology appears to involve vicious circularity.

The Husserlian argument that I do wish to stress is this: On the one hand, at least some logical principles seem powerfully evident to us—it appears obvious, for example, that if A is taller than B, and B is taller than C, then A must be taller than C. On the other hand, we also have some evidence in support of certain psychological theses concerning how people in fact happen to think. But surely at least some of our logical principles, such as the one just mentioned, are far more evident and obvious to us than are any of the empirical generalizations we find in psychology, or in any of the other empirical sciences. Thus, to attempt to explain logic in terms of psychology is to explain the more certain by the less certain. It is, in short, to commit the fallacy of *obscurum per obscurius*.[21]

Now let us apply this argument to our specimen of postmodernism —the passage by Bridges quoted above. Let us concede that there is some evidence to support many of Bridges's central contentions. Certainly there is no shortage of evidence to support the conclusion that much of our thinking is, indeed, "conditioned by gender, history, class, ethnicity," and so on. Perhaps there even is evidence to support the claim that *all* of our thinking is so conditioned, together with the further conclusion that, as a result, we cannot "contemplate things or events as they really are in themselves" (let us here waive the self-referential inconsistency objection). But the presence of some such evidence, even if it be both powerful and abundant, is not yet sufficient to sustain the conclusion. Thus, the evidence that all of our thinking is thoroughly conditioned, and in such a manner as to cut us off from all knowledge of "how things really are," together with the inference from this that our belief that 2 + 2 = 4, for example, is a thoroughly conditioned belief which, for that reason, cannot be granted transcultural and transhistorical validity, must be weighed against the evidence that, simply, 2 + 2 = 4. Similar considerations apply to the balancing of the evidence that "*q*" follows from the conjunction of "*p* implies *q*" and "*p*," or (to turn to empirical matters) that elephants are heavier than ants, and that the sun is hotter than the Earth, or, finally (and turning now to value judgments), that happiness is intrinsically better than misery, against the evidence that all of these are conditioned and relative claims, lacking in universal validity, and telling us nothing about how things really are. It seems to me clear that, however strong may be the evidence that at least much of our thinking is conditioned in the ways described by Bridges, there are at least some logical and mathematical, and even empirical and moral judgments for which our evidence is much stronger. Thus, the attempt by postmodernists such as Bridges to explain away these judgments when they run afoul of epistemological strictures less certain than are the judgments themselves is to commit an evidentiary fallacy and to reason *obscurum per obscurius*.[22]

III. The Eidetic Argument

Finally, it seems to me that Bridges goes wrong by assuming, without argument, that a knower must achieve a standpoint stripped of all particularity in order to have access to knowledge that is not thoroughly conditioned by the particularity of the knower. But an alternative possibility, defended at length by Husserl[23] but ignored by Bridges, is that it is possible, even from a particular standpoint, to see truths which transcend that standpoint, and which further transcend the particularities of what is seen, so that the knower "rubs up against" truths which are not only objective, but also universal and necessary.

Consider this example, provided by Erazim Kohák:

> When I try, unsuccessfully, to squeeze a tennis ball into a wine bottle, I need not try several wine bottles and several tennis balls before, using Mill's canons of induction, I arrive inductively at the hypothesis that tennis balls do not fit into wine bottles. One instance is enough. I see not only that this tennis ball won't fit into this wine bottle but that in principle, tennis balls do not fit into wine bottles, and, for that matter, I see that large objects do not fit into small openings. . . . [O]ur experience . . . includes not only a perception of objects but a perception of principles as well.[24]

We are now in a position to turn the tables on Bridges and ask, "if I judge that tennis balls do not fit into wine bottles, can you show *precisely* how it is that my gender, historical and spatial location, class, ethnicity, etc., undermine the objectivity of this judgment? They seem quite irrelevant to *this* judgment, though, of course, not to others." Or again, "if from the fact that A is taller than B, and that B is taller than C, I draw the conclusion that A is taller than C, how, *precisely*, does the fact that I am a historical being, living in a particular time and place and culture, preclude me from rubbing up against this truth?"[25]

Thus, it would appear that Bridges's argument depends on proceeding sweepingly on the theoretical level, and on prescinding from close consideration of any of the billions and billions of particular cases of experiences which, like the ones I have cited here, at least seem to fly in the face of his prescriptions. If we are to make sense of the ways in which we are influenced in our thinking by our particularity, it will not do to operate in this high-flown manner. Rather, we will have to emulate Husserl in looking at specific instances carefully and in detail, remaining alive to the possibility that, while our particularity might influence our thinking here, distort it there, and utterly close us off from the truth in another instance, it might not at all undermine our ability to arrive at objective truth in yet another case.[26] All of this deserves much more careful consideration than it has usually received from contemporary postmodern relativists.[27] Should such careful consideration soon be forthcoming, it might yet become possible in the twenty-first century to dispense with the business of repeating Husserl's most fundamental insights, and instead get on with the task of criticizing, refining, and building upon them.

7

The Constitutional Problematics of Nonrelativity or How to Dump Garbage in Nobody's Backyard

Lester Embree

The expression "nonrelative" (and derivatives) is offered here as an alternative to "objective" (and derivatives) in one of its significations, "objective" being excessively polysignificant in current philosophical English. In constitutive phenomenology, "constitution" refers to the explanation of objects in terms of intentive processes or encounterings and is accomplished through fictive as well as serious reflective theoretical observation performed upon the pertinent noetico-noematic correlations. Since the set of problems pertaining to nonrelativity is quite extensive, only an outline of it is ventured in this essay. Outlines omit details and lesser structures but are concerned to delineate the whole and its greater structures.

There is need for an outline of this problematics because most discussion within constitutive phenomenology of what is here called nonrelativity suffers from excessive emphasis on cognitive personal human life. The emphasis on *human* intentive life will not be challenged here but equal emphasis will be placed on the affective and conative as upon cognitive strata in all encounterings and also upon communal as upon personal life, personal life being, after all, abstract while collective life is concrete. This more balanced emphasis is evident in figure 1, which will be followed in the body of this exposition from the bottom upwards as well as from left to right, row by row and letter by letter.

Figure 1
Outline of Problematics of Nonrelativity

	interoccasional	interpersonal	intercommunal
conative	G.	H.	I.
affective	D.	E.	F.
cognitive	A.	B.	C.

A running example may aid the following exposition. Suppose that there is an urban sprawl that extends over several adjacent counties in a state, that an agency of that state proposes to locate a garbage dump in one of the counties, and that there are a series of counterefforts by concerned citizens making up groups such as Hiasson's Mothers of the Wilderness (the "Mowistas") and, far to the left of them, the dreaded "GRD" (Gordon's Reef Defenders). How is this prospect made aware, believed in, valued, and willed by concerned individuals and groups?

The problematics of nonrelativity needs to be distinguished from those of truth and justification. "Truth" applies to propositions only in the case in which the states of affairs referred to in them are affirmed or denied.[1] There can then be truth that is subjective or relative and nonrelative or objective according to whether the matters are thus posited by one or more than one person. "Justification" applies not to propositions but to positings and depends on whether or not positings are immediately or mediately founded upon and motivated by evidencing of the matters posited. There can then be relative or "subjective" and nonrelative or "objective" justification according to whether the same states of affairs or matters in question are evidenced by one or more than one subject in the way most original for objects of that region.

"Skepticism" would seem prima facie to apply to the position or positions whereby there can be no truth and no justification, but showings that there is subjective truth or subjective justification would not seem sufficient to defeat skepticism; nonrelativity is also required. For example, if someone reports in all sincerity the nightmare of having married a real estate developer, that report can be taken as true for that person, but nobody else perceived or can remember that dream and the representational awareness of it on the basis of the person's report is not an original mode of evidencing for objects of the region in question.

For another example, if the preponderance of evaluation within a group is that garbage dumps are intrinsically good, then the positive value of garbage dumps is, for that group, nonrelative, although few outsiders would, it seems, accept that the positive valuing of garbage for its own sake can be justified. (The contention that dumps are the best method of disposal is based on extrinsic as well as comparative valuing.) Then again, the positive valuing of health for its own sake might be nonrelatively justified by outsiders as well as the insiders of a health-valuing community and thus justified intercommunally, provided the pertinent conditions of evidencing are fulfilled.[2] It may also be mentioned, but not pursued, that justification can be naive or critical according to whether the encountering in which objects are constituted is reflectively observed, analyzed, and described in a worldly or in a transcendental attitude. With the differences of nonrelativity from truth and justification borne in mind, the problematics of nonrelativity can now be outlined.

I. The Cognitive Level

The cognitive level consists, for present purposes, of the awareness of realities and the believing that accompanies it and, correlatively, the real objects and their belief characteristics, which characteristics can be discerned when objects as they present themselves are reflectively observed. The cognitive level includes but is not confined to linguistic or predicative intentiveness. There are also nonreal or ideal objects, such as propositions, which are of course expressed in the statements that make up this essay, but they are—for the sake of simplicity—excluded from consideration here. We are not made aware of some real matters, such as the intentive lives of other animals, in a strictly sensuous manner, but we become aware of them representationally, in close relation with sensuous awareness, which is direct.

As for belief, there is the stratum of believing in the intentive process, on the one hand, and there is a belief characteristic, discernible reflectively in the object as it presents itself, on the other hand. This believing and the correlative belief characteristic can be positive, negative, or neutral; as positive and negative it can be firm ("certain") or shaky ("probable"), and it might be extrinsic (as well as intrinsic) when objects, such as causes or effects, are believed in for the sake of other objects, such as effects or causes. The question, again, of whether the belief is justified is excluded from the present sketch. Moreover, the question of whether the expression of belief is true is also excluded and the focus is on encounters as pre- if not nonpredicative.

A. *Interoccasional Cognition.* The first time an individual encounters a garbage dump the stench is overwhelming in what is then a predominantly olfactory perceiving of it. That this smelling motivates a negative valuing and even willing of some sort, e.g., to get away from the stink, will be returned to presently. At this point, it is plain that the dump as stinking is believed in. If this happens only once to an individual, then the encounter is merely occasional or, in traditional terms, subjective in the extreme. If the dump is smelled two or more times, it comes to have the minimal nonrelativity or, again in traditional terms, objectivity. This seems best called interoccasional nonrelativity.

Interoccasional nonrelativity of the cognitive sort is constituted within an individual conscious life. Most broadly considered, the smelling of the dump a second or subsequent time is retrotentive to the earlier predominantly olfactory perceiving and through identificational-differentiational synthesis it is constituted as the same smelly dump. Furthermore, it is automatically protended so that if that individual approaches that dump again, then she will smell it again or, equivalently, it will have the same smell for her. Finally, just as believing in the smelly dump was immediately motivated by the smelling of it, so too the believing that the dump previously smelled and, under pertinent conditions, will be smelled again as the same smelly dump is believed in automatically. (The fascinating constitutive phenomenological issues concerning how similar stenches on different occasions cannot only be intended to as pertaining to the identical dump but also can be intended to as different from one another are beyond the scope of this outline.)

B. *Interpersonal Cognition.* The individual may well not approach her first dump alone. If not, then she may well not only become aware of the stench but also become aware that her companion is smelling and disvaluing the stench along with her. Whether or not this is also conveyed verbally, it can readily be observed representationally on the basis of a normal companion's behavior in such a situation. This is social intentiveness. For there to be a group, the intentiveness needs to be reciprocal, at least in a marginal way. It can be retrotentive to earlier joint encounterings and protentive to more of the same or others to come. Already in the case of the two mutually intentive dump encounterers, a first level of intersubjective constitution of the smelly dump occurs and, correlatively, of the nonrelativity of that which is smelled obtains. It seems best to entitle this interindividual nonrelativity.

Strictly speaking, there are now four types of constitution recognized, for the occasional/interoccasional and the personal or individual/

interindividual distinctions intersect. Without attempting to decide whether interoccasional/individual or occasional/interindividual forms are the more nonrelative, it can be recognized that occasional/individual cognition is the most and the interoccasional/interindividual cognition is the least relative of the mentioned compound forms. Again, there are interesting questions about individual differences in, e.g., the ability to smell, which will not be pursued here because they might distract attention from the big picture, but it may be mentioned that matters like the smells of dumps are so regularly constituted as interindividual that the first interesting question may not be how that is possible but rather how it is possible for us to discern personally relative smells.

C. *Intercommunal Cognition.* Our two mutually aware dump smellers can constitute a minimal group. Humans form and participate in various ways in numerous groups and there can be cooperation as well as conflict between groups. Suppose, for example, that a group of concerned citizens seeks to become well informed by consulting experts.[3] Verbal communication is required here and, on the basis of a modicum of science, they come to believe that a garbage dump includes (and can generate) concentrations of toxic substances (which may or may not be sensuously perceived) that so contaminate the air and ground water that organisms of various orders, humans included, and even entire ecosystems located downstream in their toxic flow patterns can be harmed or killed. Here causal connections come to be cognized, but the point is that the effects of dumps on life is nonrelative in a third way, which can be called intercollective, one collective being the group of concerned citizens who have become well informed and the other collective being the scientific community in which this knowledge about garbage dumps is discovered. For both groups, dumps have the same specific effects.

II. The Evaluative Level

The phenomenological issue of relativity/nonrelativity has tended to be focused on scientific objectivity, which pertains to the cognitive level. Yet, because the evaluative and conative levels were clearly recognized by Husserl at least since *Ideen I*,[4] this ought to have been a matter of emphasis rather than of essence. The evaluative level involves, noetically, valuing, which can be positive, negative, and neutral—as positive and negative it can be firm or shaky ("ambivalent")—and it also involves valuing objects for their own sakes or for the sakes of other objects. Overall, it can thus have correlative values qua noematic pathothetic characteristics objectivatable in objects of the nine sorts established through analysis of pathic positionality in figure 2. This analysis is subject to refinement with respect to the natural determinations of the value objects, e.g., rose scent and dump stink both have firm intrinsic values, but one is positive and the other negative. That this analysis parallels those possible for belief and volition has not helped keep them distinct, although the differences between (1) believing and disbelieving, (2) liking and disliking, and (3) willing for and willing against should be clear.

Figure 2
Gross Taxonomy of Values

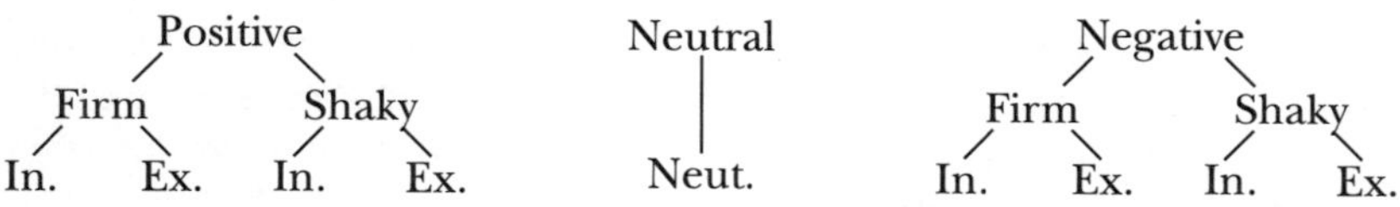

D. *Interoccasional Evaluation.* There is relativity and various stages of nonrelativity to the values of objects constituted in the evaluative stratum of the intentive process. The first valuing of the scent of a nicely cooking compost pile might be shaky as well as occasional but can become interoccasionally firm. It may furthermore be intrinsically negative but extrinsically firm. It may also be intrinsically negative but extrinsically positive in value as one cognizes it as a nonpolluting way of disposing of yard and kitchen waste and also of generating solid and fluid organic fertilizer, compost, and mulch. The first degree of nonrelativity is not dependent on the valuing of something for the sake of something else but upon the repeated valuing of it as the same. It may also be mentioned that to become a person who approves of composting does not imply that the value of composting is objectivated, much less that propositions about it are formulated. Interoccasional or individual evaluation is originally prepredicative.

E. *Interpersonal Evaluation.* The members of a household, neighborhood, town, county, etc., can positively and firmly but especially communally value compost facilities of various sizes in the same intrinsic and extrinsic ways. Like wormeries, composting is a partial alternative to garbage dumps. Cognition is involved, for the valuing is immediately motivated by believing, and believing is immediately and mediately motivated by observing or evidencing of various sorts and degrees of sophistication. Moreover, there is mutual intentiveness, evaluation as well as cognition included, among what thereby become members of the group. This mutual encountering is usually relevant if not marginal rather than thematic. The point is, however, that a nonrelative positive and firm value can be interindividually constituted where composters in at least a partial preference to garbage dumps are concerned, i.e., leaders of a community can speak on behalf of the group and say "We prefer composting to dumping" or "Composting is better than dumping." This is nonrelative, but relative to a community rather than to an individual or an occasion. From within, however, it is quite "objective." And the question needs to be asked whether something that is nonrelative to all competent individuals, and communities, i.e., omnirelative, is still relative in a serious way.

F. *Intercommunal Evaluation.* In the case under analysis, however, a county is confronted with the problem of the state planning to impose a new garbage dump upon it. To the well-informed and concerned citizen groups of the county, this is nonrelatively bad. For the sake of the discussion, let us suppose that all such groups in the county in question form a coalition to oppose the siting of the dump. They might even rally under the flag on which it is inscribed "Not in our backyard!" The political plot would then thicken, but the phenomenological point at this stage is that there would be an intercommunal negative valuing correlative to which the dump siting would have intercommunal negative nonrelative value, some of it intrinsic with respect to the stink and other ugliness, but most of it extrinsic with respect to the adverse health impacts.

An intercommunal intersubjectivity has not only mutually encountering intentiveness within it between persons but also between communities. This involves mutual awareness of various representational sorts, mutual believing in various ways, and mutual evaluation. In an alliance or coalition, the persons and communities like their fellow persons and communities for, among other things, their valuings, in this case their disliking of new dumps in the county, and this is also not unilateral but mutual. Coalitions and even communities are sometimes not stable, especially before participation and support become habitual and also when based only on one negative valuing. An interesting question that, like the questions of the justification of valuing, can be left for another occasion concerns the conditions under which communities and coalitions are stable.

III. The Level of Action

From a cognitive and even from an evaluative standpoint it is almost too easy personally to take up a standpoint outside of interoccasional, interpersonal, and intercommunal forms of intentiveness and the correlative relativities and nonrelativities constituted in them. To do so with respect to action, however, is simply to be neutral and thus not act, something theorists may overlook. Others, individual and collective, are allies, opponents, or nonparticipants. One only acts from a subjective or relative standpoint, which can still be justified, and as one participates in intersubjectivities, various nonrelativities are constituted. If one acts for or against a present actual or future possible situation, i.e., to preserve, destroy, create, or prevent, one must act personally alone, as a participant in a community, or as member of a coalition of persons and communities, and the nonrelativity or "objectivity" of ends and means is constituted in that "subjective" or in one degree or other "intersubjective" action.

In action, the means that is always willed is somatic movement, whether I-engaged or habitual, and other matters are willed as ends also others as means. This is done at least on the basis of believed-in causal connections, so that believed-in possible effects are willed as ends and then causes or, more generally, conducive circumstances, are willed as means. The ends can be positive, negative, or neutral, as positive and negative they can be firm ("resolute") or shaky ("hesitant") and, according to whether the matter willed is already actual or not, they can be preservative or destructive or creative or preventative. The countywide antidump coalition is resolutely devoted to preventative action.

G. *Interoccasional Action.* One can recognize the most relative action to be occasional. For example, upon the first sniff of a dump in her life the individual turns heel and flees breathing through her mouth but beginning already to believe that the stinking mess will still be there after she gets away, and thus not only the cognitive but also the evaluative and the conative or practical nonrelativity begins to be constituted immediately, even though it is most conspicuous when there are successive and intentively interrelated occasional encounterings. It is also reflected in situations of vacillation. Interoccasional action is personal action. This can become habitual in the case of driving routinely on the upwind side of the dump or purchasing bottled water and it can also consist of consciously chosen actions.

H. *Interpersonal Action.* As a rule, personal actions do not make much difference in larger situations; most persons who seem effective are effective only as leaders and leaders are as much participants in communities as followers are, although the mutual encounterings and roles in planning, decision making, and task execution vary. One can will in connection with others against either an already existing garbage dump in one's area or against the siting of a proposed one there. This is interpersonal action. Persons reciprocally act on one another and are affected by earlier actions within the community and projected communal actions, i.e., plans and policies. Quickly, however, when up against the state and on an issue with such broad and adverse impacts, communities seek allies and thus engage in intercommunal negative action. Alliances are formed, mutual support occurs, etc., and then the forces of evil might even be slowed down a bit, maybe.

I. *Intercommunal Action.* The problem that arises for intercommunal action is that if the dump is not sited in this county it will be sited in one of the other counties in the region. Not in my backyard seems, at least to the unthoughtful, to entail somebody else's backyard. After all, it will be said by those who site new dumps, all this garbage is produced and must go somewhere. And if larger and larger intercommunal antidump alliances, even intercounty, statewide, interstate, national, and international ones, keep being formed, the backyard out of which the dump would be kept just gets larger and larger and the rest of the finite area left in Gaia gets smaller and smaller. Carrying this through all the way, the entire intersubject is humanity and the big backyard is called Earth and there is no nonbackyard. Or is it feasible to dump waste into the sun? Then again, must waste disposal necessarily entail dumping?[5]

The concern in the present essay is merely to show that the problem of nonrelativity holds on practical and evaluative as well as cognitive levels and for intercommunal as well as interpersonal as well as personal lives, but it might still be suggested that ultimately the nonrelative (or omnirelative) practical goal is to have no dumps in anybody's backyard or, in other words, no dumps anywhere in "our" backyard. Means to that end would include personal and communal composting of yard and kitchen waste, but it would also require reduction in the use of other materials, e.g., packaging, the reuse rather than dumping of, e.g., building materials, recycling and the prevention of the use of nonrecyclable materials, etc., which are matters of wider and wider intercommunal, interpersonal, even interoccasional personal action but then also evaluation and cognition.

Conclusion

To show that this sketch plainly invites further phenomenological investigation, some questions may be raised. (1) While the problem of the nonrelativity of the values of ecosystems, including animals, human and nonhuman, has been intimated, there is the question of the possibility of multispeciel, interpersonal and intercommunal life as constituting nonrelative items, as happens, for example, when a human hunter and her dog pursue game together. When the nonhumans involved in intersubjective life are incapable of language, such nonrelativity must be interestingly prepredicative in conspicuous respects. (2) While already addressed to some extent in the phenomenological tradition, the interoccasional, interpersonal, and intercommunal constitution of ideal matters, e.g., mathematical and logical structures, would contrast with the present sketch, which is devoted to real matters. And (3) the present sketch has focused on the constitution of present and future nonrelative real matters, leaving the constitution of nonrelative past events still to be considered, e.g., our future communal memory of the nonrelative facts of how we succeeded in eliminating the institution of garbage dumps.

8

The Desire of Reason: A Plea for a "Practical" Response to Skepticism

Brice R. Wachterhauser

I

Skepticism is a recurrent cultural phenomenon. Wherever philosophy is pursued, sooner or later skepticism rears its hydralike head. Like the hydra, skepticism has a way of regenerating itself in every historical period. And, like the hydra, skepticism has more than one head, more than one face as it were. Plato confronted a version of it in Sophists like Gorgias and Protagoras; Augustine did battle with the academic skeptics of his day; Descartes attacked it as the most serious challenge to his search for a secure foundation for the sciences; Kant was shaken out of his dogmatic slumber by the urbane skepticism of Hume; Hegel even claimed to find skepticism in Kant's distinction between things-in-themselves and things-for-us; Husserl confronted it in a version he called "psychologism"; and today we see both a resurgent Nietzschean version going under the name of "deconstruction" and a pragmatic version of it in Rorty's repudiation of the usefulness of "truth talk." What all these versions of skepticism have in common is the refusal to recognize a nonrelative, nonhistorical truth.

The apparently deathless character of skepticism is not due in my opinion to its truth. As many philosophers have pointed out, skepticism's denial of truth always presents itself inconsistently as a nonrelative truth. Logically speaking, skepticism's denial of truth already undercuts itself whenever and wherever it asserts its own truth-claims. Human beings cannot consistently deny their capability for knowledge if for no other reason than that the very denial of knowledge itself is an explicit knowledge claim. Moreover, the skeptic always offers reasons to disavow knowledge. Thus, even the denial of knowledge presupposes some set of true knowledge-claims about the grounds for this denial. In fact, they are often far-reaching claims about the human condition and its prospects, claims, for example, about the nonverdical nature of sense perception. Or other skeptics might maintain that language and our linguistically conditioned concepts place an insurmountable barrier between us and the nonlinguistic world. Still others might insist on the cultural relativity of all knowledge-claims, a relativity that supposedly precludes a transcultural truth. And so it goes, thus showing the deep inconsistency of skepticism. All these arguments for skepticism wish to establish that human beings know no truth and some even celebrate this claim as a great good.

If I am right that every skeptic is an implicit knower this obviously shows that skepticism is internally inconsistent. I think this is so but I also think that establishing the logical inconsistency of skepticism is not sufficient to dislodge the skeptic. While such refutations are sufficient to show that the fundamental propositions of skepticism are not true, they are not sufficient to change the skeptic's mind. The skeptic is often not moved by the charge of internal inconsistency because, for one reason, there is in her mind a question about the real value of rigorous consistency. Of course she knows that if she wishes to make any sense at all to herself or others she must not contradict herself. But her conversational contexts change (even the ones she carries on with herself) and as they change she often feels compelled to maintain first one viewpoint and then another. The skeptic is often someone who has brought this fact to self-consciousness. She is aware that she cannot consistently maintain both points of view, but it just isn't clear to her which viewpoint is true or even if there is a non–question begging way of deciding the issue. This quandary certainly prevents her from elaborating a systematic philosophy and it leads her to the further doubt of whether reality can be adequately described in a coherent system. Perhaps reality is just a "concatenated" whole, as James maintained, and not a systematic, logical whole, like Plato and Hegel viewed it.[1]

I think these issues and doubts are common and widespread. In my opinion, something like them contributes to the resurgence of skepticism in every historical epoch. I think this requires the nonskeptic to think more carefully about skepticism's seemingly undying appeal. This paper is in part an exploration of what I take to be some of the important sources of skepticism in our culture. My purpose is to show that it is more difficult to put skepticism to rest than many would think who see the skeptic's position as a nonstarter. While I do not share the skeptic's doubts, I think there are genuine issues that the intelligent skeptic has put her finger on. These issues are not sufficient to vindicate the skeptic but they do make the position in my opinion an attractive one in some respects. I offer this observation not as a surrender to the skeptic's position but because I think it is important that we nonskeptics not overstate our case. A dogmatic antiskepticism seems almost as extreme to me as the skeptic herself. Antiskepticism itself has a tendency to attempt to overwhelm its opponents with arguments that are supposedly beyond all possible doubt. We often dream of conquering the will of the skeptic with apodicticity, as Husserl frankly confesses in the *Crisis.*[2] I think, however, the nonskeptics desire to coerce and control needs to be replaced by the desire to converse and persuade. Nonskeptics would be better served by arguments more modest in tone and more insightful about the common predicament of the skeptic and nonskeptic. Instead of the imperious tone of coercion, I think that what we need is a "practical" argument against skepticism, an argument which places the skeptic and nonskeptic on a similar footing of a shared understanding of our condition and its prospects. Such an argument would be "practical" both in its emphasis on the practical consequences of skepticism, as well as "practical" in its argumentative structure. What the nonskeptic needs to do is go beyond the formal refutation of skepticism to develop an argument that is geared at helping the skeptic develop beliefs that resist skepticism's allure. Although we can always present arguments but never guarantee their effects, we need, nevertheless, to be more concerned with their probable effects. In short, logic needs to rejoin forces with rhetoric (perhaps along the lines Plato recommended in the *Phaedrus*) if the skeptic's ascendency is to be reversed.

As a beginning, I think the nonskeptic's case would be strengthened by recognizing that skepticism as a cultural phenomenon is not reducible to a set of "pure" epistemological propositions, but a complex gestalt of issues with epistemological, metaphysical, and ethical components, perhaps even psychological ones as well. At the very least, skepticism is both metaphysical and ethical in nature in that any compelling response to it will have to be committed to some far-reaching claims about the world and its intelligibility in principle, about human nature and its relation to that intelligible world, as well as the human good and the place of knowledge in it. I think the skeptic is often worried about these far-reaching metaphysical and ethical issues more than the epistemological ones. Hence the epistemologist's attack often misses the mark, at least as far as these sources of skepticism are concerned. While the "pure" epistemological arguments must be part of what I am describing as a "practical" response to skepticism, such a response must also address the metaphysical and ethical concerns of the skeptic. Such a response must learn to weave together the epistemological, metaphysical, and ethical issues at stake and present them in a persuasive argument which appeals to the intellect, emotions, and will of the skeptic. The ultimate aim of such an argument is human flourishing of a certain kind. The nonskeptic must set out to show that skepticism is not as conducive to our well-being, corporately and individually, as nonskepticism. Nothing less will suffice to unseat skepticism's growing influence.

In order to set the stage for a more in-depth consideration of this strategy, let us now turn to some common sources of skepticism in our world today. In developing this analysis, I will rely on my own perceptions of general cultural trends, illustrated often by references to Husserl's phenomenology. It should become evident that I see Husserl's legacy vis-à-vis skepticism as "mixed," in that he contributes in my opinion both to the problem of skepticism's growing influence and, in different respects, to a helpful strategy for skepticism's defeat.

II

In my opinion, there are two main sources of the skeptic's worries about logical consistency and truth. The first I'd call the "incompleteness of reason" and the second I'd call "human fragility" or our tenuous hold on the conditions of our own well-being. These two recurrent sources of skepticism reciprocally reinforce each other, making them very difficult to refute or come to terms with, at least as far as the skeptic is concerned. Nevertheless, the nonskeptic must learn to understand both these sources of skepticism more deeply and to address her argument against skepticism to them more self-consciously. Let us begin by looking at the first of these motives for skepticism.

Reason is "incomplete" in the sense that it has not been able to give an account of "the whole," of the general logical structure of intelligible reality. This is not simply to say that human reason has not yet achieved "omniscience," that it has not yet come to know everything that is knowable. This is obviously true and will always be true. But the question cuts deeper than this in that the possibility of knowledge itself presupposes that reality has an internally coherent intelligible structure.

How can the world be knowable in principle if different accounts of different finite aspects of reality suggest contradictory conclusions about the whole? Could a god make sense of an internally incoherent world? Such a world seems unknowable in principle. Yet, if the world does "make sense" in principle, we can rely on that rational structure as we gradually amass on ever-increasing internally consistent body of truth. How can we know upfront that the world makes sense in this fundamental way? Can we ever establish this claim empirically?

We confront reason's incompleteness in many ways, but one example of it is the failure of science, specifically physics, to provide a universal language of physical reality, capable of translating, as it were, all diverse scientific languages, like those of ecology, genetics, or geology into one comprehensive, cohesive language of the natural world.[3] This ancient dream of a unified science sounds quaint and hopelessly dated today. The fact that it was so inspiring to the founders of modern science and philosophy, men like Galileo, Newton, Descartes, and Leibniz, strikes many as a mere culturally contingent artifact. In my opinion, however, the search for a unified science reflects a regulative demand of reason itself for a coherent, systematically related account of all that is. Nevertheless, it seems to many intelligent observers today that we are as far from this dream as ever. Not only do the different sciences (to different degrees) function with different conceptual languages and methodologies, but physics itself, the most likely source of such a unifying vision, has evolved to a point in quantum mechanics that defies traditional binary logic. In such a setting, consistency seems to many to be indeed the hobgoblin of small minds. Perhaps James was right: reality is a mere concatenation of logically unrelated particulars. My purpose is not to endorse this conclusion—far from it—but to point out that the state of science itself seems to many to mock the ancient claim that the truth is one. The fact that disillusion with this dream is so widespread shows I think the extent of the crisis. Many people doubt whether we can even claim to be "on the way" to such a unified vision of reality.

Other examples could be cited as well. The phenomenologist's defense of the irreducibility of intentionality to physical laws is gaining wider acceptance in the intellectual community today.[4] This growing realization certainly represents a triumph for a fundamental Husserlian thesis. But it also represents a major enigma, in that no one has a coherent account of the relation between intentional structures and the physical world. Dualism once again is gaining a hearing, albeit a dualism of mental states and not necessarily of mental substances. I take this to be a step in the right direction. Human knowledge must follow the things themselves even if they thwart our attempts at a coherent vision. For the past fifty years physicalism seemed to many the best hope for a coherent account of the mind-body relationship. Nevertheless, coherence must not be purchased at the cost of distortion and falsehood. The refusal to acknowledge the stubborn reality of intentionality was just such a distortion in my opinion. Nevertheless, the fact that intentionality cannot be explained in physical terms (at least as we understand them today) carries along with it the specter of incoherence. Perhaps someday we will understand this relationship, but today it is one source for doubt about whether the world is a coherent whole or at least a doubt about whether human thought should aspire to ultimate coherence. It seems to many today that the vision of an internally unified reality is hopelessly passé. Still, I think it is the case that reason demands a coherent, clear, and compelling account of the various "regional ontologies" (to borrow Husserl's phrase), i.e., of how the various aspects of our world are coherently integrated into a single unified reality.[5] In fact, the refusal of physicalists to acknowledge the irreducibility of intentionality is a testimony to the strength of reason's demand for unity. Despite the fact that physicalism does not appear to be the path to unity in this area of inquiry, its refusal to give up its quest to solve the mind-body problem in physical terms shows the force of this recurrent regulative ideal. Be that as it may, in light of mounting evidence that intentionality cannot be explained away many will wonder whether skepticism is not the proper response to this enigma. To many the problem seems to be the very basic drive for logical consistency in this domain. Perhaps we can't make logical sense of this problem because we have no internally consistent set of concepts to adequately describe all its various aspects. Perhaps we can hope for no better than a patchwork of linguistic accounts each of which is illuminating in its own limited way but each of which is also inconsistent with the other accounts. In such a situation, the viability of the demand for logical unity, even as a regulative ideal, seems suspect.

But the incompleteness of reason presents itself in ways that provide even more troubling propects for the nonskeptic. Put generally, the problem is that reason cannot guarantee its own results. It seems that knowledge-seekers have a choice; either they use reason as the situation seems to dictate and accept its results *at face value* or not. There is nothing other than reason itself that we can appeal to when we wonder if reason is capable to bringing us ever closer to a true view of the world and our place in it. Reason seems circular in that if we ask how can we know if reason is a reliable guide to truth, there is nothing other than reason itself that can be appealed to in order to develop an articulate answer. To the skeptic this seems like question begging of the worst kind. Of course we can chose to trust reason, to take it at face value, but the warrant for such trust can be had only from inside a rational perspective. There is no way to substantiate this trust prior to exercising it. As Hegel noted against Kant, the demand to know the conditions of knowledge prior to entering actual situations of knowing is like demanding to know how to swim before entering the water. Nevertheless, the skeptic wonders under these conditions whether she should go swimming at all.

Oftentimes the nonskeptic appeals to self-evidence or to a so-called self-grounding truth-claim to silence the skeptic once and for all. It is as if the nonskeptic is saying: "Here it is. You can't possibly doubt it. There's simply nothing more anyone can say." Husserl appeals to the "luminous" certainty of truth established by direct insight, rather than inference of any kind. He has in mind the most basic truths of logic and math, which insight supposedly tells us can only be denied at the cost of being charged with absurdity, *Unsinn.*[6] The skeptic, however, is often left untouched by such moves. The skeptic counters that it is just such appeals to self-evidence that she finds suspect. Isn't it *possible* that the force of what we take at face value to be obviously true and unassailable is simply due to unknown prejudice, prejudices so deep that we are not conscious of them? After all the conditions of consciousness and human reason are never completely transparent to us. Will they ever be? How can *all possible* doubt be ruled out by appeals to the unique intentional character of certain cognitions? As powerful as I take Husserl's appeals to "luminous" certainties to be, it is a claim that claims too much for itself; it is a claim that ultimately rests on trust and not on presuppositionless seeing, whatever that might be. The obvious metaphorical appeal to "luminous" certainties or even to "immediate intimations of truth"[7] really only suffices to circumvent the problem rather than solve it. How can we really be sure that we are in the presence of such luminous certainties and not their false surrogates? How can we explain the difference between the feeling of such certainty which is compatible with complete error and actual presence of such certainty which is not? Despite the fact that Husserl claims that these luminous certainties are not recognized by the presence of a certain "feeling" in consciousness he fails in my opinion to adequately describe in concrete phenomenological terms the difference between cognition of truth and their deceptive surrogates. While I share Husserl's respect for truth and even agree with him that there can be no more basic appeal than to this type of seeing, I doubt that such faith is completely immune from the skeptic's doubt.

The *locus classicus* of this problem is, I think, Descartes's "First Meditation." Descartes's run-in with the mere possibility of a malicious, powerful deceiver is sufficient to raise the specter of a truly profound skepticism. Even though mathematics and logic seem self-evidently true, self-evidence itself is called into question by the mere *possibility* of an evil genius, whose malicious power could turn self-evidence into a mere dream or illusion. Descartes, of course, got caught up in trying to prove the impossibility of this metaphysical illusion—a mistake that we know as the Cartesian Circle—but the mythical story of the possibility of an evil genius should not distract us from the realization that Descartes was dealing with a profound and recurrent problem for rational thought. It is the problem of whether rationality is really self-grounding and, if so, what this means.

Could it be that reason rests on something other than itself? Thinkers like Derrida are arguing this today. But even Husserl came to recognize this as a problem, perhaps the profoundest problem of reason. Of course, he never surrendered his appeal to self-evidence, but he does probe into the source of this self-evidence with ever-increasing radicality. For example, Husserl complains in the *Crisis* that the post-Cartesian philosophy of Leibniz and Wolff lapsed into dogmatism because it took the testimony of self-evidence for granted (*Crisis*, 92, 93). Even Kant, who sets out to overcome this naiveté, doesn't satisfy Husserl's insistence on the need for a more radical grounding. According to Husserl, Kant himself took the relationship between synthetic a priori knowledge and the self-evidence of the "lifeworld" for granted (*Crisis*, 100, 101). The real issue is not how to account for the conditions of objective science. Important as this is, Kant and his predecessors ignored the fact that the objectivity of science rests on a type of certainty and self-evidence encountered by everyone in their everyday experience of the lifeworld. According to Husserl, Kant and his predecessors take this self-evidence for granted instead of making it *the* problem, the problem of the very ground of reason itself in the broadest possible sense. The result was a naive concept of self-evidence, which Husserl calls "theoretically no better than an appeal to an oracle through which a god reveals himself" (*Crisis*, 188, 189).

Predictably, Husserl sets out to overcome this naiveté in a radical transcendentalism. Unfortunately, Husserl's transcendental idealism, even his most mature statements of it in the *Crisis*, which seeks to understand the ground of the most basic form of evidence in the lifeworld, doesn't really solve the problem. In fact, I think the reduction of all being to the "absolute" being of the transcendental ego, a pure residuum of consciousness (as Husserl puts it in the *Ideas*)[8] actually compounds the difficulty. Husserl's insistence on the phenomenological epoché, with its "bracketing" or "suspension" (not to be mistaken for denial) of the world understood as standing in itself, real in itself without any necessary connection to our experiencing, seems to make possible an awareness of a world of "pure essences," the world "as meant," reality as the various modalities of its givenness to consciousness, etc., etc. But this same epoché, Husserl's starting point for the supposed solution of all philosophical problems, raises an insurmountable difficulty concerning the relation between this sphere of meanings, which the epoché opens up, and reality as it exists on its own terms, prior to experiencing. As Husserl puts it: "In so far as their respective senses are concerned, a veritable abyss yawns between consciousness and reality. Here, an adumbrated being, not capable of ever becoming given absolutely, merely accidental and relative; there a necessary and absolute being, essentially uncapable of becoming given by virtue of adumbrations and appearances."[9] Despite Husserl's insistence that we have no business worrying about this problem because only the experiencable world, the world as correlate of the transcendental ego, is a world we can begin to understand, the problem remains; it is as if the world and even my own individual existence gets swallowed up within the ego. At times, Husserl himself saw this as a major stumbling block. He writes in the *Crisis*: "But precisely here lies the difficulty. Universal intersubjectivity, into which all objectivity, everything that exists at all, is resolved, can obviously be nothing other than mankind; and the latter is indeniably a component part of the world. How can a component part of the world, its human subjectivity, constitute the whole world . . . ? The subjective part of the world swallows up, so to speak the whole world and thus itself too. What an absurdity!" (*Crisis,* 179, 180).[10] Yet Husserl is not daunted by this absurdity, this phenomenological paradox par excellence. He thinks that by evermore "consistent regressive inquiries" (*Crisis,* 181) he can span the "veritable abyss."

This never happens satisfactorily in my opinion. Much like he does in the *Logical Investigations,* Husserl appeals to "a sphere of self-evidence," which in his opinion is "of such a nature that any attempt to inquire behind it would be absurd" (*Crisis,* 188). Unfortunately, the appeal to self-evidence fails in my opinion to deal with the problem of the self-grounding of reason because it exists only in essential reality, in the sphere of the transcendental ego, whose relationship to the world simpliciter is simply left unclarified. One wants to know what the relationship is between the cognitive structures of rationality and the world as such. Of course, Husserl insists that our apprehension of the factual world, the real world, depends on an eidetic or ideal grasp of a realm of essences which makes reference to the real world as an intelligible world possible but doesn't really solve the problem. We are still left with the unmistakable impression that we are dealing here with two worlds, the world of rational experience and the world as such.[11] Specters of Aristotle's criticism of Plato begin to haunt Husserl at such points, not to mention Kant's problem with the thing-in-itself.

As Robert Sokolowski has recently noted,[12] Husserl himself seems in part to have created this problem for himself by adopting a consciousness/world dualism in the Cartesian tradition—even while he combats a specific representational model of that dualism. This dualism, which has trouble shaking the images of a hermetically sealed consciousness and transcendent world in itself, cannot help but frustrate any compelling account of truth. Of course, Husserl insisted that consciousness is not in principle sealed off from the world, and his account of intentionality has even contributed significantly to overcoming that dualism in philosophers who have rejected Husserl's idealistic account of knowledge. Nevertheless, Husserl's insistence that the sphere of meaning which the epoché opens up for the phenomenologist is not grounded in the "merely existent" world makes his claim about the "worldly" character of consciousness hard to hear.[13]

Nevertheless, I do think that Husserl's *intentions* are realist in nature. At times he even speaks of an "absolute correlation between world and world consciousness," a correlation which makes it possible to say that we are not presenting a "view" or "interpretation" bestowed upon the world but one which allows all views to be "ground[ed] in the pregiven world" (*Crisis,* 152).[14] But the nature of this grounding always eludes Husserl. As it turns out, it's not the world that grounds the ego and its knowledge but the ego and its knowledge which grounds the world, i.e., which makes the world intelligible in the first place. Given this Cartesian starting point, with its idealistic development, it's no wonder that Husserl's realist intuitions remain nascent. In this context, I can't help but wonder if Husserlian self-evidence is not itself much like "an appeal to an oracle through which a god reveals himself."

Of course, if one accepts the absoluteness of transcendental subjectivity, the *Unhintergehbarkeit* of phenomenological evidence, then Husserl's positions makes sense. But it is precisely the *Unhintergehbarkeit* of experience that is difficult to accept. Our sense of living in a world whose being and intelligibility are not our creation, either individually or corporately, i.e., through "intersubjectivity," is simply too strong to accept the absoluteness of Husserl's account of transcendental rationality in any of its versions. The sense that all reality has a dimension of standing in itself, of being other than an ego-relative reality, extends not only to the entire natural world but also to the ethical world of other human beings, both as physical and conscious beings. If there is anything we cannot go behind, as it were, it is this sense of the independent existence of the world and others. For both epistemology and ethics it is ultimately the independent reality of the physical universe and of other human beings from which we take our measure and must take our measure even when we self-consciously and self-critically seek to ascertain the ego's role in these endeavors. Reality is never a dumb presence waiting to have a meaning ascribed to it; it is always already meaningful. It reaches out as it were to human reason and demands recognition. It is not our creation, but our discovery. Husserl, to his credit, acknowledges this issue with some regularity, but his solution, in my opinion, suppresses one of the strongest intuitions we have by denying the meaningfulness of the world itself and claiming instead that all meaning is constituted in the ego.[15]

These issues will occupy us again at the end of the paper, but before turning to them one last time we need to examine the other motive for skepticism that I mentioned above—namely, our tenuous hold on the conditions of our own well-being.

III

There is perhaps no older motive for skepticism than human vulnerability and the deep fear that our neediness and our relative powerlessness in the face of a seemingly indifferent universe strikes into our hearts. We are born absolutely vulnerable and needy and even the mature skills of an adult human being in her prime only offers a very modest, relative control over life. This awareness of our fragility has always accompanied human consciousness; one finds it in all the world's great literature and in all honest conversation. Fragility is a basic, transcultural fact of the human condition.

Of course, one response to our plight has often been an aggressive defense of our prospects for knowledge, particularly as that knowledge issues in the technological manipulation of the world. Since the days of Plato and Aristotle, a version of this antiskeptical program has been pursued, partly as an antidote to our vulnerability to chance. In saying this, however, I do not wish to endorse Heidegger's reductionist vision of Western intellectual history. It is much too one-sided to maintain that technology has always been the telos of Western rationality. But certainly Heidegger and others like Martha Nussbaum[16] are right in thinking that *one* motive, a very strong motive, for defending human knowledge is our need to gain some measure control over our fragile position in the world.

But the skeptic responds to our fragility in a different way. In such a tenuous situation the skeptic abhors dogmatism of all sorts. Better to keep one's doxic options open by cultivating skepticism. Skepticism claims to allow the person to respond with greater practical flexibility to the changing appearances of the world and the various threats to and opportunities for well-being they present. The skeptic asks why she should commit herself to strict epistemic rigor when such a program might curtail her freedom to respond with sensitivity and human ingenuity to both the social and natural world around her.

I take it that some argument like this has perennial appeal for the skeptic. It can often be seen in the arguments of the ancient Sophists, like Gorgias and Protagoras. It was their genuine humanism and concern for human well-being that compelled them to make this case. Not all Sophists evinced the nihilism of a Thrasymachus or Callicles. We find this concern for human well-being in Sextus and the Pyrrhonists. *Ataraxia* is primarily a practical ideal, not just an epistemological one. The skeptical tropes are designed to achieve this practical state and not just to refute opponents. Close to our own day, I think we see a modern version of this kind of humane, practical skepticism in Montaigne and Hume.[17] And is it not the case that it is often precisely this sense of human frailty and the need for an open, flexible attitude in the face of it that in large part leads many scholars in the humanities today to resonate sympathetically with positions like Nietzsche's and his poststructuralist cousin Derrida? It seems to me that this is an understandable and plausible motive for skepticism, even if one has doubts, as I do, that the recognition of our own frailty requires skepticism.

Nevertheless, this same awareness of the tenuous nature of our grasp on the good life leads to an awareness of the *occasional* nature of our grasp on the conditions of our own flourishing, and thus to a kind of cultural relativism. The familiar argument runs something like this: every culture and perhaps every person is situated uniquely in terms of physical and psychological capabilities, natural resources, financial means, cultural history, political history, etc. All these factors contribute to who we are, how we think, what we value, etc. So it is that every culture and perhaps every person in it develops their own "truth" relative to their own search to lead the best life they can. Once we recognize this then the only humane response is to recognize, as it were, the "absolute relativity" of such "truths," including one's own, in order to "live and let live." Despite the logical paradox of such a situation, the skeptic argues that only skepticism can save us from the parochial dogmatism which inevitably results when one mistakenly equates one's relative coping mechanisms with absolute truth. Instead of a rigid dogmatism, with its implicit or explicit cultural imperialism, we should recognize difference as irreducible and celebrate diversity as a source of inexhaustible human ingenuity.

Although I do not think that skepticism is required for tolerance it is nevertheless important to note that it often has been effective as a kind of mantra or ethical technique for keeping one's own limited enthusiasms within acceptable, humane bounds.[18] Quite plausibly, if we repeatedly remind ourselves with the help of skeptical formulae that there are no absolutes we will be less likely to ascribe certainty and necessity to those beliefs and practices that are least certain and most occasional. In such settings, logic is sacrificed (or perhaps merely bracketed) for the sake of a more humane practice. If I have to choose between being consistent and being decent, the skeptic argues, I will choose to be decent. Moreover, I will adopt whatever practical strategies are most conducive to the ethical imperatives of decency, tolerance, and respect for difference. Ergo skepticism.

IV

What then is the nonskeptic to do? If the nonskeptic finds herself in a position vis-à-vis the skeptic of not being able to offer any response that does not beg important metaphysical and ethical questions, how then should she respond to the skeptic? Is the nonskeptic without philosophical arguments and perhaps even morally bankrupt? Should she go over to the skeptic's side, conceding the self-delusive character of her previous "refutations" of skepticism? Should she simply declare a truce, allowing the skeptic to go her way unchallenged but persisting in her own nonskeptical convictions?

Certainly the first response is unacceptable. Nothing that has been said entails skepticism. The second response recommends itself as a practical response to the fact that the skeptic is not likely to go away in our culture, and some way to allow the skeptic and nonskeptic to coexist is always needed. But ultimately the resignation implied by leaving skepticism intellectually unchallenged in order to do justice both to our awareness of our own limits and the practical imperative of tolerance exacts too high a price. While we often have need of tolerance, especially in the face of deep and stubborn human problems, like skepticism, tolerance does not require intellectual resignation.

What tolerance does require is a strong but provisional ascription of good will to one's opponents, modest self-assessment, and self-critical reflection. In my opinion, the skeptic mistakes an irrational skepticism as the ground of tolerance and forgets that tolerance is a *rational* virtue, rooted in a critical awareness of the limits of one's own reason. The rational person is able to recognize her own merely contingent concerns and habits and is on her guard against ascribing to these same concerns and habits an unwarrantable truth. Intellectual modesty does not require skepticism but it does require the recognition of a second-order truth, i.e., a truth about the limits of some of one's beliefs and practices. Far from entailing skepticism, this recognition of a second-order truth avoids the logical paradox of ascribing "unconditioned conditionedness" to all practical and theoretical claims. Such a self-critical awareness shows a *proper* respect for both one's own particularity and that of others and it holds out the further prospect of discovering *common* truths shared between participants of diverse cultures. Rather than precluding such common truths by an antecedent denial of their possibility, the nonskeptic searches for them and believes in principle that they cannot be ruled out and are even likely to be found, if only we look with sufficient care and proper attention to complexity, difference *and* sameness.

Thus, for the nonskeptic there is simply too much at stake to concede the debate to the skeptic. Not only does the nonskeptic wish to avoid explicit contradiction, but the possibility of discovering transcultural truths about the human situation is also on the line. While it can be conceded that skepticism as an *ethical mantra* has often been effective in combating dogmatism, the nonskeptic sees the cost associated with its consistent employment simply to be too high. The sacrifice of logical consistency and common truths in the name of tolerance and diversity is not only not required either logically or ethically but such a sacrifice would entail the surrender of logic and truth as normative ideals. The skeptic seems to forget that as normative ideals logic and truth have a long and distinguished history of urging human beings away from dogmatism, superstition, parochialism and even an overweening intellectualism itself. Like any ideals, logic and truth can be and have been abused, but when properly applied they contribute to human flourishing in unmistakable ways. Even diversity itself can only be given its proper due if we pay attention to the *logical* distinctions between contingent and necessary truths, probable beliefs versus merely possible beliefs, normative claims versus descriptive claims, etc. While I disagree with Husserl's transcendental strategy in combating skepticism, I agree with him that nothing less than the direction of human culture itself hangs importantly (but not exclusively) on the choice between skepticism and nonskepticism. This is not simply a personal choice, but one that will ultimately effect our institutions, particularly those involved with education and government, in profound ways. But before developing this observation further, I want to discuss more explicitly the methodological assumptions behind the approach to skepticism I am advocating.

I think it is evident by now that my approach to skepticism is practical in at least two senses. First, I am concerned with the practical issues at stake between the skeptic and nonskeptic. I think more needs to be said about the kind of culture(s) and society(ies) implied by both the skeptic and nonskeptic. Only by doing this kind of exploration can we responsibly weigh the value of each position. Such a task is by no means easy. What is needed is nothing less than an "ethics of truth." Such an ethics must explore not only personal truth-telling, but more importantly it must explore the value of truth as a normative ideal for culture. I obviously cannot supply such an account here, but only such an account will begin to do justice to the "humane" concerns of many skeptics.

Secondly, my argument is practical in a more fundamental way. I think an adequate philosophical response to skepticism, even its epistemological and metaphysical components, should be structured in some important respects like an Aristotelian practical argument. First of all, it should follow Aristotle's advise in the *Nichomachean Ethics* not to be overhasty in ascribing certainty to positions that really do not warrant it. One should take one's cue from the "things themselves" and ascribe certainty only insofar as the things themselves warrant it. I think this has consequences for a theoretical response to skepticism. Unlike many thinkers in the epistemological tradition, I think claims to necessity and certainty are not sufficient by themselves but assume metaphysical claims and perhaps even a certain kind of mystical experience. The fact that claims to strict necessity and certainty terminate in deeply appealing but deeply mysterious, perhaps ineffable appeals to "luminous self-certainties" makes such appeals metaphysical and perhaps ultimately mystical in a certain sense. They are metaphysical in that they often carry with them the conviction that one is looking into, as it were, the deep rational structure of reality. This conviction is ineffable in the sense that it is impossible to find anything more basic than this to appeal to in order to justify it, but it is also extremely elusive in that its full force is not experienced equally by all minds. Thus, it seems that even these basic convictions can be doubted, albeit at a great cost. Far from conceding the entire case to the skeptic such a move allows us to meet the skeptic more honestly with a less coercive agenda. Such a recognition of the metaphysical depths of appeals to certainty and necessity allows us to situate such appeals in a more tenous, but more fitting grasp of our own experience and its limits. This suggests to me that what the nonskeptic needs to do is to mount an argument whose *overall import* seeks to *persuade* the skeptic on a number of different levels rather than to *coerce* with logic. The nonskeptic's dream of coercing the will of the skeptic with apodicticity needs to be replaced by a more complex strategy, an argument whose many components addresses the many faceted metaphysical, epistemological, and ethical concerns of the skeptic. Such a persuasive argument would include appeals to rigorous reasoning, but its overall import would be rational in the broad, practical sense of trying to understand how these different concerns can be understood in a coherent pattern of meaning whose ultimate cash value would be its anticipated practical results. The nonskeptic's argument would begin with a defense of the claim that her position offers that coherence in a way that the skeptic position does not, but it would go on to make an ethical appeal about the value of a nonskeptical position. Just as Aristotle concedes that ethical argumentation cannot be value neutral but must make its case for ethical truth by offering to make the best overall sense of our given moral intuitions, so the nonskeptic should not argue from the presumption of theoretical or value neutrality but from the perspective of lived experience, i.e., from a perspective that claims in a fallibilistic spirit to make the most sense out of the whole gamut of conflicting intuitions regarding skepticism. Such an argument demands that we surrender the claims of epistemology to autonomy or purity vis-à-vis ethical concerns and insist instead that epistemological concerns are inseparable from value considerations.

We can further explicate this practical strategy by referring to Rawl's method of "reflective equilibrium," a method which, despite its use in Rawl's generally Kantian framework, draws its inspiration from basic Aristotelian sources. Generally speaking, this would mean that the nonskeptic would begin to approach the skeptic by challenging her to examine her intuitions about the validity of knowledge and its place in our lives. While her intuitions in this regard could turn out to be intractably skeptical, more likely she will discover that she actually has conflicting intuitions about the possibility of truth and the importance of this truth for human well-being. Assuming she will find conflicting intuitions, it's now a question of carefully articulating these intuitions and deciding which intuitions are the "deepest," i.e., which can she least imagine herself as living without. Careful work needs to be done to show that our most consistent and strongest intuitions are nonskeptical. It then becomes a question of how best to validate these intuitions with a deeper understanding of how they fit into a general sense of what our life is about and how best to encourage each other to act on them. What is needed here is a "metaphysics of knowledge" or an account of our capacity to know which offers a coherent but frankly speculative framework that allows us to make sense of this capacity to know by situating it in a "likely story" about human reason and its place in the world. Such a story could claim neither a priori certainty nor could it claim to be a simple descriptive account of the empirical "facts" of our existence. Rather, its claim on our reason would be "hermeneutical" in that it would offer an interpretation of our experience that brought cohesion to our experience by showing how the various pieces of our experience can be viewed as a coherent whole.

The strategy of reflective equilibrium asks the skeptic to consult her own experiences, her own intuitions about whether or not she can know reality as such. The appeal to experience is of both ethical and psychological importance. Ethically, it is important if we are to satisfy the moral imperative of self-responsibility, which Husserl repeatedly reminds us is an appeal implicit in all philosophical calls to examine oneself; often such an appeal is implicit in the defense of skepticism as well. Psychologically, it is important as well if the skeptic is to be convinced to repudiate her skepticism. If she cannot be convinced that some version of nonskepticism offers a better account of *her* experience, she cannot begin to see its *universal* validity.

Of course, this strategy assumes that the skeptic will discover conflicting intuitions about the possibility of knowledge of reality as such. This assumption seems to me highly plausible, given that we not make the mistake of thinking that the process of examining one's intuitions is a simple one of merely making certain assumptions thematic that were always transparent prior to the examination. Making our intuitions clear to ourselves is a highly *dialectical* and *intersubjective* process. We need not only to confront conflicting positions on the major issues but we need to see how others understand and respond to these positions. This is what it means to discover ones "own" intuitions; they need to be thought through in light of both the relative immediacy of one's experience and the highly mediated sense of one's place in a historically formed culture. Even a great philosopher's account of her intuitions is "always already" dialectical and intersubjective. Of course this means that such intuitions are always culturally conditioned, but this need not mean that they cannot contain truth. It's fully possible for culturally conditioned learning to discover transcultural truths, a possibility Husserl defended from the *Logical Investigations* through the *Crisis.*[19] A reading of the so-called pure epistemological account of skepticism, pro and con, belongs to this context of preliminary, dialectical exploration. Far from making these epistemological accounts the last word in the debate on skepticism, they need to be a first word, a starting point for broader considerations.

Now that one has uncovered these conflicting intuitions the next step is one of deciding which of these intuitions are the "deepest," i.e., which intuitions deserve priority and preservation because she can least imagine her life without their regulative influence. Such considerations are, of course, explicitly practical. It is here that the nonskeptic can appropriately introduce questions about the indispensability of logic for any meaningful communication whatsoever. Here the case can be made for the *value* of respecting the law of noncontradiction for communication. Such an appeal would be explicitly ethical in that it should point to the social value implied by the concept of *communication* and even the individual practical imperative of making sense to oneself. This is not to say that the meaning of logic is exclusively ethical. The *ordo cognescendi* need not be confused with the *ordo essendi.* It is to say, however, that the ability to see the full essential meaning of logic is often contingently dependent on appreciating its moral payoff. Perhaps no one in our day has tried to bring this to our attention more than Habermas, but certainly we find this kind of ethical argument also in thinkers like Plato, Aristotle, Kant, Hegel, and Husserl, although in these thinkers it is an argument of secondary importance. I am suggesting that the communicative value of logic be given center stage in a response to skepticism that is preeminently practical.

Such a consideration about the value of logic leads naturally to broader considerations about the value of accepting the possibility of valid knowledge-claims for one's life but also for culture and humanity at large. What this requires is something on the order of what I called above an "ethics of truth." I'll say here in my opinion that the form such an "ethics" should take is teleological. I think this is so first of all because we are historical beings, embedded in a past and projected toward an unknown future. Nonskeptics have often overlooked this fact in their preoccupation with necessary and universal truths. Such an oversight opens them to the charge of a fundamental distortion of the human condition. If, however, we recognize our historicity, then we need a teleological account of reason to descry patterns of meaning in the flux of history, patterns that will help us discern both reason's triumphs and failures in the past, as well as its plausible directions in the future. Such teleologies are explicitly ethical in that there is no way to construct such a narrative from a value-neutral standpoint. The ordering of all the "relevant" data involved is always done in light of value-laden norms. In fact, I would argue that all histories are teleological and hence ethical in this way. I think helpful hints for such a teleology can be found in thinkers like Hegel, Husserl, and Habermas. While not pretending that their respective philosophical agendas are the same, they nevertheless share a deep ethical sense of what is at stake between the skeptic and nonskeptic.

But we need this teleology for the even more important reason of counteracting the negative teleologies of reason that seem to be dominating the philosophical discussion today. I mean the negative teleologies of Nietzsche, Foucault, and Derrida. Without minimizing their differences, I think one thing these thinkers have in common is a similar tendency to reduce reason to power. They see all cognitive disagreements as attempts at power plays, i.e., infinitely various strategies of self-aggrandizement.

When applied to their own positions it seems to me that such reductionism makes their own claims vacuous and morally questionable.

But such well-justified complaints against these positions are also in danger of missing an important feature of these positions, a feature which makes them compelling to so many. I think that each position appeals to an erotics of sorts. I mean by an erotics an appeal, either implicitly or explicitly, to a kind of deep desire. It is this desire, barely articulated but pervasive in the rhetorical force of their writings, which carries a large burden for convincing the reader. We need to look again at the real rhetorical force of their appeal. In Nietzsche, I think we see a deep appeal to the erotics of artistic creation, particularly as a model of what it means to be a self, to lead a fully human life. Foucault shows us an erotics of the flesh, an account that understands our social institutions as strategies of coercion and control against the anarchy of individual pleasure. And Derrida puts forth what I would call an erotics of the word, a kind of reveling in the rush of the linguistic flux, the flood of words that results when one argues that the context for understanding any writing is always an infinite one. However different each of these "erotic" positions is, I think each presents a facet of a broader erotics of freedom which has considerable appeal. It is the deep appeal of freedom of various sorts which, in my opinion, accounts in large part for the widespread success of such positions. In a culture that increasingly leaves little room for individual self-expression it is no surprise that "freedom" can be valorized, even at the cost of logic.

As sympathetic as I am to the value of freedom, I am not willing to give up logic and truth to defend it. It seems to me that the skepticism behind each of these positions can only be effectively counteracted by an erotics of reason itself. This erotics of reason needs to be part of the teleology I called for above. The skeptic needs to be argued against on numerous levels, not the least of which is an attempt to show what is concretely desirable about the life of reason itself. If reason is to be recognized as an "infinite task," a valid moral ideal for all human beings, we need to think more about why a human being with limited time and a variety of possible practical goals would choose the life of reason. Certainly Plato is a helpful starting point for such an endeavor. The goal of personal enlightenment, so erotically portrayed in the "Allegory of the Cave" and dialogues like the *Symposium* needs to be rekindled in our discourse. And even Husserl can wax lyrical about the "final harmony" (*Crisis*, 72–73) of viewpoints envisaged by reason, suggesting, I think, a genuine social value to reason that needs explication and defense. Such an "erotics" of reason needs to explore both the personal and social dimensions of reason's appeal to us.

If we turn for a minute to the social value of reason, we are reminded that reason offers us the possibility of reconciling conflicts in terms of common rational insight. I think the adjudication of practical disagreements in the light of reason is a genuine moral vision for all humanity to embrace. It is a moral vision which exhorts us to repudiate force and adjudicate conflict, wherever possible, in light of a common pursuit of truth.[20] One does not have to think that all moral goals boil down to this question of a final truth in order to endorse *this* goal as valid. Moreover, one does not have to think that it is a sufficient response to all moral evil simply to diagnosis its irrational roots. Not all moral problems are problems of truth and its recognition.[21] Nevertheless, I think the ideal of truth is often necessary to an acceptable strategy of confronting evil. Many evils begin simply by the stubborn refusal to see and accept the truth. Moreover, such evils need to be resisted in the name of truth if such moral confrontations are not going to degenerate into the mere clash of wills. The notion of truth is a normative one and one to which we must learn to subordinate our irrational impulses.

It is lamentable that in some quarters of academe today there is so little respect for this ideal of truth and its regulative role in human interaction. If this repudiation of truth continues, the very ideal of a university as a community of scholars seeking the truth is threatened with extinction. The dignity and respect accorded to each member of this community rests in no small part on their common pursuit of truth. When our very real differences of opinion are taken out of this ethical light and seen, as they are today by many, as nothing more than various strategies of political maneuvering, then the solution to these differences can take no other imaginable form than a gratuitous power play. If our intellectual life comes to this sorry state, as it has already in some quarters, the civilizing, irenic effect of a common pursuit of truth will be eroded, and perhaps destroyed altogether by a barbarism of either the right or the left.

If this happens first within academe in a truly pervasive way, then I doubt that the broader, more important democratic ideal of reasoning together about common problems can survive much longer. Such an ideal presupposes in principle a common ability of human beings not only to recognize truth but to recognize that truth is normative for many pursuits, not the least of which is simple justice. The very ideas of both distributive and retributive justice presuppose the ability of human beings to accurately describe the situation in question, a description which can claim to be true and not a self-serving projection of the powerful against the powerless. Without this basic capacity for truth, real disagreements cease to be looked on as failures of reason (which I think they truly are) and are seen instead simply as rhetorical strategies in a power game whose real solution is impossible *in principle*, because every move is nothing but another vibration in the ubiquitous web of power.

In a world and society that is threatened by increasing "tribalization" and "balkanization," I think we need to heed the call of reason's quest for unity in the light of a common truth. To make this goal practically effective in the minds of the majority of educated people more attention needs to be placed on the erotics of reason. To accomplish this task, philosophers need to recapture a feeling for the potentially complimentary tasks of intellect and emotion. The so-called purity of the intellect and its principle guardian, traditional epistemology, must be questioned and placed in a broader, practical context where real human beings live their lives.

I think one possible consequence of rediscovering an erotics of reason, or the complimentary intentional structure of intellect and emotion will be nothing less than a renewed interest in metaphysical concerns. I think metaphysics is a part of the practically driven teleology I called for above. Human beings not only need to situate themselves in as deep and wide an understanding of reality as they can, it turns out that we always do this even when we repudiate this need because it goes under the name of "metaphysics." Metaphysics, like eros, is concerned with "wholeness," i.e. by our need to discover "what is" and "what is good"; it is driven by our need for a compelling account of reality, our place in it, and our prospects in light of our situation.[22] Such a metaphysics responds to both practical and theoretical issues that arise from experience but cannot be answered by appeals to experience alone.

In the context of confronting skepticism, I think one of the most important metaphysical issues to arise is whether or not the human mind has the ability, as it were, to rub up against the "real" world in all its enormous, fascinating, and frightening complexity. This question involves nothing less than the need to take a stand on the relation between our rationally structured experience and reality as such. Such a stand would be openly speculative in frankly admitting that it had no a priori or empirical insight into this relationship. We cannot miraculously leave our experience behind for a short time in order to see how experience as such is related to reality as such. Nevertheless, we need to answer this question explicitly or otherwise it will be answered implicitly and the skeptical consequences will be drawn. Such an answer can still claim to be rational in that what it seeks is nothing less than coherence between our strongest intuitions of ourselves as "sources" of reason and the independent reality and reason of the world. This implies I think that the nonskeptic's answer to this question of the relation between experience and the world must be openly realistic in nature. In my opinion nothing less than realism will do justice to both ourselves as "sources" of reason and the independent reality and reason of the world. In my opinion nothing less than realism will do justice to both ourselves as "rational centers" and the world as somehow coming out, as it were, to greet that rationality with its revelation of itself. Nothing less than realism does justice to our sense that we discover the world and do not create or "constitute" it, even in its intelligibility.[23] Finally, I think nothing less than realism will be able to combat the contention that the intelligibility of the world is not a function of the will but a function of the things themselves. If it is the will that is behind the various ways the world presents itself to us, if it is the will that is the final source of our disputes, then it seems that all our differences are simply reflections of the will to power. This recognition ultimately drives us to skepticism. It should come as no surprise to those who know the history of recent European philosophy that skepticism is so widespread today.[24] Nothing less, in my opinion, than a return to "the things themselves" holds out hope for a resurgence of reason. Nothing else rekindles the wonder that has always been the starting point for rational inquiry and nothing else provides us with its proper touchstone.

9

Meditations of a Russian Neo-Husserlian: Gustav Shpet's "The Skeptic and His Soul"

George L. Kline

Russia was the first country outside of Germany in which Husserlian phenomenology was taken with full philosophical seriousness, although the earliest Russian commentators tended to interpret Husserl as an ontologist, a theorist of the *eidē*—almost a Platonist—rather than as a theorist of transcendental subjectivity.[1] The most forceful and original of the Russian philosophers influenced by Husserl was Gustav Shpet (1879–1937), who attended Husserl's seminars in Göttingen in 1912–13 and carried on an active philosophical correspondence with him between 1913 and 1918. Shpet had an unusually keen sense for what was fresh and exciting in contemporary philosophical thought. He unfailingly recognized—as did the Pole Roman Ingarden, his fellow student at Göttingen—that in 1912 Western Europe could offer no philosophical mind more powerful or original than Husserl's.

I

Half a dozen publishing events in the first two decades of this century marked the emergence of a deep and fruitful interest in Husserlian phenomenology among Russian philosophers.[2] The very first translations of Husserl's works were into Russian, and long predated the first English and French translations. An authorized Russian version of the first part of the *Logical Investigations: Prolegomena to Pure Logic* (1900) was published in 1909,[3] and a translation of the long and seminal essay "Philosophy as a Rigorous Science" appeared in the Russian edition of the *Logos* yearbook in the same year as the original publication in the West European edition of that yearbook.[4]

A certain amount of Russian discussion of Husserl's ideas appeared as early as 1906.[5] Major articles on Husserl began to appear three years later,[6] but the most important publications date from the five-year period 1913–17. It was in 1913 that the first Russian monograph on Husserl appeared.[7] And it was in 1914 that Shpet published his lively and highly original meditation on Husserlian themes—themes drawn mainly, though not exclusively, from *Ideas I*.[8] In 1917 Lev Shestov published his provocative, penetrating, and in some respects idiosyncratic attack on Husserl's theory of knowledge.[9] In April 1928, by the way, Shestov and Husserl met in Amsterdam (by then Shestov was living in permanent exile in Paris) and soon became very close. Husserl's seven letters to Shestov (1928–33) and one letter from Husserl's wife Malvine are included in Husserl's recently published correspondence.[10] They offer ample evidence of Husserl's respect, admiration, and affection for Shestov and his family—despite their deep disagreements about the role of rationality and of universal validity (*Allgemeingültigkeit*) in human life. The salutation of one of Husserl's warmest letters to Shestov is revealing: "Verehrter *Freund* und *Antipode*."[11] Shestov survived his friend by only a few months; his last, posthumously published, essay was a generous, eloquent, and moving tribute to his distinguished philosophical adversary.[12]

There seems to have been a strong mutual attraction, both personal and intellectual, between Husserl and Shestov. Husserl was only seven years older than Shestov. He was *twenty* years older than Shpet, and there was perhaps a touch of fatherly concern in his respect and affection for the younger Russian, and a touch of filial piety along with respect and affection in Shpet's relation to his beloved master Husserl.

II

Since Shpet is not yet well known to students of phenomenology in general or of Husserl in particular, the following details of his life and work may prove helpful at this point.

Gustav Gustavovich Shpet was born on 25 March (Julian calendar, or 7 April, Gregorian calendar) 1879, in Kiev, to a single mother whose brother adopted the boy, a step which made it possible for him to be enrolled in good season at Kiev University. Shpet's ethnic background was Polish, his confession (at least in his youth) Lutheran. His mother was poor and he had to help support himself (which he began to do as early as age thirteen, working as a tutor) as a student in the Classical *Gymnasium*, where, among other things, he acquired the solid mastery of Greek and Latin that was to serve him well in his later philosophical and scholarly work. After graduation in 1898 he entered Kiev University, but his radicalism got him into trouble with the authorities. He was expelled after two years at the University, and sent into internal exile (in 1899). He was permitted to return to Kiev and to reenter the University in 1901, at which time he transferred from natural sciences to humanities (the so-called Faculty of History and Philology). His degree, received in 1905–6, was an "external" one; but his graduation essay, on Kant's relation to Hume, was awarded a "gold medal"—the Russian equivalent of *summa cum laude*—and published in a university periodical.

In the early 1900s Kiev University had on its humanities faculty such luminaries as Prince Eugene Trubetskoi, Sergei N. Bulgakov, and Georgi I. Chelpanov. Shpet was selected—along with one or two of the other most promising graduates in his class—for further study, some of it abroad, in preparation for an academic career. But his repeated brushes with the state authorities led to his being barred from teaching in institutions under the jurisdiction of the Education Ministry. For a time his teaching was limited to private secondary schools and the *Vysshie zhenskie kursy* or "women's universities."

When in 1907 Shpet's mentor, Psychology Professor Chelpanov (1862–1936), was invited to Moscow to join the university there and set up an Institute of Psychology, he took Shpet with him. In 1910 the two made a tour of psychology institutes in Germany, examining procedures and institutional arrangements that might be worth introducing in Moscow. From 1907 to 1912 Shpet not only continued his graduate studies in philosophy at Moscow University while working at the Institute, but also taught at a Moscow secondary school, the Moscow "women's university," and Moscow University itself, where in 1910 he completed his M.A. and was appointed a *Privatdozent*. Boris Pasternak was a member of his Hume seminar.

Shpet traveled abroad to do further research on his doctoral dissertation during the summers of 1910 and 1911 and the academic year 1912–13, including the 1913 summer semester at Göttingen, where, inter alia, he took Husserl's seminar on "Nature and Spirit." He worked in major research libraries in Berlin, Paris, and Edinburgh. In 1916 Shpet defended his doctoral dissertation *Istoriia kak problema logiki* (*History as a Problem of Logic*) and was named a professor in the "women's university" and a *Dozent* at Moscow University. He was promoted to professor at the University in 1918. During this period he taught a wide variety of courses, ranging from aesthetics and logic to the philosophy of history and the history of philosophy.

By the end of the academic year 1921–22 the teaching of non-Marxist philosophy had been banned and Shpet was dismissed from his university posts. Between 1920 and 1922 he passed up two chances to leave the country. First he and his family were offered Lithuanian citizenship and passports. Later, in November 1922, when more than a hundred distinguished non-Marxist writers and thinkers—including Lossky and Nicolas Berdyaev—were deported, Shpet's name was on the original list of deportees. But Shpet's personal appeal to A. V. Lunacharsky, People's Commissar of Education in Lenin's government, was granted and his name was removed from the list. His loyalty to the new Russia was soon to prove fateful.

Shpet, perhaps surprisingly, was allowed to remain culturally active in Moscow during the first decade of Soviet rule. He was an influential member of the Linguistics Circle, where his ideas had a powerful impact on fellow member Roman Jakobson. He held various offices in Councils and Academies concerned with the study of the arts. But in 1929 he was dismissed and forbidden to teach or to publish his own work. The only activity in which he was permitted to engage, through the mid-1930s, was the translation of and commentary on various literary and philosophic texts, mostly English, including works of Berkeley, Shakespeare, Byron, and Dickens.

After sharp ideological attacks on him in Soviet periodicals, beginning in 1930, Shpet was arrested in March 1935 and sentenced to five years of internal exile. He spent eight months in the Siberian town of Yeniseisk but was then transferred to the Siberian university city of Tomsk (in December 1935). Although his requests for formal ties with the university were denied, he was given limited access to the university library, which he made use of in completing an impressive new Russian translation of Hegel's *Phenomenology* (which was not published until 1959). He was arrested again on 27 October 1937, and sentenced to ten years' imprisonment. But on 1 November he was twice interrogated in secret. The protocol of the first session contains nonincriminating information and each of its pages bears Shpet's signature. In contrast, the protocol of the second session teems with seriously incriminating but quite fantastic charges; the signatures pedantically set down on each page of this second protocol are evident forgeries. On 6 November Shpet was sentenced, in secret, to death; a terse secret-police document dated 16 November reports that the sentence had been carried out. Shpet had been shot, apparently on that same day.[13]

When, after repeated urgent requests, Shpet's family finally was officially informed of his death, the death certificate which they received (in 1956) stated, falsely, that Shpet had died of *pneumonia* on *23 March 1940.* That fabricated date has been widely repeated, e.g., in the Soviet *Filosofskaia entsiklopediia* (*Encyclopedia of Philosophy*) of 1970 and the Husserl *Briefwechsel* of 1994, where both the year of birth (given as 1878) and the year of death (given as 1940) are wrong (cf. vol. 10, 76). It seems that 1937 was a particularly bloody year for political prisoners in Stalin's gulag; when the time came in 1956 and the following years to "rehabilitate" them, the announced dates of death were routinely shifted to later years, in some cases as much as half a dozen years after the actual death, although in Shpet's case only three.

Unfortunately, Shpet's *juridical* rehabilitation was not accompanied by any *cultural* or *intellectual* rehabilitation. Another thirty years were to pass before his works began to be republished and discussed in Russia. Shpet was a prolific author. In a fourteen-year period (1914–27) he published seven books. He also completed an eighth (in 1918) but was barred from publishing it.[14] The seven books are: *Iavlenie i smysl* (*Appearance and Sense*), 1914; *Istoriia kak problema logiki* (*History as a Problem of Logic*), part 1, 1916; *Filosofskoe mirovozzrenie Gertsena* (*Herzen's Philosophical Worldview*), 1921; *Ocherk razvitiia russkoi filosofii* (*An Outline of the Development of Russian Philosophy*), part 1, 1922; *Esteticheskie fragmenty* (*Aesthetic Fragments*), part 1, 1922, parts 2–3, 1923; *Vvedenie v etnicheskuiu psikhologiiu* (*An Introduction to Ethnic Psychology*), 1927;[15] and *Vnutrenniaia forma slova* (*The Inner Form of the Word*), 1927.

Shpet was the founding editor of a philosophical yearbook, *Mysl' i slovo* (*Thought and Word*), which, between 1918 and 1921, when it was suspended, published remarkable essays by Vladimir Solovyov and Lev Shestov as well as several by Shpet himself, among them "Skeptik i ego dusha" ("The Skeptic and His Soul"), 1919, to be discussed in section IV, below.

Shpet's philosophical position has until recently been characterized as "orthdoxly Husserlian" by both Soviet and Russian émigré commentators.[16] But in fact it would be more accurate to call him a "neo-Husserlian" (as I have done in the title of this essay), since on central philosophical issues he was closer to both Plato and Hegel than to (early) Husserl. After an initial enthusiasm for the powerful current of Neo-Kantianism—represented primarily by Hermann Cohen and Heinrich

Rickert—that dominated Russian intellectual life in the first decades of the twentieth century, Shpet turned sharply away from both Kant and the Neo-Kantians. He was unimpressed by the parallel current of positivist "empirio-criticism" of Mach and Avenarius and their Russian followers, a position which, like Neo-Kantianism, wrongly elevated epistemology to the status of the key philosophical discipline.

In Shpet's eyes both the Neo-Kantians and the "empirio-critics" stood in the tradition of what he called "negative philosophy," which included Locke, Hume, J. S. Mill, and Spencer. In contrast, Husserl stood in the tradition of what he called "positive" or "affirmative" philosophy (*polozhitel'naia filosofiia*), which included Plato, Leibniz, Hegel, and Lotze. Shpet is here rendering Hegel's expression *die positive Philosophie*, which he sets in sharpest opposition to Comte's *philosophie positive* or positivism. Negative philosophers are one-sided and reductionist. Although relatively strong in their criticism of rival positions, they are unacceptably weak and narrow in their own "positive" or "affirmative" contributions.

Shpet had thoroughly assimilated the Western tradition of affirmative philosophy from Plato to Husserl, but he remained essentially "Russian" in his insistence (with Vladimit Solovyov and Solovyov's teacher P. D. Iurkevich) that philosophy should be a full and integral knowledge that deals with the complex richness of lived human experience, and not just with its intellectual dimensions. Moreover, with Hegel and Solovyov, Shpet maintained that what is whole and concrete (in Hegel's speculative sense, namely "many-sided, fully-related, adequately mediated") is also social and historical, active and dynamic. This stands in sharp contrast to the position of the early Husserl—the Husserl of the *Logical Investigations*, "Philosophy as a Rigorous Science," and *Ideas I*—which was of course the only Husserl that Shpet knew when he wrote such works as *Appearance and Sense* and "The Skeptic and His Soul." None of Husserl's early works contained the stress on intersubjectivity, history, and the "lifeworld" (*Lebenswelt*) which Husserl introduced in such late works as *The Crisis of the European Sciences and Transcendental Phenomenology* (published in part in 1936 and in full—posthumously—in 1954).

Still, Shpet found much to admire in the early Husserl, above all the powerful critique of relativism and "psychologism," i.e., of the attempt to reduce what is logical to its psychological causes or conditions. However, in the early works Husserl, while rejecting psychological individualism, continued, in a sense, to accept a methodological and phenomenological individualism. And Shpet found both kinds of individualism unacceptable, insisting instead that we cannot adequately understand a society, community, people, or "ethnic group" simply by studying the individuals who make it up. In other words, there is a Hegelian *objektiver Geist*—

a complex of cultural traditions, institutions, practices, and products—which must be studied as a coherent system of signs and symbols. Another way to put this point is to say that, for Shpet, a "hermeneutical logic" of history is an indispensable and central philosophical discipline.

III

The recently published Husserl correspondence contains a rich harvest of letters, mostly *not* previously published, from Husserl to Shpet, from Shpet to Husserl, and from Malvine Husserl to Shpet and to his wife.[17] Husserl's six letters to Shpet were written between May 1913 and May 1914. Shpet's five letters to Husserl were written between November 1913 and June 1918. Malvine's note to Shpet and his wife is dated May 1913 and her final letter to Shpet's wife is dated September 1918. Up to now, only brief excerpts from a few of these thirteen letters have been published, mostly in the original German, with a scattering in English translation.[18]

Shpet's letters are written in fluent and forceful German. In preparing them for publication the editors of the *Briefwechsel* have had to make only a few minor corrections to Shpet's word order and grammar (mostly endings). Only once did Husserl indicate that he had had any difficulty in following Shpet's German: one of Shpet's philosophical objections, he says, wasn't entirely clear to him, in part because of Shpet's sentence construction. Husserl goes on to make a little joke about the difficulty of the "wretched German language" (*das böse Deutsch*).[19]

The correspondence makes it clear that the relations between the two men, and indeed their families, was marked by great respect, admiration, and affection. Husserl's first note expresses his deep concern about the "harrowing adventure" that Shpet had had to endure the night before (i.e., on 8 May 1913). We have no details about this "adventure"; but what in any case is most striking is Husserl's evident concern for Shpet's welfare. He reports that he has already spoken with the Rector, urging him to remove the cause of the unpleasantness, and invites Shpet to visit him for a private conversation the following morning, adding that he has canceled all of his academic exercises scheduled for that day. The salutation of Husserl's letter is "*Lieber Herr von Spett*"; the complimentary close is "With collegial greetings and best personal wishes" (*Mit collegialem Gruss und besten Wünschen für Sie*).[20]

Malvine Husserl's note dated 13 May cordially invites both of the Shpets to join the Husserls for an afternoon walk followed by coffee "out of doors" (*im Freien*) the next day.[21]

On 30 August Husserl sends Shpet, now in Edinburgh, a postcard from his holiday retreat in Mürren (in the Swiss alps). He reports that he has been working hard on the revisions to volume 2 of the *Logical Investigations* and hopes to be able to send him a copy of the "completed work"[22] by the end of October as a "return gift" (*Gegengabe*) for Shpet's gift to him of Jakovenko's Russian monograph on Husserl's philosophy, and also as a remembrance of their "semesters at Göttingen."

Shpet, now settled for a time in Paris, writes to Husserl on 23 November 1913, addressing him the way any German university student of the time would address his professor: "*Sehr geehrter Herr Professor!*" He uses this same salutation for all of his letters until the last (June 1918), at which point he adds one word to make the salutation "*Sehr geehrter* lieber *Herr Professor!*"[23] But as early as March 1914 he had closed his longest letter to Husserl with the words "With complete respect and much love" (*Mit voller Achtung und grosser Liebe*).[24]

Expressions of warm regard were mutual. Husserl began his letter to Shpet dated 29 December 1913: "Valued Friend!" (*Werter Freund!*) and used the same salutation in his letter of 28 March 1914.[25] Between these two is a letter (15 March 1914) with the salutation "Dear Friend!" (*Lieber Freund!*).[26] Although Husserl's last letter to Shpet (to have been preserved), dated 17 May 1914, uses the more formal salutation "Highly Respected Colleague!" (*Sehr geehrter Herr College!*), it is permeated with Husserl's joy and excitement at the prospect of Shpet's return to Göttingen for an early visit, something to which Shpet had referred in his letter of 4 May. Husserl urges Shpet not to make his visit too short and to give him advance notice so that he will be able to arrange his schedule to allow ample time for Shpet.[27]

By November 1913 Shpet, in Paris, reports to Husserl that he has made good progress with his book *Appearance and Sense*, inspired by *Ideas I*. (It was to be published in Moscow the following year; see notes 1 and 7, above.) As Shpet puts it, despite the charms of Paris, his "phenomenological hunger" is stronger than his "touristic curiosity." He adds that he had completed, but not revised, a draft of the book in Moscow. Apparently Shpet returned to Moscow between leaving Göttingen in late June or early July and arriving in Edinburgh in late August. He mentions having stopped in Berlin, presumably en route by train between Moscow and Paris.[28] *Ideas I* had been available to him for only a few months; it is astonishing how quickly he had absorbed the rich content of this difficult book to produce a sound and yet highly original interpretation and reinterpretation of central Husserlian themes.

He now tells Husserl that in addition to tightening his entire presentation, he plans to carry out major revisions, focused on two key points: (1) the problem of the intuition of ideal essences and the linked problem of the relation of what he calls *Präsentativismus* (which he vigorously defends) to *Repräsentativismus* (which he flatly rejects);[29] and (2) the problem of nominalism. Shpet expresses the hope that these changes will make clearer to his Russian readers the general significance of phenomenology and of the phenomenological "turn" (*Wendung*) in philosophy.

He also speaks of his growing interest in finding phenomenological ideas and insights in earlier thinkers—"before the birth of phenomenology." He mentions Plato in this connection, but adds that for the moment his anxiety—presumably about misinterpreting Plato's position—is saving him. ("*Vor Plato habe ich vorläufig die rettende Angst.*")[30] He reports his excitement upon reading the statement in a here unidentified French source (possibly Bergson?) that for Maine de Biran "*la véritable invention en philosophie consiste uniquement dans la détermination exacte des données immédiates de la conscience.*"[31]

Shpet writes again from Paris on 14 December to thank Husserl for his kindness and consideration in sending him the two volumes of the revised *Logical Investigations.* They have, he says, brought him both great joy and much worry. "The [philosophical] riches from which I must select are truly inexhaustible." He is now dividing chapter 5 of *Appearance and Sense* into two separate chapters in order to be able to expand his discussion of the concept of *Bedeutung.* Noting that revised volume 2 ends with Investigation 5, Shpet indicates that he is now awaiting Investigation 6 so as to be able to bring his own book to an appropriate conclusion.[32]

Shpet goes on to raise his first (written) objection to a Husserlian position. His question is about "presuppositionlessness" (*Voraussetzungslosigkeit*).[33] He asks whether the requirement of *Wissenschaftlichkeit* (roughly, "scientific or systematic character") isn't itself a kind of presupposition. And wouldn't such a requirement rule out the otherwise desirable phenomenological investigation of religious and in particular mystical language, say, in the writings of Santa Teresa, Jakob Böhme, or Thomas à Kempis? Finally, Shpet asks whether *Wissenschaftlichkeit* shouldn't rather emerge in the course of, or as a result of, phenomenological investigation. "[O]n the *threshold* of phenomenology we do not yet know whether it will be constituted as a science or in some other way."[34]

In his response of 29 December Husserl admits that the passage about the requirement of *Wissenschaftlichkeit* was taken over from the first edition and might better have been omitted. He did not, of course, have in mind a presupposition of *Wissenschaftlichkeit* in the sense of a preexisting norm, in the style of the Marburg Neo-Kantians. He admits that the very idea of *Wissenschaftlichkeit*[35] requires preliminary clarification. Here it really amounts to "rationality" (*Vernünftigkeit*), something which is "understandable in an exemplary way and is directly self-evident" (*die exemplarisch und in direkter Evidenz verstehbar ist*).[36] Husserl adds that on problems such as this his *Ideas I* offers much more than even the revised *Logical Investigations.* But he does suggest that Investigations 3–5 in their revised form will be especially useful for Shpet's work on his new book, even though in preparing the revised edition he "had to leave in place much that was imperfect" (*manch Unvollkommenes stehen lassen musste*).[37]

Husserl's letter, however, begins with a heartfelt expression of the joy which Shpet's letters from Paris have afforded him and his wife. He goes on to wax uncharacteristically lyrical:

> It refreshes my heart to see that the upland [*Hochland*] of phenomenology in all its grandeur, beauty, and philosophy-generating strength stands as vividly before your eyes as [it does] before mine, and that you too . . . do not shun the immense labor [*die unsäglichen Mühen*] that everyone who wishes to make himself at home there must take upon himself.[38]

Husserl adds that he is delighted by what Shpet has told him about his methods of working and his plans for further work. "Only full and complete devotion [to one's work]," Husserl writes, "will produce anything of permanent value, anything truly fruitful." Husserl goes on to insist that the world must see how seriously we (phenomenlogists) take phenomenological investigation. We will deserve whatever blame we get if, instead of working seriously, we indulge ourselves in babble and chatter (*schwätzen*). However, only a few months later (on 28 March 1914) Husserl was warning Shpet against *over*work. "Don't overwork, so that you may continue to be spared the nervous set-backs [*Rückschläge*] which often slowed me down and inwardly depressed me when I was your age."[39]

Although, in the letters we have, Shpet had said nothing about Bergson, Husserl ends his letter with the rhetorical question: "Do you really mean to pass up the chance to meet a thinker of genius like Bergson?" He adds that if Shpet should decide to look Bergson up in Paris, he will be glad to write him a few lines of introduction.[40] My own guess is that Shpet the rationalist and passionate defender of "affirmative" philosophy did not really want to meet Bergson, the eloquent critic of reason and passionate defender of what to Shpet amounted to a "negative" philosophy—however much of a "genius" he might have been. In any case, we have no evidence that Shpet ever had any personal or professional contact with Bergson.

The next two letters which Shpet sent Husserl from Moscow (on 11 March and 4 May 1914) and Husserl's responses (15 March and 28 March) are quite long and filled with discussion of technical points in Husserl's philosophy, such as the relation of *Erlebnis* and *noesis* to *noema*, of sense (*Sinn*) to content, of the abstract to the concrete, and questions about the controversial status of what Husserl called the "transcendental 'Absolute.'" Since these topics have no direct bearing on our main theme, they will not be discussed further here.

Shpet reported that in Moscow he had found a gratifying increase, "in all philosophical circles," of serious interest in Husserlian phenomenology, even though the recently published *Ideas I* had not yet been much studied or discussed. "The assessment of phenomenology in all quarters is high and favorable; phenomenology is viewed as a serious new step in philosophy." Shpet reports the success of his own public lectures, including one at the Moscow Psychological Society where the audience numbered nearly two hundred, in which he presented phenomenology as a fundamental science. Despite the difficulty of the material he was presenting, the lecture aroused "lively interest and close attention." The critical responses from such invited discussants—all well known in Moscow philosophical circles—as Ivan Il'in, Boris Jakovenko, and Lev Lopatin, were, Shpet claims, mostly based on an inadequate grasp of the principles of phenomenology. Shpet felt that he had met all of their objections squarely.[41]

In his letter of 28 March Husserl thanked Shpet warmly for the detailed report of his "powerful" efforts on behalf of phenomenology, which have strengthened the already active interest in that position among the Moscow philosophical public. But he goes on to warn:

> The main thing is that your countrymen, who are so given to enthusiasms, should realize that this is not a new doctrine of salvation [*Heilslehre*], faith in which will make them happy, but [rather] a new science [that] has been opened up, an infinitely fruitful soil on which to work, one that is endless and fruitful like the Russian steppe, but which will bear a rich harvest only as a result of irksome labor [*mühevoller Arbeit*]. . . .[42]

At the end of his letter of 11 March, reporting on the progress of his work on *Appearance and Sense*, Shpet had said: "I should be happy if you would permit me to dedicate the book to Professor and Mrs. Husserl."[43] Husserl's answer came at the end of his long letter of 28 March (he admitted that it *should* have come at the beginning): "I hardly need say that it is a heartfelt joy for me to be honored through the dedication of a scholarly [*wissenschaftliche*] work by a man whom I have learned to value so highly, both as a person and as a scholar." Husserl adds that his wife was pleased by the kind offer to include her in the dedication, but felt that she should not accept, given that this is a purely scholarly book. "Since she will not budge [from her decision], all that remains for me is to let you know this and to accept the dedication for myself with heartfelt thanks."[44]

Shpet replied on 4 May that he was delighted to know that Husserl welcomed the dedication, adding that Mrs. Husserl's response had not "embittered" him. "I fear," he added, "that my request was perhaps indiscreet . . . perhaps it was 'all too' Russian . . . yet [it was] heartfelt and cordial [*herzlich und innig*]!"[45]

Iavlenie i smysl (*Appearance and Sense*), when it was published in Moscow later that year, bore the dedication (in German): "Dedicated to Professor Edmund Husserl with heartfelt respect [*in herzlicher Verehrung*]." The presentation copy which Shpet sent to Husserl bears the additional handwritten dedication (also in German): "To Professor Husserl, my dear master, with gratitude. Gustav von Spett."[46]

During and after the First World War certain philosophers and ideologists in Russia—as in the United States—produced a number of ill-conceived and hastily prepared pamphlets, books, and articles in which they laid partial or, in some cases, almost total blame for twentieth-century German militarism on the philosophical ideas of such diverse eighteenth- and nineteenth-century German thinkers as Kant, Fichte, Hegel, Schopenhauer, and Nietzsche.[47] It is against the background of such philosophical propaganda, as well as that of the frightful mass slaughter of the previous four years, that Shpet's letter to Husserl of 6 June 1918 is to be understood. Shpet writes:

> I am seizing the first opportunity to send you and your family my most heartfelt greetings. The madness of mankind in its old age is, it would seem, far from over, and we do not know what the immediate future will bring. But I may say with assurance that nothing that has happened could change my evaluation of German philosophy, and there is nothing in the world that could shake my deepest devotion to you personally. During these four long years there has not been a day when I have not reflected on phenomenology and rejoiced in my spiritual and intellectual bond with its creator.

Furthermore, says Shpet, he has constantly thought, with gratitude, of Husserl's truly human and humane interest in his own, and his children's, fate. He adds, obviously not yet knowing the dreadful news about Husserl's son Wolfgang that Malvine Husserl's letter of 20 September

1918 will bring: "I venture to hope that the general unhappiness has not touched your family directly and that your children are with you."[48]

Malvine Husserl says in her 20 September letter to Shpet's wife that her husband is answering Shpet's letter (*mein Mann* [*beantwortet*] *den Brief des Ihrigen*).[49] But there is no such Husserl letter in the *Briefwechsel,* the Shpet (Spett) section of which in fact ends with this moving letter of Malvine Husserl.

IV

Both Hegel and Husserl took skepticism seriously, devoting careful, detailed, and insightful discussion to it.[50] Shpet wrote a sixty-page essay, "The Skeptic and His Soul," the subtitle of which is "A Study in Philosophical Interpretation." It *is* that, but it is also (1) a study in *metaphilosophical* interpretation, focused on the relations between negative and "affirmative" philosophy, and the relations among rationalism, empiricism, relativism, and psychologism; and (2) an original and penetrating psychological account of the "skeptical state of mind" and of the skeptic as a character type. It is a quite remarkable essay. In the words of a recent Russian commentator: "The author's polemical style . . . , the biting wit crowning a professor's fundamental erudition, makes this study a literary masterpiece." Moreover, Shpet's "moral strength" is exhibited in this essay in his deep "understanding of creativity itself."[51]

Like Hegel, whose treatment of ancient skepticism he calls "unsurpassed,"[52] Shpet draws heavily for his account on Sextus Empiricus, quoting many of the same passages that Hegel quoted, both those concerning skepticism in general and those dealing with the various "tropes" (*tropoi*) used by the skeptics to undermine opposing positions. Shpet comments on all of the tropes (see esp. 120ff., 137, 138) and in fact quotes Sextus Empiricus more often than any other author. However, I shall not pause here to review the various tropes. The interested reader will find a clear and informative account in three encyclopedia articles by Philip P. Hallie.[53]

Shpet's treatment of skepticism differs from Hegel's in two significant respects. First, he treats as central the skeptics' principle of the *isostheneia tōn logōn,* the "equipollence or equal force of [opposing] claims or theses." In the *late* texts to which Shpet refers, Hegel makes no explicit reference to this principle. However—as Shpet seems not to have been aware—in a very *early* text Hegel had a good deal to say about the principle of equipollence.[54]

In any case, for Shpet it is precisely this principle which launches the skeptic on his hopeless quest (*zētēsis*), leading to suspension of judgment (*epochē*) and ultimately to imperturbability (*ataraxia*). Shpet points out, with a quite Hegelian irony, that, despite their loud talk about suspending judgment, skeptical authors have managed to fill up entire treatises with their (unsuspended) judgments (112; cf., 113, 116, 133, 135, 136, 146, 155, 156).

Second, Shpet disagrees with Hegel (and, as we shall see, with Husserl) about whether skepticism counts as a *philosophical doctrine.* Hegel referred to what he called "thinking skepticism" as a "dialectical phase [*Moment*] within philosophy itself,"[55] one which had been *aufgehoben* ("preserved, canceled, and raised to a higher level") in the subsequent dialectical development of Western, including Hegelian, philosophy. Shpet objects that the skeptic's characteristic answer to a philosophical question: "Maybe yes, maybe no," or "Maybe it's true, but then again, maybe it's false," disqualifies skepticism as a philosophical doctrine. Such an answer is static and nondialectical; it stands outside the general dialectical development of thought. Shpet insists, with greater emphasis and consistency than Hegel, that skepticism cannot be refuted or overcome by philosophical means (113).

In a long footnote focused on sections 32 and 33 of the *Prolegomena,* Shpet mentions Husserl's contrast of "logical" and "noetic" skepticism, on the one hand, and "metaphysical" skepticism, on the other, but then discusses mainly the former, a position which rejects the logical and noetic conditions for the very *possibility* of theory.[56] What Shpet emphasizes is Husserl's association of this kind of skepticism with *empiricism,* which he interprets as implying that empiricism would, along with skepticism, be denied the status of a philosophical theory. This Shpet rejects, insisting instead that empiricism *is* a philosophical theory, though a thoroughly *negative* one, in the sense that stands in contrast to "positive" or "affirmative" theories (114n.).

Shpet offers four separate though related arguments in support of his claim that skepticism is not a philosophical doctrine or theory, and that it fails to make philosophical claims. He refers, in this connection, to Emerson's remark that the skeptic takes up his position in the "*vestibule* of the temple" of knowledge (108).[57]

1. Skeptics have no arguments that are specifically or uniquely their own. The arguments they use—e.g., deducing the inaccessibility of truth from the limitations of the knower, or deducing the *inevitability* of error from its *possibility,* or deducing the lack of any necessity from the presence of a given contingency (135)—are borrowed from the negative philosophical doctrines of empiricism, subjectivism, and relativism. To

refute these skepticism-generating doctrines involves what is now called "rooting out psychologism," and this (Husserlian) project has generally been a success (110, 113, 136).

2. The skeptics have not, since ancient times, come up with any new arguments for their position, nor have they developed any of the traditional arguments. Thus, skepticism exhibits an absolute "completedness" or a "finished state" (*zavershennost'*) which is something *not* found in any philosophical doctrine (111n.–112n.).

3. The principle of equipollence (*isostheneia*), which is central to skepticism, is *not* to be found in any philosophical doctrine; therefore, skepticism is not a philosophical doctrine (113).

4. The internal (logical and methodological) *self-contradiction* which is central to the skeptical position cannot be a feature of any philosophical doctrine; therefore, skepticism is not a philosophical doctrine (112, 113; cf., 114n.–115n., 115, 118, 144).

What then *is* skepticism, in Shpet's view? He characterizes it variously as a "mood" (*nastroenie*) (110, 111, 129), an "attitude" (*otnoshenie*) (117), an "act of experiencing" (*perezhivanie* = *Erlebnis*) (115n., 129), a "psychic state" (*dushevnoe sostoianie*) (143), a "state of consciousness" (*sostoianie soznaniia*) (112), a "structure of consciousness" (*uklad soznaniia*) (118, 144), and a "psychological superstructure" on a philosophical base (134). It follows, according to Shpet, that philosophical arguments cannot refute skepticism; as Hegel noted, such arguments fly harmlessly past their target. After all, how could one expect to "refute" a mood, an attitude, or the state of consciousness that springs from disillusionment with one's projects or with the failed results of exhausting labor at a task that has proved to be beyond one's powers? (110).

Shpet sees the experience of failure as the ultimate source both of the individual skeptical consciousness and of skepticism as an historical school or movement. Ancient skepticism, he suggests, arose as a reaction to the failure of stoicism,[58] and the modern "theory of knowledge" (in Locke and Kant), which is simply "skepticism erected into a principle," arose as a reaction to the failure of (dogmatic) metaphysics (143n.).

Shpet makes the points listed above (157–58) quite explicitly. What he appears to assume implicitly, and without explicit mention or elaboration, is the claim that the various theoretical "blunders" of psychologism, which he joins Husserl in repudiating when they are applied to *philosophical doctrines* or *claims*, turn out to be quite justifiable when they are applied to skepticism as mood, attitude, state of consciousness, etc. Here Shpet appears to have picked up and developed in his own way a clue in Hegel, who had noted the element of *choice*, *decision*, or *desire* in the process by which a skeptic becomes a skeptic. (Little if any theoretical reflection is involved.)

> [I]f anyone actually *desires* to be a Skeptic [*schlechterdings ein Skeptiker sein* will], he cannot be convinced [or "prevailed upon," *überwunden*], or be brought to a positive [in Shpet's sense "affirmative"] philosophy, any more than he who is paralyzed in all his limbs can be made to stand. Skepticism is, in fact, such paralysis—an incapacity for truth [*eine Unfähigkeit der Wahrheit*].[59]

Shpet paraphrases this passage, though without giving any specific reference to Hegel's writings, and goes on to compare skepticism not only to paralysis but also to indigestion and toothache! (110).

The contemporary (Husserlian) critique of psychologism attempts to compromise it by revealing its skeptical consequences. But this approach backfires; the skeptic turns it to his own advantage, eagerly supporting psychologism, and thus attempting to strengthen his claim that skepticism *is* after all a philosophical theory (134f.). What Shpet calls the "fallacy of psychologism" is two-pronged: (1) it confuses the *object* of perception and judgment with the *acts* of perceiving and judging directed at that object; and (2) it confuses the pure act of consciousness in its intentionality (Husserl!) with the individual acts of experiencing (*perezhivanie* = *Erlebnis*) of a given judging and perceiving subject (135).

The "psychologistic paralogism"—the most general formulation of which is "We do not assert something because it's true; rather, it's true because we assert it" (110)—is a failure in philosophy; subjectivism in knowledge is "a lie" (138), and the skeptic has a distorted "psychologistic soul" (137). Shpet adds, with his characteristic biting irony, that the skeptic shares with middle-of-the-road common sense the "virtue" of "public falsehood" (151).

Psychologism includes as a special case what Shpet calls "geneticism" (the Russian form of the Greek term is *genetizm*) (123, 124). This is not just a doctrine of origin and development; such a doctrine is accepted by affirmative philosophy, which, in the person of Hegel, even views the process of historical development as a realization of the truth. Rather, geneticism involves replacing the (Husserlian) pure study of cognitive acts with genetic explanations of those acts and their content (124). As a critical method this sounds rather like what has come to be called "the genetic fallacy," i.e., the assumption that it is sufficient to reveal the sources, causes, or motives of a given doctrine or value to invalidate that doctrine or discredit that value.

To put the point a bit differently: Shpet is entirely in agreement with Husserl in denying that the discovery of the sources or causes of a given doctrine or claim invalidates that doctrine or claim. But he goes beyond and, in a sense, against Husserl with respect to skepticism, asserting that the discovery of the sources or causes of a given attitude or state of mind *does* discredit that attitude or state of mind, along with the conduct, including speech, that issues from it.

The "psychologistic" and "genetic" approach that Shpet considers uniquely justified in its application to such a position as skepticism involves the asking of such questions as: What motivates the skeptic? How did he get that way? Is he sincere? Always? Sometimes? Never? Is he a hypocrite? Always? Sometimes? Never? etc., etc. The point could be put in terms of "unmasking," the reductionist procedure made current in the nineteenth century by Marx and Nietzsche and in the twentieth century by Freud. Shpet would repudiate the unmasking of *doctrines* or *theoretical claims* (something enthusiastically practiced by all three of the "great unmaskers" just mentioned), but he endorses, and enthusiastically practices, the unmasking of the *moods, attitudes,* and *states of consciousness* of the skeptic. He speaks of the "skeptic and his soul" but not of "the *rationalist* and his soul" or "the *empiricist* and his soul," and this distinction is a matter of principle for him.

His unmasking of the skeptic is not, of course, either Marxian or Freudian. But it does contain elements that could be called "Nietzschean," e.g., the stress on the skeptic's envy and resentment of the affirmative philosopher and of the latter's successes, relative as they may be, as a source of the skeptic's attitude and conduct.

Although Shpet mentions Nietzsche several times in other connections (e.g., 150, 157, 159), he fails to make explicit his tacit "Nietzschean" assumption that "Truth is a *woman.*"[60] The generalized model of the skeptic's soul, for Shpet, is one of failure and frustration, accompanied by envy and resentment. The more specific model is that of the rejected lover. On both models, the skeptic, for Shpet, is an uncreative, reactive, negative, envious, and spiteful human being. "The philosopher, according to Plato, is a man in love. The skeptic may be called one who is disappointed in love [*neudachnik v liubvi*]. Skepticism is the jealous torment of the unsuccessful lover who has been rejected by truth" (154; cf., 149).

"Rejected by the truth, the skeptic feels as though he has been hurled into solitude, and in that solitude, alongside his secret sense of failure . . . there develops a sense of wounded conceit and arrogance" (150–51). This conceit develops into a passion to demean others, to uncover their (secret) faults and failures, and to probe the causes of those failures (152, 153). The skeptic, Shpet adds, is "stunned by the fact that he has been rejected when others have *not* been rejected" (154;

italics added). He comes to suspect that they have in fact been rejected but refuse to admit it.

At this point it is clear that the skeptic, on Shpet's account, is engaged in "unmasking" the dogmatist and perhaps the "affirmative" philosopher as well. The skeptic doesn't care much about the truth of what the dogmatist is saying. Rather, he focuses on the condition of the dogmatist's "soul": Why does the dogmatist say what he says? In what tone of voice? With what inner feelings? etc. (156).

In at least a few passages Shpet appears to fall into the error of which he has accused both Hegel and Husserl, that of treating skepticism as a philosophical doctrine. At least he claims that the despised "thesis of representationalism" (*reprezentativizm*) is accepted by skeptics as well as by dogmatists and negativists. This thesis combines aspects of several "negative" doctrines, maintaining that the contents of human consciousness are only impressions or reflections of things in the world (124, 144). As a result we can know only our own states of consciousness, and we can't even say that our ideas "resemble" things in the world; how on the representationalist account, could we possibly know whether they do or not? (125). The "terror" of the representationalist thesis has often poisoned, and sometimes paralyzed, the philosophical activity of individual thinkers (123, 118).

The contrasting "thesis of presentationalism" (*prezentativizm*), favored by affirmative philosophers, sees not two widely separated worlds but only differences among the elements which are "there" *prezentativno* ("by presentation" or "as presented") in the "*one and only* given world of things and events" (125).

Turning to the skeptic's practical philosophy, Shpet notes that the longed-for *ataraxia* brings with it a kind of gratification or pleasure that contrasts sharply with the torments of failure and rejection. This pleasure, treated as an "end-in-itself" (*samotsel'*) makes the skeptic a *hedonist* of sorts (145). Despite his indifference to the truth, the skeptic yearns for the kind of satisfaction that affirmative philosophers experience when they attain the truth. But the search for truth "requires labor, creativity, and the strength to endure the sufferings and torments that are connected with all of these." Shunning hard work, lacking creativity, deficient in strength, the skeptic emerges as lazy, uncreative, unfree, weak, and timid—in short, as a *failure* (146).

V

In the above discussion (section IV) of Shpet's rich and provocative text, I have failed to include a number of points that perhaps deserve at least brief mention here. These are of three kinds: unproblematic but not directly relevant characterizations of skepticism and the skeptical character; puzzling, though sometimes intriguing, comments about philosophy in general and about skepticism in particular; and, finally, troubling critical and polemical comments about what Shpet views as "Eastern" (*vostochnyi*) and "Christian" intrusions into philosophical theory and interpretation. I shall consider each of these in turn.

1. Shpet makes several comments about skepticism as a whole and about the personality of the skeptic, which, though unproblematic, are not directly relevant to the main themes which I have been discussing. Among these are his characterization of skepticism as the "wrong side of dogmatism" or an "inside-out dogmatism" (*iznanka dogmatizma*) (158) and his criticism of both ancient and modern skeptics for being unduly "serious" and lacking any saving sense of humor (161ff.).

2. Shpet speaks, puzzlingly, of the element of "bestialism" (*bestializm*) in skepticism (133, 134, 139, 140, 144) and, using a quite different and perhaps ironic, but no less puzzling expression, of a "skepticism touched by Grace" (*blagodatnyi skeptitsizm*) (158, 159, 161, 168). He harshly condemns metaphysics, whether speculative or empirical, as an attempt to pass off mere opinion (*doxa, mnenie*) as "rigorous knowledge." Yet he adds, unperspicuously, that he is not at all opposed to metaphysics as a "form of literary creativity" (114n., 119).

3. In several passages Shpet makes such troubling remarks as that it is somehow "Eastern" and "Christian"—and clearly unphilosophical—to mix myth and opinion with knowledge, something that happens, he alleges, when commentators who take Plato's *myths* with full seriousness treat what for Shpet is Plato's "affirmative" philosophy—presumably, the theory of forms—as a mere "appendage" (*privesok*) for the "amusement" (*zabava*) of certain German Plato specialists! (142). Shpet has similarly polemical comments about Christian agape (142; cf., 158) and Christian "positive morality"—I assume that he means the morality of the Good Samaritan (162). In such passages Shpet sometimes sounds not only very "Western" and secular but also anticlerical, anti-ascetic, antireligious—and a bit "shrill."

On the other hand, he frequently expresses his sympathies for mysticism (132, 159, 165), as he had in his letter of 14 December 1913 to Husserl, quoted above. Nine years later Shpet made an intriguing and, I think, quite valid point about the close relationship between rationalism and mysticism. He spoke of philosophies which, though "rationalistic in principle," are "filled to overflowing with purely mystical enthusiasm [*pod"em*]." His examples are the philosophies of Plato, the neo-Platonists, Johannes Scotus Erigena, Malebranche, Spinoza, and Hegel.

Shpet denies that what he calls the "mystical overtones" of these philosophies are mere "chance accompaniments." Rather they are—he insists—"necessary complements, which, like a kind of inspiration, accompany the subtlest analyses and most exalted flights of the purest and most perfect work of *reason* alone."[61]

I suspect that at least some of the points which puzzle me would also have puzzled Husserl, and that the points which I have found troubling would have troubled him as well. In any case, I am *certain* that Husserl would have been delighted by most of Shpet's work, including major portions of "The Skeptic and His Soul." It is a great pity that Husserl, who knew Shpet so well as a student, a fellow phenomenologist, and a philosophical correspondent, should have been denied the opportunity to know him as a philosophical *author*.

Unlike such of his Russian contemporaries as S. L. Frank, who wrote several works directly in German, or Berdyaev, Shestov, and S. N. Bulgakov, many of whose Russian writings were promptly translated into German, Shpet wrote and published *only* in Russian. To be sure, the German-language publications of the Russian thinkers just mentioned date mainly from the period of their permanent exile from Russia, when (after 1922) they were living in Germany or France. If, instead of remaining in the Soviet Union, doomed to suffer a ghastly fate, Shpet had joined Berdyaev and other leading intellectuals when they were banished from Russia, we can imagine that he might have gone on to write some of his philosophical works directly in German and to supervise the German translation of his Russian works. And we can vividly imagine Husserl's excited and sympathetic response to any work of Shpet's that might have been made available to him in German.

In bitter fact, as we have seen, the close ties between Husserl and Shpet came to a permanent end in 1918. Twenty years later Husserl, in the days before his death on 26 April 1938, must have remained blankly unaware that his former precocious student, lively correspondent, and valued friend—a man twenty years his junior—had been brutally swallowed up by Stalin's Siberian gulag more than five months earlier.

10

Skepticism and Dialectic

Errol E. Harris

I

Hegel's review of *Kritik der theoretischen Philosophie* by Professor Gottlob Ernst Schulze in the *Kritisches Journal der Philosophie* of 1802 is an early and somewhat immature work, largely sarcastic polemic of the chosen author; but it gives significant presage of Hegel's insights into the nature of dialectic and the relation to it of skepticism, a relation which he later emphasized and explained with greater clarity and systematic precision in his *Vorlesungen über die Geschichte der Philosophie.* The earlier work is remarkable for the evidence it shows of the young Hegel's grasp of the significance and power of negation, which is the inner principle of his dialectic, and this is what he develops more fully in the *Lectures on the History of Philosophy* and in the *Logic.*

Contemporary and recent skepticism, as represented by Herr Schulze's critique and earlier by Hume's radical empiricism, Hegel decries as unspeculative and restricted to the limits of the understanding. It rests uncritically on sense-certainty, rejects the supersensible as illusory, and undermines the coherence of knowledge by rejecting the universal. All this, however, is the result of accepting as final the limits of the finite and of failure to recognize the complementarity of mutually determining phenomena within the whole which constitutes the truth.

The thought of the ancient skeptics, in Hegel's view, was much more speculative in character, much more aware of the significance of the negative, and gave promise of the understanding to a more adequate grasp of the whole that is the ultimate object of speculative reason. But the ancient skeptics failed to get beyond the negative aspect of rational analysis, and so fell short of the comprehension and concreteness of the Idea.

What impressed Hegel about the ancient skeptics was their insistence on the freedom of thought (whether explicit or implicit) and its prerogative to suspend judgment, refusing to affirm any thesis, or either one of two opposite assertions. Such freedom, for him, is the essence of Spirit, its own self-reflective capacity, which empowers it to grasp its own relation to its other, to recognize its identity with, and to find itself at home in, its opposite. This self-determination of thought is the guiding thread of Hegel's treatment of skepticism in all its forms, as it is intrinsic to his whole system.

II

There are different kinds of skepticism, motivated by different reflective considerations. The first, of which we should dispose at the outset, is not skepticism per se, but is no more than a heuristic procedure characteristic of philosophy as such, or what Hegel would be disposed to call *Wissenschaft.* Unlike the empirical and reputedly exact sciences, philosophy sets out to eschew all presuppositions, and one way of doing this is to begin by rejecting all opinions which there is any pretext to doubt. This was the procedure adopted by Descartes, and that it was not skeptical in intent Hegel points out.[1] It is merely, Hegel contends, to insist on beginning from thought as such, and to suspend all presuppositions. In fact, by calling in question all beliefs that can be doubted (for whatever reason), Descartes seeks to discover a firm, indubitable insight that can serve as a clue to an assured criterion of truth enabling him to distinguish unerringly between the true and the false—the kind of criterion the possibility of which the professed skeptic denies. For Descartes, therefore, the rule (quoted by Hegel), *de omnibus dubitandum est,* is no more than a means to certain knowledge, the very opposite of what the convinced skeptic is willing to admit.

Another position often termed skeptical is the distrust expressed by some philosophers of the evidence of the senses. Such distrust of the senses is common to both Plato and Descartes, as well as to some empiricists, who point to illusory sense perception and perspectival distortion as grounds for rejecting sensible evidence in its immediacy as presenting objective truth. This, however, is not necessarily a denial of the possibility of knowledge, but only the rejection of one alleged source.

Plato elevated intellectual apprehension of ideas above the deliverances of the senses as the faculty of knowing, as did Descartes, who called it "the natural light." Empiricists use the so-called argument from illusion to establish the existence of sense-data, which they regard as the primary source of objective knowledge, although they usually require some kind of coherence test to establish its truth (for example, what Berkeley calls "the settled order of nature"). Here again, then, mere distrust of sensible evidence does not amount to skepticism.

Entertaining doubt or denial as to the existence of a world external to the mind has, by some, been called skepticism. This usage would apply eminently to Berkeley, yet oddly enough he adopts it himself to describe his opponents, who maintain, he says, that matter exists independently of consciousness and thus is out of the reach of knowledge. It is also applied to Descartes's initial scruples about belief in the existence of external things, even including his own body (among other considerations, because of the lack of any differentiating characteristic between dream and waking). The same usage would be appropriate to Kant's restriction of knowledge to phenomena, leaving things-in-themselves beyond the range of the understanding. This was a major consideration prompting the skepticism professed by Schulze and ridiculed by Hegel. But, again, this is not skepticism proper, and the term is used in this way only by dogmatic (naive or critical) realists, who accept without question the presupposition of external existence as an article of faith. Those who doubt the existence of the external world, moreover, do not reject truth as such; some resolve the doubt with a counteracting proof, and others develop as a positive position some form of idealism.

Hume's skepticism differs from that of the ancients by his acceptance of sense impressions and ideas (their paler copies) and the relations between them as knowable intuitively. For him, what undermines the validity of reason, of belief in a sensible world, and in the existence of the self, is his failure to discover any necessary connection between impressions or ideas, his conviction that "whatever objects are different are distinguishable, whatever objects are distinguishable are separable,"[2] that "our distinct perceptions are distinct existences," and that "the mind never perceives any real connection among distinct existences."[3] Consequently, all necessity and universality in knowledge is dissolved away, all systematicity disintegrates, neither reason nor experience can supply any criterion for decision where apparent contradictions occur, and belief can rest on no better foundation than custom.

Hegel includes Berkeley with Hume under the rubric of skepticism, differing, he says, from the ancients in that the underpinning of their doctrine is their certainty of reality[4]—that is, the reality of sensed objects, which both philosophers include within the field of consciousness. Skepticism, Hegel asserts, is the return of thought to itself, at first in the formal sense of individual self-consciousness, so that all reality is included in the activity of the subject, as with Berkeley and Hume. The outcome is a subjective idealism which in its reliance on the primacy of sense-given particulars excludes universality, and so dismembers and dissipates truth. The skepticism of such empiricist thinkers (and their followers, including Kant) Hegel held to be tainted with dogmatism because of their unqualified acceptance of sense perception.

III

The primary motivation of skepticism is the relativism that results from reflection on the diversity among and conflict between moral attitudes and philosophical views at different times and in different societies. Hegel begins his *Lectures on the History of Philosophy* by discussing the common reaction to this variety of opinions and the claims by successive philosophers to refutation of their predecessors. Common to the skeptics is their despair of finding any criterion by which to decide between all these conflicting truth-claims, a criterion (they contend) which no philosopher has hitherto succeeded in establishing, and which is not subject to dispute and subsequent rejection.

In his long introduction, Hegel draws attention to the common view of the history of philosophy as a fortuitous succession of opinions, the very multiplicity of which seems to mark them as mere opinions in contrast to truth; and the impossibility of finding any assured way of deciding between them, or of knowing which is worthy of acceptance, leads to a belief in the futility of the entire philosophical enterprise. Such a belief, however, he explains here, is simply the result of a misconception of the nature both of history and of philosophy. The first is not just a series of fortuitous events, but is a dialectical progression; the second is no mere succession of arbitrary opinions, but is the development of the one philosophy, the whole which is the truth, and which is only genuinely whole and true in and as its own self-development—as he puts it in the Preface to the *Phänomenologie*, "*hierin eben besteht seine Natur, Wirkliches, Subject, Sichselbstwerden zu sein.*"

Nevertheless, it was just such an approach that was the original source of skepticism in the ancient world, beginning with the Sophists, who saw no way of deciding between the different systems that had been advocated by various philosophers and schools prior to the fourth century B.C. So they maintained that the sole aim of argument was to make one's own case appear the stronger, no ultimate test of its truth being available—hence, the relativism expressed in the declaration of Protagoras that "man is the measure of all things" and the radical skepticism of Gorgias, who denied all existence and all possibility of knowledge.

Another pretext for the denial of knowledge, not unconnected with this, was the interpretation of Heraclitus's doctrine of universal flux by Cratylus. Heraclitus himself did not reach a skeptical conclusion, for he insisted on the harmony of opposite tensions and the truth of his "word." He declares that all things are one—"Wisdom is one thing. It is to know the thought by which all things are steered through all things" (frs. 1 and 19, Bywater's version). But Cratylus inferred that, if everything was constantly subject to change, it was impossible to make any assertion about anything that would not immediately be refuted by subsequent alteration, so that one was unable to make any statement that could ever be maintained. The diversity of philosophical views may be regarded as a product of this continual change.

The same sort of considerations motivated the later skeptics of the Hellenistic and Roman periods. Hegel maintains that the philosophers of the New Academy, Acesilaus and Carneades, adopted a position which is barely distinguishable from that of Sextus Empiricus and Diogenes Laertius. I shall not go into the detail of the separate arguments of the different philosophers, for what I am concerned with in this paper is only the general principles, as Hegel saw them, activating the procedure of the ancient skeptics. For him, they represent genuine skepticism, much more philosophical than the modern variety, and not, as is commonly held, opposed to philosophy proper. Skepticism, he avers, is philosophy, although it stops short of the Concept and does not get beyond the negation of dogmatism. It fails to recognize the negation of the negation in the Idea. Nevertheless, it presents us with the true dialectic of the finite, which is the first step beyond the rigid distinctions and separations typical of the understanding.

IV

The primary principle of skepticism is self-consciousness and subjectivity, hence relativism; for what simply appears to the subject is purely relative to that subject and to whatever might condition its cognition. This is true both of ancient and modern skepticism, the latter arising out of one form or another of subjective idealism, and the former from the inward-looking individualism of Stoicism and Epicureanism.

In the *Phänomenologie* Hegel contends that the concept of independent consciousness is represented in the history of philosophy by Stoicism: self-consciousness withdrawn into itself, but failing to find itself in and to identify with its external other. Skepticism, he says, is the realization of this self-withdrawal, as the negative attitude to all otherness. In the *Lectures on the History of Philosophy* he maintains that skepticism completes the outlook of Stoicism immersed in and asserting the subjectivity of all cognition. This subjectivity relativizes all judgment and makes any universal truth unattainable. It thus denies and destroys all being (opposed to subjective self-awareness) and all objective knowledge. Consequently, Hegel points out, it amounts to a paralysis of thought, insofar as it demonstrates the incapacity of consciousness to attain truth and rests in mere uncertainty.

The more sophisticated, philosophical and thinking, skepticism, however, demonstrates the instability and self-contradictory character integral to the nature of all determinate and finite being. In so doing it exhibits the dialectical movement which, in the *Phenomenology*, conducted consciousness from sense-certainty, through perception to understanding, which holds the distinct and determinate elements apart as absolute and self-contained, despite their evident dependence for their own intrinsic nature upon the other which they negate and exclude. Consequently, such determinate elements contradict themselves and one another. So the skeptic rightly rejects them as mere appearance, and refuses to assent to any as reliable or true. But he (or she) stops short at this point, failing to perceive the reconciliation of opposites achieved in their being-for-self as the Concept, in which their mutual dependence is grasped and they are identified in the coherence of the whole. Hence, Hegel avers, speculative philosophy, which recognizes this outcome of the dialectic of the finite, includes skepticism within itself and is immune from the skeptical assault, because the Concept contains the negative within itself as one moment, and negates it by uniting the opposing finites in systematic interrelation.

Every conviction persuasive to the person who holds it, so the skeptic argues, is as good as every other; and he bases his case on this equivalence or equipollence of opposing positions. Whichever of two opposite assertions is maintained, the other can be defended on equally plausible grounds. One is therefore not justified in accepting either and should withhold one's assent from both. The best that one can claim is that what is asserted is merely what appears to the speaker to be the case. Seeming is thus substituted for fact, and nothing should, therefore, be positively affirmed. This suspension of all commitment and indifference to all affirmation is called *epoché* and results in complete emotional detachment and imperturbability, or *ataraxia.* The epoché, therefore, Hegel contends, evinces the self-assertion by thought of its own freedom.

Hegel applauds the ancient skeptics, who, unlike their modern counterparts, sought to be fully consistent and went the whole distance, declaring even their own assertions to be unworthy of assent. Yet, in so doing they cut away the ground under their own feet and remained mired in self-contradiction. It is to this self-stultification that Hegel refers when he says that skepticism is the paralysis of thought, for either the skeptic positively affirms the equipollence of opposing views and the legitimacy of his (or her) own epoché, maintaining this position dogmatically and so contradicting the central skeptical exhortation to refrain from dogmatism, or, to be finally and utterly consistent, must desist from any assertion whatsoever—the consistent skeptic can only (as Spinoza contends) remain silent.

V

Sextus Empiricus tells us that the later skeptics did not strictly constitute a "school" and, as they held themselves aloof from all dogma, maintained no positive position whatever, describing themselves as seekers. What they sought, apparently, was not truth, but intellectual repose in *ataraxia.* Their philosophy is thus not a system or doctrine but simply a method—a way or mode of procedure, in accordance with certain prompts, which they called tropes (*tropoi*). Of these there were two sets, ten which were adopted by the earlier Pyrrhonists and five which were propounded by the later, in Hegel's view more philosophical, skeptics.

The first ten tropes concern sense perception and morality, and are all aspects of relativity in one form or another. Sextus Empiricus divides them into three classes: those referring to the judging subject, those referring to that about which the judgment is made, and those referring to both.

The first trope points to the diversity of animal anatomical organization, relative to which different species perceive the same object differently (and this in lesser degree can, of course, apply to differences in human physical condition). Hence, the second refers to differences of human sensibility, disposition, and the like, which cause different persons to perceive the same objects differently (one man's food is another man's poison). The third refers to differences in the deliverances of different organs of sense (e.g., in a picture, what appears to touch as smooth, appears to sight as raised). The fourth refers to differences of circumstance and conditions, in which the perception of the same thing may vary (as when the same thing appears red in daylight but black in moonlight, or differently when the perceiver is moving from when he or she is at rest; so also judgments of the same situation or object differ as the person judging is sober or drunk, or moved by different emotions). The fifth trope refers to differences of position and distance (perspectival distortions, appearances varying with distance, and the like). The sixth refers to intermixture, as nothing comes to the senses unmixed, or is unaffected by the structure of the sense organ, so the perception varies accordingly and no firm judgment can be made as to the nature of the thing perceived. The seventh refers to the size and cohesion of materials, which appear differently when in small quantities from how they appear when larger (compare ground glass with blown glass, or small drops of water with lakes and the sea). The eighth trope refers directly to relation—what is large in one set of relations is small in another (as, in the *Phaedo,* when Socrates compares Simmias as tall in comparison with himself but short as compared with Phaedo), and nothing can be assessed out of all relation. The ninth trope refers to judgments of value, which vary according to scarcity and abundance; and the tenth refers to the variability of law and custom in different places and at different times, conflicts between law and morality, and differences of moral judgment according to different circumstances.

Clearly relativity is the principle operative in all these tropes, and it is relativism of one kind or another that motivates the skeptical stance. That nothing can be judged out of relation to some other is the key statement: everything is related to something else. So what these ten tropes illustrate in diverse ways is the key statement: everything is related to something else. So what these ten tropes illustrate in diverse ways is the dialectic of determinate being (*Dasein,* in Hegel's logic). The quality and nature of determinate being is what it is only as determined by what it is not, by its relation to something other. It is therefore being-for-another and essentially alterable. Every determinate entity is something, and is opposed to, or related to some other. As each is equally other than the other (*aliud, aliud*) they are equipollent, or, as Hegel says, identical. This dialectical relationship is common to all stages of the dialectic. Every moment is determined by its opposite and each opposing thesis is equally valid and important. Hence, they cancel one another out, and, if we go no further, justify the skeptical attitude.

Hegel is somewhat contemptuous of these ten tropes, considering them naive and relatively unphilosophical; but he was clearly not unaware of the dialectic involved. They mostly (all but the last two) concern perception, and the Doctrine of Being in Hegel's logic is explicitly said to be the logic of the immediate: being as presented in *Anschauung*. Thus, the first division of that Doctrine applies to the perceptual. This is not, of course, to say that the Doctrine of Essence is irrelevant, for that is the logic of relation, per se. It is *Ansichsein*, which gives rise to *Füranderssein* and *Änderung*, and they are the grounds of the skeptical attitude.

The later tropes Hegel holds to be more important and more speculative. These refer directly to differences of philosophical opinion and the methods of supporting and criticizing philosophical positions. "They belong more to the thinking reflection," Hegel says,[5] "and contain the dialectic which the determinate Concept has within it."

The first rests on the diversity of philosophical opinions, a primary motive for skeptical doubt, suspension of judgment, and refusal of assent. Each opinion is declared by its proponent to be the truth, each is supported by equally persuasive argument, yet each repudiates and contradicts the other. There being no independent criterion of justification, suspension of judgment is the only permissible course. Against this conclusion, however, Hegel warns us again that the idea of philosophy, as such, is nevertheless the same for all philosophers (even though they themselves may not be aware of it), and that the different opinions are related dialectically as stages in a development. If each is one-sided (and from this he does not exempt skepticism), the truth is yet to be reached in the totality.

The second trope is the infinite regress, into which a philosophy falls when it gives a reason for any assertion, which again needs justification by a further reason, and so on ad infinitum. There being ultimately no solid foundation for any of these reasons, suspension of judgment is the only option. In modern times this criticism has been brought against the Aristotelian syllogism, which Hegel himself rejects in its sheer formality as inadequate to express speculative truth.

The third trope is again relativity. Whatever is asserted can be defended only in relation to other considerations, which may be rejected by other thinkers, so each view is relative to the thinker holding it. Thus, any such view is only appearance and nothing appears as it is in itself.

The fourth trope draws attention to the arbitrariness of philosophical presuppositions. In the quest for a foundation some first principle is announced, which is a mere presupposition, and axiom, the opposite of which can be as easily postulated and with as good a ground, for really neither has any ground at all, and both are unproven.

The fifth is reciprocity, or circular argument. As what is maintained requires some ground, and that again another, to avoid infinite regression appeal is made to the original assertion as the basis of the assumed ground, and the argument becomes circular. That which is proved is used as the reason for that by which it is proved, as when the question is raised: What causes a certain phenomenon? And the answer is, force; and when asked for the evidence of the force we are again referred back to the phenomenon.

The diversity of philosophical systems (the first trope of the second set) is what constitutes the history of philosophy. And skepticism has its own history. The Pyrrhonists claimed that Homer was a skeptic, and there was much discussion in the New Academy as to whether Plato himself was not one. Socrates always denied that he knew anything, and the Socratic dialogues of Plato commonly end negatively, in the conclusion that neither Socrates nor his interlocutor know the answer to the question from which the discussion began. We have seen that historically skepticism can be traced back at least as far as Heraclitus and Cratylus, and in the early essay on the relation of skepticism to philosophy, Hegel maintains that the origins of skepticism are to be found in Plato's *Parmenides.* He claims, further, that skepticism is an essential moment in philosophy and that the history of philosophy is a dialectical development. It follows that the successive differences of philosophical opinion are partial and one-sided moments complementary one to another, which, being partial and restricted points of view, fall into contradiction with one another and within themselves, and are thus grist to the mill of skepticism. But this relationship is superseded by a reconciliation in which the opposites are united and the contradictions are *aufgehoben.*

In his *Lectures on the History of Philosophy,* Hegel presents Greek philosophy as a whole as a dialectical triad:

> We begin with thought, as it is in a quite abstract, natural or sensuous form, and we proceed from this to the Idea as determined. This first period shows the beginning of philosophical thought, and goes on to its development and perfection as a totality of knowledge in itself; this takes place in Aristotle as representing the unity of what has come before. . . .
>
> After the concrete Idea was reached, it came forth as if in opposites, perfecting and developing itself. The second period is that in which science breaks itself up into different systems. A one-sided principle is carried through the whole conception of the world; each side is itself formed into a totality, and stands in the relation of one extreme to another. . . .
>
> The third period is the affirmative, the withdrawal of the opposition into an ideal world or a world of thought, a divine world. This is the Idea developed into totality.[6]

This tripartite division corresponds to that in the logic of Being, Essence, and the Concept, and in the doctrine of the Concept to Universal, Particular, and Individual.

Looking at the details a little more closely: Parmenides opposed Being to non-Being and these opposites were united in the universal flux of Heraclitus, who declares that opposites unite in harmony. In Hegel's logic this corresponds to the identity of Being and Nothing in Becoming. The monism of the Milesians and the pluralism of Anaxagoras, Empedocles, and the Atomists represent opposed determinates, and are united in the philosophies of Plato and Aristotle. Within each and all of these, similar oppositions and sublations are distinguishable.

Further, in the *Greater Logic*, in the course of developing the subcategories of Being-for-self, Hegel generates the opposition of the One to the Void, and of the One to the Many, giving the dialectical basis for the dispute between Eleatics and Pythagoreans in Greek philosophy, and for the emergence of Atomism with Leucippus and Democritus (as well as for the Leibnizian monadology in modern philosophy).

In the *Logic*, the second moment is always that of difference and mutual contradistinction, which Hegel finds here in the opposition of Stoics to Epicureans and in the negative dialectic of the skeptics. It is to this dialectical diversity and opposition that the first trope of the later skeptics points, but it fails to recognize the progression to reconciliation and identity.

Returning to the *Logic*, we find in the Doctrine of Being that *Dasein* goes over into its other, which is another determinate being. That again does the same, and so on indefinitely. This gives rise to the false infinite, which recurs sublated in later categories of the *Logic*, in particular, in Ground and Consequent,[7] Cause and Effect, in the Doctrine of Essence. It is this infinite regress which the skeptics used as their second trope. The search for a ground always leads to the demand for an antecedent ground, and so on ad infinitum.

Relativity, we have said, is the basic principle of all the tropes. It is the reference of every determinate being to its other and its dependence, for its own being and nature, upon its relation to that other. The other is what it excludes and negates, which contradicts it, and which nevertheless defines it, so that claiming to stand on its own, in isolation and independence, it contradicts itself and turns into its other. As applied to philosophical positions, as well as to individual assertions, therefore, it affords a pretext for skepticism. This dialectic is set out in Hegel's logic, not only under *Dasein*, for it recurs and is ubiquitous throughout. Especially it is characteristic of Essence. As Hegel himself says: "in Being everything is immediate, in Essence everything is relative."[8]

The fourth trope presents the problem of making a beginning in philosophy, which requires and professes to be presuppositionless. This problem Hegel discusses at the outset of the *Greater Logic*, and in the introduction to the *Encyclopedia* he says that, as every beginning makes some assumption, "it seems as if it were impossible to make a beginning at all." In the opening discussion of the *Greater Logic*, he uses arguments similar to those of the skeptics to refute every alternative example and form of beginning, and concludes that it can only be with the purely abstract immediate that we can begin. Yet he confesses that even this is implicitly what will develop out of it and so in some sense presupposes the result which is eventually to emerge. In truth, the dialectic is ultimately circular and ends where it begins, and everything in heaven and earth (he maintains) is at once both immediate and mediate. This is because the truth is the whole, which is immanent in all its parts and moments, so that wherever one begins, the end is already implied; and the end is not just a mere phase in the process, but encompasses the process as a whole, sublating all its moments in a single unity. This is why any proposed first principle can always be countered by an opposite, which, as merely finite and abstract, it implies. And this, equally, is why such presupposition is liable to involve a circular argument, as the final trope complains. Thus, the Hegelian holism and its intrinsic dialectic can account for all the skeptical tropes, and Hegel can claim that skepticism is itself rational in character and is contained as a necessary moment in speculative philosophy.

VI

The kinship of Hegel's philosophy to skepticism in large measure stems from this quest for a beginning free of presupposition. This Hegel shares with Descartes and other philosophers; in fact it is characteristic, as he himself saw, of all genuine philosophy. The refusal to accept initial presuppositions is, in effect, the same as the skeptical epoché, an avoidance of all positive assertion (at least preliminarily). The Cartesian epoché is the provisional rejection of all opinions in any way susceptible of doubt, an abstinence from all assumption prior to the discovery of some indubitable conviction.

The skeptics accepted what appeared, as appearance, but eschewed belief in any underlying reality. They thus remained restricted to the subjective. In like manner, Hegel begins his *Phenomenology* without commitment to any ontological assertion, other than what is evident to natural consciousness and its own claims to truth, which he then allows to criticize themselves, by developing their own implications and pursuing their own dialectic. Consciousness, he maintains, provides its own criterion. The dialectic is that of skepticism, in which each successive position is found to go over into its opposite and to contradict itself, so that it collapses and gives place to a more concrete and coherent alternative, which then in its turn negates itself and is *aufgehoben,* a process which Hegel compares to a Bacchanalian revel. But for Hegel the epoché, strictly speaking, comes at the beginning and not at the end of the development.

So it is also for Husserl who more recently has revived the epoché as the starting point for genuine philosophy. For him, it is the suspension of all belief characteristic of the natural consciousness. In the first instance the Husserlian epoché follows from the Cartesian, to establish the invincible presence of the intentional object of awareness, which must be accepted as it appears. Thus, Husserl remains with the subjective, and demonstrates the transcendental constitution of the lifeworld as the essential act of the subject of consciousness. But Husserl is no skeptic in the full sense of the word, even if he shares with the ancient skeptics the epoché and the insistence on appearance, for he claims that his method establishes a strict science which results in unassailable knowledge.

In many respects, Husserl's position is closely akin to Kant's, who also seeks to avoid presupposition by contending that before we can accept the pronouncements of understanding and reason we must submit the faculty of cognition to criticism, by inquiring into the conditions of the possibility of its entertaining any object. The indispensable condition turns out, for him, to be the spontaneous activity of synthesis by the transcendental ego. This, he claims, provides us with objective knowledge, so he is not finally a skeptic. And in all this he is followed by Husserl.

Hegel, of course, criticized Kant for assuming that a critique of reason could be undertaken without using reason itself, and for tacitly presupposing the prior necessity of a manifold of sense as the material of knowledge for which the understanding provides the form, accepting, in effect, with Hume and the empiricists, the givenness of sensation. Yet again, Kant's conclusion is skeptical inasmuch as he denies the possibility of knowledge of things-in-themselves, condemns the ideas of reason as illusion, and allows knowledge only of phenomena. And, like the ancient skeptics, he fails (apart from later hints and inclinations) to go beyond the negative when he denies the competence of reason to frame constitutive ideas. Even so, as we have seen, Hegel downgrades the skepticism based on the Kantian critical approach, as comparatively dogmatic.

Husserl himself, however, repudiated subjective idealism, and his phenomenology has been defended (whether successfully need not here be considered) against subjectivism. Robert R. Williams, moreover, contends that Husserl's phenomenology, like Hegel's, is a sustained critique of immediacy, and quotes Iso Kern as saying that the Husserlian reduction is an overcoming of abstraction, limitation, and one-sidedness. He also claims that Husserl's method of imaginative variation resembles Hegel's project of identifying unity in opposition.[9] Despite Husserl's avowed opposition to Hegelianism, that his doctrine can be presented as a dialectical progression has been demonstrated by Andre de Muralt;[10] so the element of skepticism in the Husserlian phenomenology may also be seen as related to dialectic. It is, as Hegel contends, not directed against philosophy proper, but is included within the more speculative phenomenology.

VII

Present-day skepticism is represented by the deconstructionism of the postmodernists; and to bring this discussion to completion some brief attention may be paid to these developments in recent philosophy. To examine and criticize them as they deserve would take us beyond the limits permissible for this paper, but it may be useful to notice certain general features in contrast and comparison with earlier forms.

Unlike previous types of skepticism, the postmodernists explicitly abandon any semblance of subjectivism and ignore, or eschew all reference to, activity of the subject of the consciousness. They offer a fresh and extreme version of positivism, which treats every human activity as an external object for impartial observation. It should be observed, however, that positivism is a one-sided doctrine opposed to a subjective experience that it ignores; it is an offshoot of empiricism, the major figures of which, Locke, Berkeley, and Hume, were led by the inevitable implications of Locke's initial realism and representationalism to the most radical form of subjectivism. While this aspect of the earlier skepticism does not appear in postmodernist doctrine, their refusal to confront the problem of knowledge, as such, leads them tacitly to assume aspects of their subject matter that they explicitly deny, with disastrous results for the consistency of their overt theories. In common with earlier skepticism, however, these writers emphasize diversity at the expense of unity, difference by neglect or oversight of identity.

Michel Foucault reduces all human intelligent activity to "discourse," consisting of explicit uninterpreted statements, which organize themselves into "discursive formations" (which he calls "positivities") structured according to inherent and objective laws. The study of these formations Foucault calls "archeology," in a sense quite different from its common use: a purely objective science, investigating the rules governing the interrelation of statements and determining their viability, as well as of discursive formations. By these rules they are organized (among themselves and with "things") into a complex structure prescribing what can be said and how statements appear. This structure is called "the archive." In this study no appeal is to be made to commonly accepted concepts, no tradition is to be acknowledged, no causal connections sought, nor any concealed underlying meanings, inspiring ideas, or hidden psychological explanations. In fact, any appeal to authorship, to a thinking subject of awareness, or to any sort of transcendental a priori is proscribed. Meaning and truth are to be attributed to statements only as they are ascribed to them by those participating in the practices in which they appear. The notion of truth is admitted, therefore, only in a radically relativistic sense.

Despite his frequent reference to "system," "organization," and "structure," Foucault declares that what is to be disclosed by the science is not continuity, gradual change, connection, and unification, but only discontinuities and dispersions. Thus, all explanation is to be in terms of difference, and all unity and cohesion (while tacitly recognized) is explicitly denied.

Similarly, Jaques Derrida (no doubt influenced by Gadamer's reduction of philosophy to hermeneutics) essays to transform metaphysics to a question of writing; hence, for him, all law, politics, and history are regarded purely as writing, and philosophy becomes "Grammatology." Knowledge is said to be writing, and writing is law. But although law may be viewed as commandment, writing cannot, of itself, provide any criterion of validity or truth, and without that there can be no knowledge, properly speaking. For truth or validity, Derrida apparently substitutes self-presence (*présence à soi*); but whatever that may mean the effect is, once more, relativism, for self-presence must surely be individual and subjective, and cannot bestow universality on that to which it refers. Even when it is described as "the voice of the other as commandment" it remains arbitrary.

The key to all interpretation, or more appropriately for Derrida, deconstruction, is difference. All writing is said to be metaphorical—"metaphoricity itself"—metaphor being simply the Greek translation of the Latin *difference.* This contention, however, is self-destructive, because without literal meaning from which it can differ there can be no metaphor, and "metaphor" cannot itself be understood metaphorically. Derrida coins the word *différance* to indicate the source and ubiquity of differences. He says it is "an economic concept designating the production of differing/deferring"[11] and that history as *différance* is "the movement of play that 'produces' . . . these effects of difference."[12] That the interrelation of differents inevitably constitutes a whole of some sort entirely escapes this form of criticism, and that without some such whole (or system) there can be neither meaning nor knowledge is altogether overlooked. Consequently, the result of Derrida's deconstruction is the demolition and dissipation of knowledge in all its forms.

There is, of course, much more to be said about postmodernism, but for my present purpose the above brief sketch is sufficient. Although it is not admitted by its proponents, it is clear that what such postmodernist teaching offers is both relativism (which is in itself, by implication, skeptical) and outright skepticism, qua the deconstruction of knowledge. It takes not much perspicacity to guess what Hegel's response would have been. He would first have grouped this postmodernist skepticism with the modern variety of his own day. He would have criticized it as accepting too readily (if only implicitly) the absolute reality of the perceptual given, whether it be writing or speaking (discourse). He would have pointed out that it is stuck with the differences and divisions of the understanding, and that it fails to appreciate the identity of opposites recognized by speculative reason. It cannot get beyond the opposition of abstract identity and abstract difference, and stops short of their concrete unification in Ground. So the dialectic of this form of nihilism is both that of Being-in-itself (*Dasein*) and of Essence (as we find it in the first main triad of that section in the *Logic*). Finally, it contradicts itself by tacitly assuming what it explicitly denies, and is self-stultified when its own methodological strictures are applied to its own recommended procedures.[13] Hence, like skepticism in general, it represents the paralysis of thought.

11

The Phenomenological Tradition and the End of History

William L. McBride

Introduction: Phenomenology and Our Generation

Festschriften inevitably conduce to thoughts about generations of humankind. There is something very elusive about the idea of a "generation," once we leave behind simplistic mathematical formulas, such as "a period of thirty years," or whatever. To recognize this elusiveness and the reasons for it is to begin to understand why Husserl encountered such conceptual difficulties in attempting to come to grips with the phenomenon of history—or, if one prefers, with historicity—difficulties that David Carr in particular has documented with such clarity and thoroughness.[1] *Perhaps, à la limite,* one may be able to produce a plausible eidetic description of the phenomenon of generation, based, no doubt, on Husserl's and others' accounts of time-consciousness. But I have deep doubts about its probable usefulness for understanding any better the sorts of questions that preoccupy me in these times concerning the "generation" to which, in a very important sense, Jim Edie and I and all but the youngest (at the time of publication) readers of this essay belong, which I shall call "the Cold War generation."

The new sense of intellectual crisis provoked by the abrupt disappearance of all the familiar, if often depressing, landmarks that defined this generation of ours was well expressed, I thought, by one of the oldest of our philosophical consociates within it, Emmanuel Levinas, in an interview published in *Le Monde.* There, he said in part:

> Even if the Soviet State had become the most dreadful of all, it remained the bearer of a promise of deliverance, of a hope of liberation. The disappearance of this horizon seems to me a profoundly disturbing event. For it overturns our vision of time. From the Bible on, we are accustomed to think that time is going somewhere, that the history of humanity is directed towards a horizon, even through detours or vicissitudes.[2]

Levinas's observation seems to me to be obviously correct and in some sense applicable to most thoughtful members of the erstwhile "Cold War generation" from both of its major "camps" as well as from its outposts. I confess to being one of this "profoundly disturbed" multitude.

It might, of course, be possible to raise the objection that, disturbing or not, such sociohistorical considerations should not be regarded as central to the business of philosophy. An illustrative personal reminiscence that comes immediately to my mind (and that in fact has always been for me one of those very salient memories originating from circumstances and remarks that at the time seemed quite casual and contingent) has to do with my first meeting with Professor Edie. It was at an annual gathering of the Society for Phenomenology and Existential Philosophy, in the development of which he has played such a central and commendable role, and it was our mutual friend, the late John Wild, who introduced us during a pause in the proceedings, explaining to Jim Edie that I was especially interested in the later thought of Sartre and, among other *relata,* the socio-politico-historical works of Merleau-Ponty, notably *Humanism and Terror* and *Adventures of the Dialectic.* Wild then absented himself, and Jim Edie and I immediately began a friendly debate about the philosophical relevance of those two books. I, needless to say, upheld the thesis of philosophical relevance, while Edie raised doubts about it. Where, after all—so his doubts went—were the *phenomenology* and the accompanying philosophical rigor in those collections of political essays, important as they might have been as marker events in Merleau-Ponty's personal/political development and in French Cold War literature? I responded by asserting certain conceptual connections between the sociohistorical books and Merleau-Ponty's writings on perception and behavior;[3] we agreed to disagree.

In his overview study of Husserl's philosophy, Professor Edie, I think it fair to say, gives fairly short shrift to Husserl's treatment of history, noting that Husserl himself had once referred to those sections of *The Crisis of European Sciences and Transcendental Phenomenology* that deal with the history of philosophy as "*meine Romane.*"[4] I, on the other hand, published a book a few years later on Sartre's political theory[5]—an undertaking, I wish very gratefully to acknowledge here, that originated with a suggestion by Professor Edie. Thus, almost a (mathematical) generation after our first encounter, we seem to have continued to pursue our somewhat similar but importantly diverse fundamental projects. Is this a merely contingent fact? One wonders. Perhaps, *malgré tout,* there are patterns in history, if we could but discern them. Perhaps, after all of Levinas's and our doubts, history has an "end," even if "victory of the proletariat" (or whichever traditional substitute you prefer) does not name it. The brief meditations on this possibility, or on the temptation to accept this as a possibility, that follow will make reference to passages and ideas from Husserl and Sartre, in particular.

Husserl

Whatever may be the exact nature of the current crisis in which we find ourselves, the crisis alluded to by Levinas, it would not be well identified as, primarily, a "crisis of European sciences"; we are preoccupied by many issues other than the state of the sciences, issues that to many of us seem more important. But nor was "Crisis of the European Sciences" a particularly apt label for the *Zeitgeist* of the "*Lebenswelt*" at the time at which Husserl was writing his book by that name. One is entitled, of course, to raise questions concerning the very meaningfulness of "*Lebenswelt*" within the framework of Husserl's philosophy: can there in fact be many such "worlds," as my reference to the *Lebenswelt* of the 1930s implies, or should the term more correctly be restricted to certain universal and invariant features constitutive of *the Lebenswelt*?[6] My greater concern at present, however, is with the entire conception of history implied by Husserl's choice of focus, rather than with the conceptual apparatus, however important, employed in his unfolding of it. For Husserl, history appears above all to be about sets of ideas, rational ways of ordering knowledge. The "concept of 'Europe' as the historical teleology of infinite goals of reason"[7] has, for him, a specificity and a superior force that render it different from mere anthropological typologies such as those of "India" or "China"[8]—Ricoeur, like so many other commentators, has taken note of Husserl's Eurocentrism[9]—and his work as a philosopher, one of the "*Funktionäre der Menschheit,*"[10] in gaining rational insight into the meaning of life gives him a privileged position vis-à-vis history. No wonder, then, that *Geschichtlichkeit* for him conjures up a rather different set of references than it did for his former pupil, Heidegger, who during the same period was unquestionably identifying the Nazi *Bewegung* as an exciting and ultimate positive intervention into history.[11] For Husserl, in a rather typical passage, "*Geschichte ist von vornherein nichts anderes als die lebendige Bewegung der Miteinander und Ineinander von ursprünglicher Sinnbildung und Sinnsedimentierung.*"[12]

Such formulas as these have always seemed to me too insufficiently lifeworldly (despite the presence here of the adjective, "*lebendig*") to permit a grasp of what I have taken history to mean; this comment is of a piece with my earlier disparaging remark concerning Husserl's grasp of his own lifeworld. But in the wake of the *Bewegungen* inspired by Hitler, Stalin, and many lesser but still effective "influentials" of the twentieth century, one must ask, not only whether Husserl's approach to history has less potential for generating moral harm, but also whether it may not in fact be more conducive to truth, or at least less susceptible to producing massive untruths, than the approaches of the well-known "substantive" philosophers of history (Hegel, Marx, etc.) and their followers. Perhaps. Nevertheless, Husserl's approach, too, seems to me to have some very problematic aspects, not the least being his excessive individualism. Despite his talk of the "*Miteinander*" in the above citation, he constantly insists, as for instance in a footnote on the very next page, that it is only through the individual that the historical world exists as such.[13] Of course, he acknowledges the reality of groups, but he takes history to be constituted by the individual ego.[14] And he finds it marvelous that, within history as he comprehends it, it is possible for an individual to create a new *Zweck*, a new historical goal or end.[15] He fails, it seems to me, to pay anything approaching comparable attention to the role played by human collectives, such as generations, in codetermining both the goals of individuals and the direction taken by historical developments at any given time.

Beyond the problem of excessive individualism, I believe, lie difficulties in dealing with history that are inextricably connected with Husserl's entire method. A brief reference to a single text will, I hope, illustrate this. In this text, one of his *Forschungsmanuskripte,* he shows that eidetic variation permits free meditation on infinite possible worlds and on the possible alternative ideas of a finite and of an infinite world. The resulting perspective on history, then, is nothing if not open-ended: individuals can project new ends for it, endlessly. Hence, he arrives, toward the end of this manuscript, at a particularly pithy formula concerning world history: "*Die Geschichte der Welt selbst, an sich, das ist Weltgeschichte im Sinn der unendlichen Idee.*"[16] But what, he ponders, could be signified by speaking of an infinite future? Would that have any meaning, and, if so, what? In concluding this meditation, he points to the paradox involved in individuals projecting an infinite world while being inserted in actual, finite, historical reality, and he raises the issue of the relationship between the ontological structure of the individual psyche and the ontological structure of the world.

The conclusion of this brief manuscript well reflects, it seems to me, some of the fundamental tensions and even, perhaps, paradoxes involved in attempting to bring Husserl's philosophy to bear on the question of history and particularly of the end of history. On the one hand, Husserl seems, in a realist vein, to accept the notion of the unity of humanity[17] and, hence, of the unity (in *some* sense) of human history. Now, from the science-infused perspective of the natural attitude, we have every reason to think that human history had a definite beginning in physical time and will have a temporal end; this belief is reinforced today by the real and ever-present threat of worldwide nuclear (or other) catastrophe. But, on the other hand, transcendental phenomenology begins, of course, with a bracketing of the natural attitude. However much it may be justified in doing so for its *wissenschaftlich* purposes, this has the effect of making history seem, as in the manuscript that I have cited, more like a set of infinite possibilities than like the *res gestae* of a certain real, finite species that happens to be our species. In this intellectual atmosphere, it is difficult, if not impossible, to try to come seriously to grips with historical events of the sort with reference to which I began this essay. In Husserl's thought, in short, history and the question of its end always remain somewhat at a distance.

Sartre

Sartre's short treatise, *Vérité et existence,* was written in 1948 during a particularly threatening period of the Cold War, when a global atomic war that might annihilate humanity seemed a distinct possibility, as Arlette Elkaïm-Sartre notes in her editor's introduction.[18] This work is also one of the most recent of Sartre's publications to appear in print (1989), and the only one that constitutes a complete, integral whole; it has already appeared in a fine English translation by Adrian Van Den Hoven with Ronald Aronson.[19] Arlette Elkaïm stresses, to a greater degree than I think the actual text warrants, its role as a reply to Heidegger's *Vom Wesen der Wahrheit.* In fact, it is above all an honest and interesting effort by Sartre, in light of his background in the phenomenological tradition, his strong emphasis (as found on almost every page of *Being and Nothingness*) on the free, creative choice of individuals in forging and defining their world, and his then-increasing perceptions of the philosophical importance of lived experience[20] and of history,[21] to produce an acceptable and consistent notion of *truth* within his philosophy. Despite all the relativistic elements in Sartre's thought, the question of truth always remained central to him (he spoke of "finding the absolute in the relative"), and this text proves it.

Although the majority of the pages in *Vérité et existence* do not deal explicitly with questions of history, it is fair to say that it is from the perspective of history, and especially from that of an "end of history," that Sartre's central insights in this entire work take shape. Truth, which is a gift, he says, can never be anonymous: it is always delivered to specific individuals and verified interindividually. It cannot be otherwise, and to accept this is philosophically liberating. So it is with truths about the meaning of history. For philosophers, like Hegel, who attempt to produce definitive overviews of history, the end of history is postulated as internal to the historical process. But in fact it is external:[22] the truth about history, and hence about the end of history, is decided by us for our generation, without any guarantee of its eternal certitude. This truth is not, as Spengler would have it, something *merely* subjective and relative to a particular generation, so that the truth for one generation would be born and die with that generation; for the next generation will absorb, in its own way, the earlier generation's truth that has now become its destiny. Nor is it, as for Marx, something purely objective, to be viewed from the "superior" standpoint of the future generations that will look back with pity on the past; for this neglects the earlier generations' actual lived experiences of their own historical truths. In two sentences that well epitomize this entire portion of his text, Sartre says: "In a sense, I define *our* 'end of history' at the heart of a broader history; by choosing a finite history, I interiorize the limit of history. Let it be well understood that this by itself defines a future."[23] (The "*our*" here refers to "our"—one's—generation.)

There are, as one might have expected, some interesting similarities between this Sartrean approach to history and Husserl's; open-endedness is perhaps the most obvious. But there are also numerous dissimilarities of emphasis and more. The disagreement that Sartre himself explicitly mentions has to do with his own supposedly more concrete orientation; at one point, he proposes substituting the notion of "project of discovery" (*projet de découvrir*) for Husserl's "empty intentions," which, he alleges, had the effect of going beyond (*enjambaient*) the present while striving to become future to themselves—a result, he says, of Husserl's problematic theory of time.[24] Sartre clearly, it seems to me, does place a great deal more emphasis than did Husserl on concrete, lived experience as opposed to abstract truths. By the latter, he says at one point, he means unverified ones; the example that he gives to explain his own very non-Husserlian sense of "verification," an interesting one from a commonplace event, is of the difference between a judge's "abstract" understanding of the meaning of a ten-year prison sentence that he is meting out, and the prisoner's grasp of what that means.[25] Moreover, Sartre in this text shows a tolerance of, and even an appreciation for, ignorance and error that cuts deeply against the grain of Husserl's aspiration for a rigorous science; as he writes at another point, "It is therefore possible to consider the history of man as the history of his errors, if one considers stoppages of verification due to death, to the succession of generations, etc."[26] Indeed, Sartre goes so far as to state that "Freedom," which of course was always central to his entire thought, "*requires* basic ignorance of the general destiny that the world reserves for the human enterprise"[27] and even an ignorance of most, though not all, consequences of our actions.

It can thus be seen that the Sartre of *Vérité et existence* was indeed, as Arlette Elkaïm insists, very much obsessed with the idea of an end of history—in, I would add, both the teleological and the temporal senses. (The possibility of equivocating between the two meanings of the word "end" is of course always present when this topic is discussed, and I have been taking it for granted throughout this essay.) Early on, when considering the sense in which generations create their own truths about the telos of history, he reflects on the "catastrophic" aspect of the eventual cessation of history as far as the sciences are concerned, for this means that it will never be possible to know with finality, for example, whether Marxism was true or false as an interpretation of history or just what place, in some ultimate absolute scientific hierarchy, the theories of Heisenberg, Broglie, or Einstein occupied.[28] Near the very end of the text, in a series of especially cogent observations, he considers the possibility of an abrupt, perhaps quite arbitrary, contingent stoppage "of the story" (*du compte*). What would be required to write *finis* to history, he says—and not merely to give it one or several meanings (for even if history were nothing but a long series of catastrophic absurdities, then that would be its meaning)[29]—would be someone or some being outside of history "*to close the eyes of humanity*. And that someone being in principle impossible, man is the worker of a truth that no one will ever know."[30]

Vérité et existence lays a philosophical groundwork for thinking about differences of generations that one finds at least as early as the *Carnets d' un drôle de guerre* within Sartre's corpus and that was to stand him in good stead in sorting out basic questions about Flaubert's life and thought, and about the reasons for Flaubert's enormous popularity during a certain historical epoch, in *L'idiot de la famille*, Sartre's last major philosophical undertaking. It also speaks interestingly to the concerns with which I began this essay. The Sartre of *Vérité et existence* would presumably have looked upon the recent epoch-ending events that we have been experiencing with an equanimity not easily imaginable in him during the period of his most intense political commitment later on. On the other hand, I think it can plausibly be argued, as I in fact tried to do long before I was aware of the existence of the text of *Vérité et existence*,[31] that Sartre never at any time succumbed to anything approaching the self-assurance of the "orthodox Marxists" of unhappy memory concerning the alleged "truth of history," of which they were supposedly the vanguard; I do not believe that he ever repudiated the perspectival conception of historical truth or the broader idea that truth and creation coimply one another[32] that one finds here. Throughout his most Marx-influenced works, for example, he retained the distinction between ongoing historical "totalization" and the idea of history as a "detotalized totality," on the one hand, and the (for him) false and unacceptable notion of it as a "totalizable totality," on the other, that one already finds worked out on one crucial page of *Vérité et existence*.[33] The same sense that history has the meaning that "we"—understood in some large measure, though not entirely, in generational terms—give it underlies a number of remarks in his final published interview with Benny Lévy, recorded just shortly before his death, "Hope, Now." The context of his historico-political observations in this interview is one of a seemingly inexorable decline of movements on the left, a prescient anticipation of the further decline that has since ensued; but Sartre, ever the philosopher of freedom, still does not succumb to the thesis of historical inevitability.

Universality and Universals

Throughout his writings, James Edie has always shown great admiration for Husserl, particularly because of the latter's insistence on the universality of truths across all possible species. Nowhere, perhaps, is this theme more clearly or cogently defended than in his recent article, "On Confronting Species-Specific Skepticism as We Near the End of the Twentieth Century." Interestingly enough, that article ends with a citation, with approval, of a passage from the writings of Merleau-Ponty, "speaking as a disciple of Husserl," in which "the idea of a single history or of a logic of history" is said to be implied universally—"in the least human exchange, in the least social perception."[34] But as I mentioned at the outset, history presents an especially difficult challenge to the Husserlian standpoint, for it is not clear—at least not to me—just what universals, in any strong sense of the word *universal,* can validly be said to apply to all of history and particularly to all possible histories other than universals that are quite abstract indeed, such as "*Bewegung der Miteinander und Ineinander von ursprünglicher Sinnbildung und Sinnsedimentierung.*"

This question becomes particularly pointed if we consider, as Sartre does in a few intriguing passages in both volumes of his *Critique of Dialectical Reason,* precisely the possibility of species other than our own—Martians or Venutians or whatever—who might lack the conditions that Sartre has identified as especially salient in human history up to the present, notable scarcity. (The issue remains even if one finds Sartre's emphasis on scarcity unacceptable.) To push the question even further, might it not even be possible to conceive of an intelligent species whose activity lacked some or most of the "existential universal"[35] qualities that characterize Sartre's own most fundamental category of *Geschichtlichkeit* in his later work, namely, *praxis*? To such a (barely) conceivable species, might not even the universal, "*Bewegung der Miteinander and Ineinander,*" be inapplicable? (Suppose, for example, that these beings were sorts of Nietzschean *Übermenschen,* not basically dependent on one another, rather like the fictitious adults that political theorists of the right, for their own ideological purposes, pretend that the *homines oeconomici* of the "free market" actually are or at least could be. In such a world, "*Miteinander und Ineinander von ursprünglicher Sinnbildung und Sinnsedimentierung*" would, I think, mean something very different from what it means for Husserl and, to the extent to which we accept this terminology, to us.)

But overindulgence in science fiction can quickly take us uncomfortably far away from the sphere of the human lifeworld with which the later Husserl, Merleau-Ponty, Sartre, and Edie have all been most preoccupied. As Edie, who has argued convincingly for a greater similarity than is usually admitted between Husserl's and Sartre's (at least the early Sartre's) theories of consciousness,[36] well knows, Sartre himself tended increasingly in later years, as he became more and more concerned with issues of history and its putative end, to rely on a notion that he denominated "the singular universal." Its value was that it enabled him to deal with the differences between and among human individuals and groups, including historical generations, and to avoid universalism of a Platonic sort while still retaining something of the presence of universality that Edie regards as necessary to make sense of the philosophical enterprise and indeed of the concept of truth itself. (Kierkegaard's sense of the uniqueness of the human individual in history was a significant inspiration for this notion and is explicitly invoked in Sartre's important essay, "The Singular Universal.")[37] I am not sure whether this idea of the "singular universal"—roughly, that individuals and groups incarnate given qualities in thoroughly unique ways—with its strong component of nominalism, would satisfy Edie's standards for the sort of non–species-specific universality that he lauds in Husserl's thought, though it is clear that some interesting further comparisons between Sartre and Husserl could fruitfully be developed around the notion of universals and on the basis of Edie's work. In the last analysis, at any rate, I *do* remain skeptical about the Husserlian–Merleau-Pontyan–Ediean idea of a single history or of a logic of history, and I attribute some of the origins of this skepticism to my contact with Sartre's thought.

It must also be pointed out, by way of completing this brief excursus through Husserl, Sartre, and Edie into the question of the phenomenological tradition and the end of history, that beyond the method and parameters of transcendental phenomenology, which Sartre learned from Husserl and never completely abandoned, lies the possibility of an approach from Transcendence. Sartre repeatedly and vehemently ruled out such an approach more or less a priori—for example, by curtly dismissing, in his striking text about someone's "closing the eyes of humanity" at the end of history, the need to think of that someone as a God or a Demiurge; Husserl did so more discreetly. But such an approach is suggested, appropriately enough, by Levinas in the passage from an interview with him that I cited at the outset, when he refers to the influence of the Bible on "our" thinking about time as directional; it remains a viable option for many, and it should not be surprising that it is undergoing a considerable revival these days, especially in Russia—one is reminded of Professor Edie's important work in making nineteenth-century Russian thought available to American readers[38]—and other East European countries.

Conclusion

Meanwhile, some of us still hold out the hope, if only from force of habit, of being able to discern some concrete trends in addition to abstract universals in the history of the here and now. One trend about which Sartre himself wrote, in his *Critique,* and to which I have made some reference,[39] is that of a "One World" toward which many of the developments of our century seem to be propelling us, without any guarantee of its being a happy or peaceful outcome. It is also possible to hope, though admittedly with scant grounds for optimism, that there may come about a revalorizing of the life of the spirit, of culture, after the period of domination of two forms of materialism, historical materialism and capitalist materialism, that we of the "Cold War generation" have all lived through. In an interestingly anticipatory passage near the end of *Vérité et existence*, Sartre, speaking of a later generation's inevitable reappropriation of the previous generation's self-understanding, which is itself however not altogether lost in the reappropriation process, says:

> For example, the effort to interpret social phenomena by means of the economic will perhaps appear to the descendants of our epoch as the *spiritual* characteristic of our epoch: in a word, the material truth uncovered by the epoch [which is] in the process of finding itself will become spiritual truth for the generation to follow.[40]

It is interesting to recall, in this context, the brief enthusiasm that was expressed, even quite recently, for the idea that history had indeed achieved a substantive end with the triumph of free market capitalism as we now know it; the title of a book that articulated this enthusiasm was, in fact, *The End of History and the Last Man.*[41] But if there is one universal characteristic of the "logic of history" on which agreement can certainly be found among Edie, Merleau-Ponty, Sartre, myself, and many others, it is the characteristic of change. And that, to my mind, is very reassuring in the present context: it can already be said, trading on the pejorative and uncomplimentary nuance given to this expression in the contemporary vernacular, that the faddish glorification of materialist excess characteristic of the past decade or so already "*is history*"! If the coming generation *should* witness a renaissance of the life of spirit and with it the dawning of a new hope of liberation to replace the lost hope lamented by Levinas, the extensive contributions of Jim Edie to the American philosophical scene in this generation will be reckoned a significant influence.

12

A Crisis of Reason? Husserl, Heidegger, and National Socialism

Tom Rockmore

The claim that philosophy is or even can be socially relevant has been sorely tested by the events of this century. The understanding of National Socialism squarely divides two of the most important phenomenologists in our time: Husserl, who opposed it, and Heidegger, who embraced it, in their respective efforts to come to grips with, and to correct, what each regarded as the contemporary crisis of reason. This paper considers the problem and its consequences for our understanding of phenomenology and philosophy.

I. The Canonical View of Philosophy

We can start with some remarks on the familiar, canonical philosophical view of philosophical reason—mainly supported by the majority of philosophers but disputed by a minority of philosophers and nearly every one else—according to which philosophy is the sole source of reason in the full sense, hence of knowledge worthy of the name. This leads to the inference that knowledge following from philosophical reason is not only socially relevant, but even socially indispensable, and philosophers have a particular social role to play. This latter idea is deeply rooted in the philosophical view of the philosophical task, leading to the idea that when a philosopher is carrying on philosophical reflection, what a philosopher usually does, then he or she is being socially responsible in a way beyond mere mortals, say what is possible for a carpenter or a literary critic, and that philosophy is socially relevant in a way that nothing else can be.

This view of philosophy as the final source of knowledge, hence as a key player in society, is the result of sustained reflection on the Socratic claim that the unexamined life is not worth living. The two main variants of this view consist in the idea that philosophical reason grasps the nature of reality, of what is, and in the rival idea that reason itself is self-sustaining, and self-justifying under the proper conditions. The former idea relies on the mimetic capacity of philosophical reason to grasp the nature of the cosmos. It leads to what has been called "objectivism," that is "the basic conviction that there is or must be some permanent, ahistorical matrix or framework to which we can ultimately appeal in determining the nature of rationality, knowledge, truth, reality, goodness, or rightness."[1] The latter idea holds that reason itself is intrinsically relevant in the absence of an ontological reference, either through the reabsorption of theory into practice or in the more plausible subordination of theory to practice that remains the criterion of theoretical relevance.

The two main variants of this view are associated with the names of Plato and Kant. It is, then, significant that Kant claimed to know Plato better than he knew himself.[2] At a minimum, Platonism that accords a preeminent role to the philosopher in the search for truth can be understood as a view of knowledge surpassing a merely empirical awareness of the world in which we live—where things come into being and pass away—through privileged cognitive access, accessible only to philosophers, to another, stable type of object. This metaphysical scheme leads to the conception of philosophy as the science of sciences, the only source of knowledge and truth in the ultimate sense and socially indispensable. Literature and the arts in general are harmful since, as Iris Murdoch points out,[3] like Sophists, who blur the distinction between the true and the false, writers and artists lack knowledge and, for that reason, tend to lead us astray.

Kant, who denied the Platonic reference to a fixed cosmos, advanced a "cosmological" idea of philosophy. He argued that reason in the full sense of the term is intrinsically relevant to human goals[4] through two inconsistent analyses respectively subordinating theory to practice or practice to theory. On the one hand, he twice attempted to subordinate theory to practice by subordinating pure reason to practical reason and later both to a putative third faculty. His candid acknowledgment of his failure to do so made this a live issue in the later discussion. On the other hand, he simply absorbed theory into practice, as witness his analysis of their relation,[5] and his theory of ethics.

The general, canonical claim for philosophy, philosophical reason, and philosophers can be reconstructed in the following way:

1. There are degrees of reason, roughly a distinction between forms of reason that can justify claims to know internally, or need to rely on an external justification.
2. Philosophy is self-justifying, whereas everything else depends finally on philosophy for its justification.
3. Reason is socially relevant and the highest form of reason is socially relevant in the highest degree.
4. Philosophy exhibits reason.
5. Philosophical reason is the final and unique source of knowledge and socially relevant in the highest degree.
6. The philosopher has a uniquely important social role to play.

The canonical view of philosophy and philosophers has never appeared more questionable than at present. No one doubts that some forms of it are socially relevant. But everything else, including the capacity of philosophy to justify itself, its claim to exhibit reason, and the social role of the philosopher is open to question. To begin with, it is questionable that other domains, such as natural science, require a philosophical justification. Further, no one now thinks that there is an independent, unchangeable reality, or, if there is, that philosophers can know it. Foundationalism, the main epistemological strategy in modern times, now seems to have run its course. With a few exceptions (Chisholm, Apel, Habermas), virtually no one now supports the foundationalist project. The idea of the philosopher's social role derives from the supposed philosophical ability to discern the true that is sorely tested by Heidegger's adherence to Nazism and Lukács's turn to Stalinism.

II. Husserl and Heidegger

After these remarks on the canonical view of philosophy and philosophers, I come now to Husserl and Heidegger. Their theories represent additional chapters in the book still being written by many hands describing the canonical view of philosophical reason.

It is still too early to provide a final description of either the personal or philosophical aspects of their relationship. At the very least, to do so implies filling out the record. The Heidegger Archives in Marbach, which may contain relevant material, is still not open to the public; and important parts of Heidegger's *Nachlass* are neither published nor, as concerns his letters, scheduled to be published.

We can summarize the salient facts quickly.[6] The personal relations between Husserl and Heidegger seem never to have been easy, no doubt because Heidegger was already beginning to seek his own way when he first became personally acquainted with Husserl, and because of his intense personal ambition. It is known that Heidegger wanted but was unable to study with Husserl. Heidegger was a *Privatdozent* when he became Husserl's assistant in January 1919. The word "phenomenology" consistently appears in the titles of his courses from then until his appointment at Marburg in 1923. Husserl and Heidegger collaborated briefly but unsuccessfully on a planned article on "phenomenology" for the *Encyclopedia Brittanica.*[7] Husserl, who was of Jewish origin, complained of Heidegger's well-known anti-Semitism at a time when he was the Nazi rector of the University of Freiburg. Although he sent flowers, Heidegger did not attend Husserl's funeral.

It is known that each influenced the other. Husserl initially seems to have regarded Heidegger as a possible successor, whom he willingly recommended for his chair when he retired. Heidegger, who was hardly a disinterested party, suggests his early fascination with Husserl's *Logical Investigations,* as well as his conviction that Husserl fell back into the position of psychologism that he refuted in this work.[8] Heidegger further edited the notes that later appeared as Husserl's lectures on *The Phenomenology of Internal Time-Consciousness.*[9] He dedicated *Being and Time,* his main work, to Husserl, even claiming that his work was based upon Husserl's *Logical Investigations.*[10] But later in the same work, he abandoned the Husserlian concept of phenomenological truth as *veritas transcendentalis*[11] for an incompatible, hermeneutical conception of truth.[12] Husserl, who studied *Being and Time* and *Kant and the Problem of Metaphysics,* seems to have concluded that Heidegger fell back from phenomenology into anthropology.[13] His remarks about the defense of reason in the *Crisis* to which we will come below further represent a response to Heidegger's embrace of Nazism.

III. Phenomenology and the Crisis of Reason

We can summarize the respective attitudes by saying that each regards the other as unfaithful to the genuine phenomenological insight. For

Husserl, Heidegger retreats from phenomenology to psychologism. Philosophically speaking it is less interesting to note that Husserl and Heidegger differ than to discuss the reasons for their differences. I have already noted that Husserl and Heidegger continue the traditional philosophical examination and defense of reason within a broadly phenomenological frame of reference. Each is further concerned to diagnose, to come to grips with, and to correct a crisis of reason that regards the crisis to be one of reason. The differences spring finally from different views of the crisis of reason that each regards, from different perspectives, as crucially linked to the rise of Nazism.

Philosophers have often been concerned with crises of various kinds, such as the Marxist concern with social crisis and its implications, and Sartre's concern, in his early writings, with forms of social crisis due to the inability of human beings to achieve an unmediated form of community that, in his later period, he thinks is achieved in a revolutionary situation. Others have been concerned with an alleged crisis of reason. Descartes, for instance, diagnoses a crisis of reason at the beginning of modern philosophy. For he holds that since we all have the same common sense but disagree, we require a method that will produce justified claims to know.[14] But for Husserl the Cartesian and Heidegger the anti-Cartesian, despite Descartes's best efforts and the work of intervening thinkers there is an ongoing crisis of reason.

The concept of crisis that only emerges in full view in Husserl's last, unfinished work, is already present, lurking as it were in the conceptual shadows of his thought from the time of his initial phenomenological breakthrough. The term "*Krisis*" in the title of Husserl's final book can be traced to the Greek "*krisis*," meaning "choice or selection, judgment or trial, crisis or critical moment." This latter pair of meanings is well conserved in the cognate terms in modern European languages, in the English "crisis" that translates Husserl's unusual usage of the Greek transliteration "*Krisis*," as well as in the more usual German synonym, "*Krise*." Speaking broadly, Husserl uses the term to refer to a problem constitutive of rationality.

Others have seen the link between the conception of crisis and Husserl's thought. According to Merleau-Ponty, "Husserl's philosophical endeavor is basically directed to the simultaneous solution of a crisis in philosophy, a crisis in the sciences of man, and a crisis in science as such which we have not yet passed through."[15] Yet, Husserl was interested not in the human sciences, but rather in philosophy as science and in the cognitive possibilities of natural science. Like Descartes, Husserl was primarily occupied with the crisis of reason's inability to make out its claim to know. His constant concern to overcome the crisis of reason is a red thread running throughout the different phases of his theory.[16] His entire theory is oriented toward diagnosing and overcoming the crisis of reason, initially through descriptive, later, after the introduction of the concept of transcendental reduction, through transcendental phenomenology. At different times of his career, Husserl's models were Kant, then later Descartes, Fichte and Kant, then Descartes again. Throughout, his aim, as he signaled in the title of his programmatic article, is finally to realize the idea of "Philosophy as Rigorous Science" in order to defend reason and knowledge.

Husserl's initial defense of reason in the *Logical Investigations*, his first major phenomenological work, is strongly motivated by Kant.[17] "Psychologism" refers roughly to the conflation between the psychological and the logical, as in Mill and more recently in Quine.[18] In the *Critique of Pure Reason*, Kant distinguishes sharply between psychology and logic. The critical philosophy is a transcendental logic that purports to determine the conditions of any knowledge whatsoever. In his work, Husserl defends a concept of logic understood as the idea and theory of science in order to found the special sciences and defend the very possibility of apodictic knowledge. Now and later, he sees the possibility of knowledge and the good life as turning on phenomenology which, as he later claims, in a perhaps unguarded moment, responds to the "secret longing of the whole philosophy of modern times."[19] Whereas Kant desires to demonstrate the possibility of a priori knowledge, Husserl is primarily concerned to refute psychologism in all its forms.

In subsequent writings, Husserl develops, deepens, but does not fundamentally alter his initial effort to overcome the crisis of reason by diagnosing and combatting various threats to reason. In the *Logical Investigations*, he links this problem to the refutation of skeptical relativism in his critical discussion of Lipps and J. S. Mill. Here he holds that psychologism opens the door to skeptical relativism, so that in combatting psychologism he is also combatting relativism.[20] In later writings, such as "Philosophy as Rigorous Science," he reconceived psychologism as a variety of naturalism, in his opposition to naturalism, historicism, and *Lebensphilosophie*. The problem here is the realization of the idea of philosophy implicit in the writings of Descartes, Fichte, and Kant. In *Cartesian Meditations*, he represents transcendental phenomenology as a determined, largely successful effort to realize the goal of the Cartesian theory. Yet in virtue of the obvious continuity between Descartes and Kant,[21] it is not surprising that there is a clear continuity between his later, more Cartesian writings, and his earlier, more Kantian phenomenological texts. In the *Formal and Transcendental Logic*, he wrote that "Transcendental logic is the ultimate theory of science, an ultimate, deepest, and most universal, theory of the principles and norms of all science."[22]

Husserl understands phenomenology as linking objective knowledge and subjective interests. Throughout his writings, Husserl's emphasis on rigorous philosophy is linked to an implicit ethical goal which, in the first sentence of his programmatic article, he describes as "the science that satisfies the loftiest theoretical needs and renders possible from an ethico-religious point of view a life regulated by pure rational norms."[23] In the *Crisis*, he restates his concern with the crisis of science[24] that he now more explicitly than before links to human being.

The link is brought out in various ways. One is the famous, enigmatic statement that the dream of philosophy as rigorous science is over.[25] This obscure statement can be understood in different ways, for instance as referring to the present period or to Husserl's own efforts that are now drawing to a close. Then there is the clearly ethical ring of Husserl's claim that in seeking objective knowledge, philosophers are, in his term, "*functionaries of mankind*."[26] Finally, there is the claimed direct link between the defense of reason and the interests of human being. "Skepticism about the possibility of metaphysics," Husserl writes, "the collapse of the belief in a universal philosophy as the guide for the new man, actually represents a collapse of the belief in 'reason,' understood as the ancients opposed *episteme* to *doxa*."[27]

IV. Fundamental Ontology and the Crisis of Reason

Heidegger's view of the crisis of reason, particularly as expounded in his early writings, is well known, certainly better known than Husserl's. The differences between the two views are obvious and important. Speaking generally, Husserl discerns a crisis of reason due to the continued striving for, but inability to attain, the philosophical goal of rigorous science. For Husserl, the crisis is epistemological, since it concerns the claim to know in a rigorous way, of which one facet is the idea of philosophy as a rigorous science. Speaking equally generally, for Heidegger the crisis of reason is due to the turn away from the problem of Being posed authentically in early Greek philosophy but later forgotten. For Heidegger, the crisis is not epistemological but ontological. The early Heidegger, roughly through the time of the 1929 inaugural lecture "What Is Metaphysics?" maintains that fundamental ontology is transcendental philosophy, before later abandoning philosophy altogether for thought

(*Denken*) beyond either metaphysics or philosophy. But although his theory has important epistemological consequences, for instance as concerns the conceptions of truth[28] and hermeneutics,[29] the main problem with which he is concerned, both early and late, is not epistemological but ontological.

According to Heidegger, there is a direct link between the level of a science and its ability to enter into a crisis concerning its basic concepts.[30] His theory rests on a basic distinction between beings or entities and Being in general, roughly the Being of beings. In *Being and Time,* through a reference to Plato, he suggests that ever since the time of the early Greeks philosophy has been in a state of permanent crisis, since it has been unable to answer the question concerning "Being." His own effort is directed toward throwing ontology and philosophy in general into a further crisis in order to question, demonstrate, and ground their basic concepts.

Since the initial phase of Heidegger's theory is complex, but familiar, we can be very brief. His theory rests on the so-called ontological distinction, roughly a distinction between beings, or entities, and Being in general, or the Being of beings. His aim is to retrieve and complete the problem of Being as it was originally, supposedly authentically raised in early Greek thought and later covered up. Heidegger begins *Being and Time,* his first and main treatise, with the claim that we do not know and must raise again "the question of the meaning of Being."[31] For Heidegger, the problem of Being is both ontologically and ontically prior over all other problems. His clue to knowledge of Being is *Dasein,* or human being that is characterized by its concern with Being. We begin with an average, nondiscursive, or pre-ontological conception of Being.[32] Analysis of *Dasein* is said to lay bare the horizon for the interpretation of the question of the meaning of Being. A necessary step in that direction is the destruction of the history of ontology that Heidegger later came to equate with philosophy understood as a series of misinterpretations of Being. Heidegger sums up his early approach in an important passage linking together his views of philosophy, ontology, and *Dasein*: "Philosophy is a universal phenomenological ontology, and takes its departure from the hermeneutic of Dasein, which, as an analytic of *existence,* has made fast the guiding-line for all philosophical inquiry at the point where it *arises* and to which it *returns.*"[33]

For present purposes, we can roughly separate Heidegger's theory into two periods separated by the famous, but enigmatic, turning (*Kehre*) in his thought. The turning apparently consists of a number of changes, including a turn away from *Dasein* to Being, since Being, not *Dasein* is the cause of its own occultation; a new focus on the loss of the thought of Being as due to Being itself; a turn to Nietzsche, since he alone has recognized the primordiality of the event of the withdrawal of Being; a conscious decision to deepen or otherwise radicalize the earlier approach; and a political turning to undo the ravages wrought by the withdrawal of Being, in which Heidegger emphasizes the need for Germany to act on behalf of itself and the history of the West.[34] It is important to emphasize the latter point, since it might otherwise be thought that after his decision to resign as rector Heidegger had withdrawn from politics.

Heidegger's later view, after the turning, is less well known, since the *Beiträge zur Philosophie*, the main but extremely difficult text of his later period, has only recently been published.[35] The main lines of his later theory can only be sketched here in the briefest way as it relates to the crisis of reason. It has been suggested that there is a break in Heidegger's thought, something he clearly denies in insisting that the truth of Being remains his only question.[36] But there is a change in his view of truth and a general shift to history. Consistent with his deemphasis of *Dasein* in his later thought, Heidegger turns away from the subjective element while rethinking disclosure as so-called gentle releasement. In comments on the event (*das Ereignis*), he suggests his intention to differentiate between an earlier metaphysical and a later, postmetaphysical period, characterized by a new form of thought, or another beginning, different in kind from its predecessor, and based on an historical perspective lacking in metaphysics.

This view is summarized in "The Age of the World Picture." In *Being and Time*, Heidegger sharply criticized Descartes. In his essay, Heidegger argues that: metaphysics grounds our age; the fundamental event of the modern age is the picture, or representationalist view of knowledge; Descartes completes Western metaphysics in the turn to anthropology that can only be overcome through overcoming Western metaphysics. He further develops this view in a series of essays on technology in the argument that modern metaphysics leads to the dominion over beings that follows from the turn away from, the forgetfulness of, Being (*Seinsvergessenheit*).

V. Nazism and the Crisis of Reason

Husserl and Heidegger link the perceived crisis of reason to Nazism in vastly different, diametrically opposing ways. Nazism occupies a very different, minor place in Husserl's theory than in Heidegger's, for which it looms very large, larger than has often been understood in part because of the understandable reluctance of so many, deeply committed to the theory, to study its connection to Nazism in detail.[37] In part, the difference is due to a difference in age. In 1933, when National Socialism came to power in Germany, Husserl was seventy-four, with his career nearly over, and Heidegger was forty-four, with the main part of his career still to come. As Jaspers correctly points out, with Carl Schmitt and Alfred Baeumler, other academics who sympathized with the conservative revolution, Heidegger tried to use Nazism to advance within the German university system.[38] Husserl was too old to do so even had he been sympathetic to Nazism which, however, he strongly opposed. The deeper difference lies in their respective ways of understanding the rise of National Socialism which, for Husserl, was a symptom of the crisis of reason, whereas for Heidegger, from a very different perspective, it represented a way to resolve the crisis of reason.

Husserl's opposition to Nazism was based less on its avowed anti-Semitism, obviously threatening for someone with his Jewish origins, than with the intrinsic irrationality of a political movement opposed to the very idea of reason. In the Vienna Lecture, presented in 1935, on which the *Crisis* is based, Husserl opposes the idea of "the European crisis,"[39] or "European sickness,"[40] to the rational goal of the "philosophico-historical idea (or the teleological sense) of European man."[41] In a clear allusion to Nazism this austere phenomenologist stakes his claim to overcoming the rise of barbarism through a renewal of reason: "The crisis of European existence," he writes, "can end in only one of two ways: in the ruin of a Europe alienated from its rational sense of life, fallen into a barbarian hatred of spirit; or in the rebirth of Europe from the spirit of philosophy, through a heroism of reason that will definitively overcome naturalism."[42] Consistent with this view, several years later in the *Crisis* he opposes the mistaken attitude that in difficult times, marked by the rise of Nazi barbarism, "science has nothing to say to us"[43] by reaffirming the need, in a passage already cited, to defend the distinction between knowledge and opinion.

Husserl stressed the incompatibility of Nazism, regarded as another aspect of the crisis of reason, and philosophy, or the highest form of reason alone capable of bringing about a life of reason. In his reaction to Nazism, perceived as the incorporation of irrationality, with which Heidegger publicly identified, Husserl reaffirmed philosophy as the guardian of reason. Heidegger saw Nazism and philosophy as compatible. Although later opposed to Platonism, in the "Rectoral Address," in a traditionally Platonic way Heidegger sought to found politics in philosophy, or Nazism in fundamental ontology, as Jaspers correctly said to lead the leaders and assume the hegemony of the Nazi movement.[44]

Beyond personal ambition, which was obvious—he later came to think that there were only four thinkers in his sense: Anaximander, Heraclitus, Parmenides, and himself—there was a philosophical link between his turning to Nazism and his concern with Being. Heidegger applied his distinction between authenticity and inauthenticity to philosophy. Inauthentic philosophy continues a philosophical tradition that long ago diverged from the authentic problem and merely perpetuates incorrect ways of understanding Being. Authentic philosophy, later authentic thought, returned back behind the philosophical tradition to take up the problem as it was originally and authentically raised. In the same way as he held that there were only two philosophical languages, German and Greek,[45] so for Heidegger the Germans were the authentic metaphysical *Volk*, those who by their tradition were destined to think Being. He understood Nazism as a political means to realize the authenticity of the German *Volk*, the metaphysical people,[46] in order to respond to the question of Being. Despite all its inadequacies, for Heidegger Nazism was important in exposing and opposing the problems arising from the forgetfulness of Being. His continued concern, after he resigned from the rectorate, throughout his later career, with what he later described, long after the war, as "the inner truth and greatness of this movement"[47] lies in his view of Nazism's role, authentically understood, in respect to Being.

VI. Conclusions: Nazism and the Crisis of Reason

The difference in the respective views of Nazism, including its link to the crisis of reason, is clear and dramatic. For Husserl, Nazism represents unreason that can be undone in philosophical reason. His view is very close to the traditional view of Nazism as an expression of irrationalism and antimodernism.[48] Although Heidegger may have been regarded as an ordinary Nazi, and he even followed the Hitler cult,[49] even in 1933, as was obscurely recognized at the time, for instance in the critical remarks of Otto Wacker, his Nazism was not ordinary, but extraordinary, following from his philosophy.

For Heidegger, although not quite the exemplification of reason, Nazism represents the means to bring it about. It is widely recognized that Nazism made extensive use of modern technology to carry out the holocaust.[50] Although he criticized modern technology as the result of the turn away from Being, Heidegger inconsistently downplayed the reliance of Nazism on advanced technological means and modern science to carry out the holocaust in order to feature its supposed usefulness for Being. In Husserl's view, Nazism is one more example of the crisis of reason due to the failure to realize the philosophical goal. In Heidegger's view, Nazism is the way out of the persistent failure of philosophy to attain its goal.

The differences in the ways that Husserl and Heidegger understand Nazism following on their respective views of philosophy are not minor, but concern the very nature of Western civilization. Both thinkers linked philosophy and reason in the full sense. But they disagree about the nature of the philosophical tradition. Whereas Husserl regarded Western philosophy as aiming steadily toward a single, never realized idea, Heidegger divided the philosophical tradition into a later, authentic, and an earlier, inauthentic form. According to Husserl, the ancient aim of perfecting the life of reason that he identified with the goal of European man was threatened by National Socialism that represented unreason. He regarded Nazism as a clear danger to the essence of Western philosophy and, for that reason, since civilization depends on philosophy, to Western civilization. Heidegger distinguished between the Western philosophical tradition and an idea that was initially evoked but later covered up at the beginning of philosophy. He, too, linked philosophy to the goal of Western civilization. But, unlike Husserl, he held that this goal could not be attained in continuing and completing modern philosophy, which was inauthentic, but only through its rejection in favor of an earlier, supposedly more authentic tradition whose completion depended on a grasp of the Nazi means. Husserl's appreciation of Nazism was defective in an obvious philosophical way, but Heidegger's even more so. Like so many thinkers, Husserl apparently took thought for action, theory as the solution for, even equivalent to practice. He believed that the reaffirmation of reason was either a sufficient or even the only recourse available against the rise of Nazism. In our time of need, he saw no other recourse, since he apparently failed to grasp the specificity of National Socialism which, from his angle of vision, was merely another, however terrible, form of naturalism. Heidegger later distinguished thought from action[51] in order to reassure his readers, after the war, of the inoffensive nature of his theory that had supposedly evolved away from his earlier identification with Nazism. But his misapprehension, whose dimensions have probably still not been fully understood, was certainly deeper than Husserl's. Husserl, aware of the danger, believed it was sufficient to practice philosophy to come to grips with it. He mistook both the limits of philosophy and the extent of the menace. Heidegger failed to perceive a menace at all since, seen through the lenses of his philosophy, Nazism represented an opportunity to seize with both hands. In each case, a philosophical theory led the philosopher astray, but Heidegger more than Husserl, who unfortunately believed he could reject Nazism through the means of philosophy, whereas Heidegger embraced it as the means to another, better life.

13

Edie's Hard-Nosed James and the Retrieval of the Sacred

Bruce Wilshire

William James's life can be read as a cautionary tale about fame. He gained widespread acclaim at the cost of being simplistically and very misleadingly understood. This occurred as much within academia as without. He was out of step with—and I think ahead of—the dominant philosophical topics, issues, and preoccupations of his time (and later)—e.g., idealism versus realism, the supposed autonomy of epistemology, the elaborate developments of mathematical logic.

The impulses of the teacher, even perhaps of the evangelist, ran high and strong in James. He thought he (and Charles Peirce) had discovered a way, a pragmatic way, of making crucial ideas clear—truth, for example. He wanted to help needlessly confused human beings. He thought the pragmatic method was so powerful and flexible it could be applied by anybody within any metaphysical system of thought to clarify the ideas therein. He neglected to emphasize that his *own* pragmatic theories of meaning and truth could be properly understood only within his own metaphysics of radical empiricism.

And this is a metaphysics that can be grasped, I believe, only through a phenomenological reading of it, a reading that is completely foreign to most Anglo-American philosophers then and now, thinkers who seem to know only two options: skepticism or some version of dogmatic metaphysics, such as certain analytic philosophers' scientism. James Edie has contributed to the resurrection of James from the strange obscurity of his fame, because he has done the hard work of grasping James's hard work as a major creative philosopher. I think Edie shows that James's greatly humane and existential message can be rightly appreciated only through the most rigorous retrieval of the philosopher's reasoning.

It helps to recall that James seriously considered becoming an artist. He had a genius, and a deep need, for grasping the concreteness of experience. He marvelled that philosophers could so easily forget the actual circumstances within which we live, move, and inquire. He marvelled that supposedly rigorous thinkers could so uncritically reify abstractions. What do we mean by "truth," for example? Logicians need propositions to do their logic, and these must be true or false. Most contemporary epistemologists need them to do their epistemology. Propositions are "defined into being" as asserted meanings that can be true or false. They float somehow between minds (or language) and states of affairs in the asserted-about world. The actual situations in which human organisms interact with the environment and eke out some truth has been papered over. "True propositions" blur or fudge the relationship of organism and environment in which truth happens.

James helps us understand that once propositions are reified, the really hard work of philosophy is forgotten. How attractive is reification! Take, for example, "There are no extraterrestrial intelligent beings." It must be the case that the proposition is either true or false. It is probably false, but it may be true. If it is, it is true already, though we know it not. And isn't it!? Once a proposition is defined and reified as that which must be true or false then *of course* it must be one or the other. And perhaps in the many situations in which quick thought and action are required, the human mind must, as a practical necessity, believe something like this.

But James's exhaustive reflection on the conditions of human practice in general—the actual structures of reason that practice presupposes and entails—illuminates the price we pay for this greased slide. A true proposition is only as revealing as the meanings that make it up, and we can only form meanings in terms of what we can anticipate can happen within a world we can experience. We must believe to be true, James writes, whatever is necessary to form a world—a meaningful world—in our experience. But how commodious and rich is that world so formed? What if we cannot anticipate modes of intelligence much vaster than our own? Then we would not be able to recognize them even if they were all around us. Our meaning of "intelligence" would be too narrow and superficial. "Well then, if there are such super-intelligent beings all around us but going unrecognized," the reifier of propositions will say, "the proposition that there are no extraterrestrial intelligent beings is false, though we cannot know this."

But James would say that the reifier has shifted his ground. He has tacitly altered the meaning of "intelligence," and thus has altered the proposition (since a proposition is nothing but its asserted meanings). So he has a *different* proposition. He has evaded the hard work of perpetually forming meanings that are more and more adequate to a world that overflows any and all of the meanings we could ever form.

The Meaning of the Word "Truth"

James Edie writes: "[It] is the *meaning* of [James's] pragmatism which must be rescued from the oversimplified version of it which has been uncritically accepted by historians of philosophy. By reducing James to his pragmatism we risk losing the authentic genius and originality in his thought."[1] So what are the structures of reason and reasoning presupposed when organism and environment cocreate a world in experience, an experienceable world? Nothing less than the answer to this is required to actually understand what James means by truth. What is James's metaphysics of radical empiricism? Edie's great contribution is showing that these questions are best answered by regarding James as a phenomenologist, or a protophenomenologist at least—by comparing James and Edmund Husserl. I want to show that this comparative study is essential for understanding everything James did, even—and particularly—his "attack on reason" and his religio-philosophical speculations at the end of his life.

Edie illuminates brilliantly the phenomenological-philosophical significance of James's masterwork, *The Principles of Psychology*. To talk intelligibly about the ever-changing, streaming course of our experiencing presupposes a rational structure: we can know that no sensation or thought of an object can ever be exactly the same as another only because the object as we mean and intend it is held constant. There is reason to compare thoughts or sensations, and to tell that they differ, only because we know they are *of* the *same* object. This is the idea of intentionality, which is essential to building the experience of a world: "I and my thoughts and feelings can change, and the world—the larger reality—remains what it is."

Entailed is that objects *are* of certain sorts, whether we like it or not; and that they endure as objects of these sorts (for a time typical for individuals of the sort in question). Without this objectivity there could be nothing to contrast to it, no subjectivity. To have a world we must be able to conceptualize, to hold general meanings constant, and to see objects as instances of these meanings or sorts. Concepts are "teleological instruments": Again, a world of experience is possible only when things are sorted out; and things are sorted only with respect to the specific active attitudes they solicit or demand from us, the ends we must keep in view. What sorts of anticipating, coping, responding do they call out from us?

Already in the *Principles* reasoning is understood as a structured phenomenon, something in the service of doing. James speaks of "the essence" of things, the characteristics without which they wouldn't be what they are. But he keeps the word in scare quotes, for they are features that we must ascribe to things in a particular epoch of activity and interactivity if sorts are to be indentifiable and useable by us. They are no less objective and no less the work of reason for all that.

In the last chapter of the *Principles,* "Necessary Truths and the Effects of Experience," James distances himself decisively from many other "empirical" or "experiential" philosophies. Reason has a particular kind of ideality and autonomy, and sorts are sorts, regardless of the frequency or recency with which these sorts are actually encountered in the course of experience. Reasoning traces the web of a *world* in experience, because it can infer that what's of a kind must be of the kind's kind. And things must stick to their kinds with enough constancy and stability for concerted reasoning and action to be possible.

In "Necessary Truth and Perception: William James and the Structure of Appearance," Edie rightly compares James's elucidation of sorts or "essences" to Husserl's method of fictive variation or eidetic experiment. He quotes from James's last chapter in the *Principles,* "Necessary Truths and the Effects of Experience":

> Suppose a hundred beings created by God and gifted with the faculties of memory and comparison. Suppose that upon each of them the same lot of sensations are imprinted, but in different orders. Let some of them have no single sensation more than once. Let some have this one and others that one repeated. Let every conceivable permutation prevail. And then let the magic-lantern show die out, and keep the creatures in a void eternity, with naught but their memories to muse upon. Inevitably in their long leisure they will begin to play with the items of their experience and rearrange them, make classifactory series of them, place gray between white and black, orange between red and yellow, and trace all other degrees of resemblance and difference. And this new construction will be absolutely identical in all the hundred creatures, the diversity of the sequence of the original experiences having no effect as regards the arrangement.[2]

For James, British empiricism, with its air of solipsism, doesn't really come to grips with the experiencing, vulnerable, worldly self at all. Its notion of discrete sensations within a mental "sphere" is the result of analysis and abstraction mistaking itself for description of immediately lived experience. Mentalistic nouns are reified. The adjectival, adverbial, prepositional, conjunctive flowing and webbing of immediate experiencing is overlooked. The British empiricists must overload common habitual associations to have even a semblance of a world. The result is a small, tame, child's world. Edie quotes Iris Murdoch to the effect that because these empiricists restrict themselves to the world "in which people play cricket, cook cakes, make simple decisions, remember their childhood and go to the circus," they thereby exclude themselves from the adult world "in which [people] commit sins, fall in love, say prayers or join the Communist Party." Edie goes on, "The trouble with British empiricism since its inception has been that it smugly spurns human experience."[3]

Reasoning and Experience

Without the background in the *Principles* which Edie sets forth so well, James's somewhat fragmentary but immensely important last works cannot be understood. I mean his pragmatic theory of truth, metaphysics of radical empiricism, exploratory views on religion, and his notion of a pluralistic universe. All these works presuppose the structures of reason that make possible a world in experience, but they seldom make these presuppositions perfectly explicit.

For good reason, James initiated his *Essays in Radical Empiricism* with "Does Consciousness Exist?". He eschews all mind/body dualism. There can be no domain or substance called mind conceived to be independent of our total activities as organisms in the world around us. Thinking does, of course, occur, but it is a function, a "leading" within the world. This "leading" involves interest, expectation, anticipation, the activities of meaning-making. James's empiricism is radical because relationships are just as primordial as things related. And grasping the relationship between organism and environment has a certain priority if the meaning of other relationships are to be, for it is the meaning-making relationship. James describes the body as the constant "storm center," where the stresses and enticements, the "circumpressure," of the environment emerges in experience. The body's needs, interests, desires, and fears spring from this center. Interest, he says, is the a priori factor in cognition.

Reasoning, recall, for James, is a phenomenon of human life. It does have a certain essential autonomy, but it is an activity of an active bodily being involved directly and immediately through its organism with the world around it. We need a phenomenology, a disciplined description of experience in all its moments and levels. Without phenomenology reflexive reason will leap in prematurely and reify its abstractions: "proposition," "sensation," "concept," "belief," etc.—thus pulverizing and congealing the flow of what James aptly calls the flowing "much at once."

When we attune ourselves to experiencing as it actually occurs "hot off the griddle" of the world—we need perhaps an artist's eye—we see that it is "pure" or "neutral," as James says. That is, it is neither clearly "in a subject" nor "out there" in an object, neither clearly subjective nor objective. Where is the beauty of a rose, he asks, when we directly encounter it? It is neither "out there" nor "in here."[4] It's a kind of presence or "between" in "the much at once." Even the extension of something in space—Descartes's prized earmark of the objective or physical world—has its organic resonance in an actual if immeasureable extensity of visual, tactile, and kinesthetic "imagery."

We construct, or coconstruct, distinct "objective" and "subjective" realms only in retrospection, James says—though it may be exceedingly rapid retrospection. Yes, only reasoning—habitual and "instinctive" or, on the other hand, deliberate—limns the contours of the *world* and our place in it. But it must work with experiences that are primordially "pure," "neutral." The very same pure experience—of coldness, for example—can figure in two retrospectively created contexts at once. It can be "placed" in the context of the history of the world while appearing also in the context of my personal history—a context in which it can be recalled with particular intimacy, shudderingly and dreadfully, for instance.

James uses a spatial metaphor to try to clarify what he means. Imagine, he says, a point through which vertical and horizontal lines are drawn. The very same point occurs on two different lines—or, playing with the trope—occurs in two contexts of the world. He also writes that there is a "coordinate" realm "drawn through the same point"—the realm of concepts. But the account of how this coordinate realm works—how it coordinates?—is left in a fragmentary state by James, and this will return to trouble his thought.

The Grasp of the Whole

The gist of James's radical empiricism holds immense possibilities for development. We can begin to imagine how all his work in the last eight years of his life might fit together in a whole view—a view he knew he had not himself completely grasped or written down. Edie is certainly on the right track when he writes in "William James's Phenomenology of Religious Experience" that James conceived of the intentionality of the whole organic being, the whole body-self. Supposing this we can understand how the "much at once" and the "circumpressure" in its "neutrality" can be experienced. Supposing this we begin to grasp how mystical states of union are possible. Of course they are trances or trancelike: the organizing center of experience lies outside the ego-self. Of course they are typically "oceanic" and ineffable: articulation has its sure ground in one or other of the retrospectively produced contexts, and it is just these divisions that are overwhelmed in religious experience.

We can also grasp why James's radical empiricism, phenomenologically understood, must generate a "pluralistic universe." Reason is reasoning, and it is always and only something done by an organism within a context. We do make some sense of the universe, within the scope of our activities, actual and possible—activities that include our ability to imagine hypotheses. But to think that reason can withdraw within its own resources—whatever that might mean exactly—and discover on its own some single property or relation which would entail how everything is bonded to everything else—that seems to James to be prideful and unwarranted. There is a universe he thinks, but it has a "concatenated" not a "through and through" unity. That is, "'and' names a genuine reality." As far as we can tell, some things are merely "along with one another" in a way that our reason could never entail that they be. The universe allows for things to be loosely joined, from next to next; there is room for things to rattle around a bit.

And by this time we can see why James's pragmatic theory of truth can be understood only within his metaphysics of radical empiricism. He cannot think that truth is some kind of correspondence between something in the mind (or in language) and something "out there." This is to suppose an inexperienceable and occult correspondence, one that pretends to do without the primal matrix of "pure or neutral experience" and our worldly contexts. And he must think that propositions supposed to possess a property of truth are inexperienceable and occult entities. Truth for James can only mean fruitfulness of thinking, thinking that gets us where it presumes to get us within the coercive grain of the world. Part of what reason tells us is that our thinking cannot create things out of nothing. When it discovers them it *must* believe that they existed prior to its discovering of them. Again, this must be so, because we must believe whatever is necessary to have an experienceable *world,* a grand concatenated whole that endures on its own through time.

So, though truth must occur through successful leading in time, it can have a timeless quality once achieved. For example, to believe that Maggie the horse ran out of the barn at 6:00 A.M., 9 October 1993, is to believe that nothing can change that, the belief is timelessly true. Reason demands this of us. ("But wouldn't the proposition expressed by the belief be timelessly true whether anyone held the belief or not?" Reply: "*You* are imagining such a proposition, and we might have reason to believe it is true.")

Finally, we can better understand James's famous "attack on reason" at the end of his life. We sort out a world for the purposes of getting around in it, for coping and enjoying. We hold general meanings or concepts constant, as James put it in the *Principles.* He implies that for a world to be possible in experience it must be experienceable as enduring on its own through time. Essential to this is that it be composed of things that are likewise experienceable as enduring, at least for some stretch of time. The world is ordered or sorted into the sorts themselves, which are experienceable as enduring, and into the individuals that instantiate them. Indeed, we cannot individuate things, cannot count individuals, without assuming they are one-of-that-sort. As to horse, say—one, two, three of that sort. As to human, ten in all of that sort, etc.

All this was implied from the very beginning of James's reasoning about the world and our place in it. The assumption emerges unmistakably in his *Essays in Radical Empiricism*: primal experience is neither "objective" not "subjective." There must be formative principles or structures in terms of which the general history of the world, on the one hand, and our personal history as occasionally conscious beings, on the other, are composed.

Now, when James hit upon the idea of pure or neutral experience, it was as if he had poked his hand deep into a hole in the ground and encountered something strange, intriguing, and disturbing that he could not get a good grip on, pull out, and inspect. More and more in his last years he tries to grasp immediate experiencing in its prereflective integrity. More and more he tries to advance his insight born in *Varieties of Religious Experience*: the intentionality of the whole body-self, as Edie puts it, that composes a unified, absorbant, pulsing context in "the much at once," a context that is anterior to, and in a real sense more fundamental than, the conventional, retrospectively produced contexts of "subjective" and "objective" history of the world and personal history. He knows he has put his hand on something primal, labile, fundamental, but he doesn't know quite what to make of it.

This primal experiencing of flowing, unpredictably burgeoning, numinous and powerful life engenders some of James's most eloquent, questing, and powerful writing.

> [T]he real units of our immediately felt life are unlike the units that the intellectualist logic holds to and makes its calculations with. They are not separate from their own others, and you have to take them at widely separated dates to find any two of them that seem unblent . . . my present field of consciousness is a centre surrounded by a fringe that shades insensibly into a subconscious more. . . . Which part of it properly is in my consciousness, which out? If I name what is out, it already has come in. The centre works in one way while the margins work in another, and presently overpower the centre and are central themselves. What we conceptually identify ourselves with and say we are thinking of at any time is the centre; but our *full* self is the whole field, with all those indefinitely radiating subconscious possibilities of increase.[5]

This fullness of life, this immediate sense of the simplest bits of immediate experience flowing into one another, budding and burgeoning out of one another, captivates James. So captivated is he that he writes, "Not only the absolute is its own other, but the simplest bits of immediate experience are their own other, if that hegelian phrase be once for all allowed."

Everything is its own other!? This threatens to totally undermine reasoning, and the experienceable world we build up out of it. Reasoning, as James knows, requires most basically the law of identity: each thing is identical with itself, each thing is itself and not another thing.

But without reasoning and the sense of the world around us built up retrospectively (no matter how rapidly) and in some manner conceptually, how could James even try to attune himself to this burgeoning, personal, *pre*reflective life? Without some rational structure, how could there be the contrast requisite for recognition of the prereflective? So captivated is he by his insights into the flow of pure experience that he denigrates conceptualization and "intellectualist logic." "Our intellectual handling of [experience] is a retrospective patchwork, a post-mortem dissection, and can follow any order we find most expedient."[6] "Expedient"—there is no word more dangerous for James to use. It does not distinguish what works for our *thought* in the *world* anticipated by that thought, from what works for us as *beings who wish,* and who can fall into self-deluding *wishful thinking.* Using the word "expedient" uncritically at times, he plays into the eager hands of the critics of his pragmatic theory of truth.

At the end of James's life his whole intellectual career is thrown into crisis and, because he is an intellectual, it is also a personal crisis. The reader can, at times, hear from him the clear sounds of desperation. For example, the critics of his pragmatism show, he says, an "inability to understand him that is almost pathetic."

He has some sense of where the great problem lies. It appears in his *Essays*, where he suggests that concepts are "a coordinate realm of reality" that intersect at a point along with the "lines" of world history and personal history. But how does this coordinate realm coordinate, how does it function in building up a sense of the enduring world and our place in it? This was left undeveloped, and the lacuna remains to haunt him. In his very last work, the unfinished *Some Problems of Philosophy: The Beginning of an Introduction to Philosophy*, he devotes many pages to "Percept and Concept." He tries to explain how the two work coordinately: they require each other as do "the two blades of a scissors." But the book is left unfinished, and in no merely accidental way.

I think he is only partially aware of some of the resources of his own past thinking. Given *his* understanding of concepts, which goes back at least to the *Principles*, why should he denigrate them? They have their proper work in building up the indispensable contexts of the history of the world and of our place in it. Concepts do not mirror the showcase of finished and eternal forms as they did for Plato. They are teleological instruments that we find indispensable for identifying things and dealing with them during stretches of world time, sometimes very long stretches. But "essence" is always kept in scare quotes. We needn't pretend that things are absolutely delineated and captured by concepts. What we *mean* by an *actual* thing is its "overflowingness," as James himself insists. The law of identity as James understands it pragmatically is a highly useful ideal, fruitful and true within its proper domain.

Again we must consider James's desperation. He dreads "intellectualist logic" wielded by philosophers that does not remain within its proper domain, but invades and violates the precious domain of the body in its total organic intentionality: our immediately lived personal life, its numinousness and power, the surging juice of our lives. His great fear, he said, was of becoming desiccated. When we look at what many philosophers actually do, James's fears are reasonable. But it is too bad that his fears had to be so strong.

Thought beyond Thought

Edie's hard-nosed James is indispensable for grasping the total background against which James's thought emerges, and without which we cannot further develop it. The horizons for development are bright but difficult to traverse. We must avoid some of the deepest prejudices of Western dualistic, logistic, and atomic-substantialistic thought. In retrieving flowing, organic intentionality within a "neutral" "much at once," this particular Western philosopher was breaking into the archaic, universal culture of humankind. The body-self in first-intention is unpredictable, snakelike, powerful, labile, precious, disturbing. It can bring unspeakable interfusion, support, vitality. It seems to grasp aspects of our reality ungraspable in other ways. But the very discontinuity with conventional life is shocking. The body really lived and understood is fascinating, both attractive and repelling. It is taboo. Age-old religious practices were erected to house it, practices now fallen into disrepair for most people, secularized as they are. We are left with the great task of learning again to live with our power. The threat is mere wildness and violence. Or, on the other hand, stultifying repression of the gamut of our feeling life—a gray, faceless, relentless violence, actually. Witness, for example, most academic philosophy in the United States today.

At the close of "Does Consciousness Exist?" James writes: "The 'I think' which Kant said must be able to accompany all my objects, is the 'I breathe' which actually does accompany them." James always adopts a polemical attitude toward Kant. But he is making some profound points. First, James does not think that the "I think" is in fact capable of accompanying all our objects of thought. For stretches of time we are too absorbed in the prereflective "much at once." Second, breathing is integral to feeling of self, and to psychical and spiritual life.

To affirm something's existence is not just to perform a "mental act inside a consciousness" or "inside language" (a "propositional attitude"?). It is to allow the thing to exist with us in the same world, to allow it to be at a place that I and others can share, that is, to allow it to compenetrate and interfuse with the body. One can take its presence into one's body through the inhaling, inspiring breath. To deny is the reverse. We feel the dissonance as we try to simultaneously deny something's existence and inhale.

James's creative religious thought and his phenomenology of the breathing body join at this point, recalling how spiritual arts were once called pneumatic. Note how a contemporary's experience is illuminated. Conger Beaseley recounts accompanying an official of the Alaska Department of Fish and Game in an expedition on the Bering Sea. The goal was to shoot four seals so that biologists could analyze blood and tissue samples for toxics, trace minerals, and parasites. Revolted by the experience, Beaseley clutches for some redeeming qualities in it. After a seal is shot, its vivid blood boils up around it in the icy water. But the redeeming feature is there: for the first time he realizes viscerally his consanguinity with seals. He is bonded to a fellow animal. As they open up the seal's abdomen and extirpate its vital organs, Beaseley notes,

> I developed an identification with the animal that carried far beyond mere scientific inquiry . . . the abdomen of an adult harbor seal is approximately the size of an adult human male's. Each time I reached into the tangled viscera, I felt as if I were reaching for something deep inside myself. As I picked through the thick folds of the seal's heart collecting worms, I felt my own heart sputter and knock.[7]

As they extirpate the seal's vital organs, Beaseley realizes, viscerally, that "the physical body contains functional properties, the proper acknowledgment of which transforms them into a fresh order of sacraments." Coiled intestines intertwine resonantly with coiled intestines of all animate things. Visceras interfuse and bond in experience. In the recoiling intake of air, in the body's gasp of awe, we pay tribute to the wilderness mana and taboo energies that our bodies share with all animals. In the gasping intake of breath we let these animals into our being. The sacrament is the involuntary acknowledgment of our kinship and our common preciousness—an acknowledgment that resonates, nevertheless, through our voluntary consciousness and career. It is sacrifice in the sense of sacrifice of ego: the acknowledgment of all that we do not know and cannot control, and upon which we depend. It names the sacred.

The Final Dilemma

James could not keep up with the revolutionary implications of his thinking. Probably we today cannot. Though it has been one of my major points that James's later thought builds centrally on his earlier—and that Edie helps greatly in grasping this—James did in fact abandon a key earlier idea, and with very disturbing consequences. In the *Principles* he denied that there are enduring mental atoms that can be summed into larger wholes in consciousness. Consciousness is an ever-changing streaming; only its objects in their various domains are constant and summable. Though he attacked British empiricism, he still held to a generic form of psychophysical dualism: Each person has one body and one consciousness, and this consciousness—though linked to the intended world essentially—is private and personal.

This psychophysical dualism collapses in his last works. Consciousness is no kind of domain or substance. Mentation of various kinds goes on, but it is a function, a "leading" of a body in an environment. He can no longer speak of gulfs dividing minds. In the second *Essay* he writes, "whatever differing contents our minds may eventually fill a place with, the place itself is a numerically identical content of the two minds. . . . The receptacle of certain of our experiences being thus common, the experiences themselves might some day become common also."[8] A place is a "receptacle" we share. When I hold you by the arm, we share that, we interfuse and compenetrate to some degree as feeling, conscious beings. James so often writes of "the excitement of reality."

We are tempted to interpret his questioning thusly: Since we share the same "at" experienc*ed*, why shouldn't our experienc*ing* of this be shared or shareable somehow? But there is a vestige of dualism here, a distancing of body-self and world. James is suggesting a radical intimacy of body-self and world, suggesting that we completely rethink the intentionality of organic body-self caught up in the world. On the level of pure, not yet conventionally contextualized experience, we can share experiences. Why shouldn't they be "summed" into transpersonal wholes?

In the fourth and fifth lectures of *A Pluralistic Universe* James seriously considers Gustav Fechner's hypotheses about plant-souls, animal-souls, even Earth-Soul. What if mind and soul are not something hidden away inside bodies (and only in human bodies, as intellectualism likes to think), but occur as the most intimate leading, greeting, and fusing of bodies at places numerically identical for them? For James to consider this is for him to consider the most ancient religious practice we know: shamanism. He invites us to try to understand our human ancestors when—while hunting seals, for example-they "shape shifted" and "became a seal." These powerful blurrings of identities between "individual beings" of all sorts still go on today, I believe, but typically furtively and unacknowledgably and often destructively. Think of tacit group fusions and mob phenomena, e.g., "ethnic cleansing" occuring in many places today, or highly specialized academic professionals who purge "alien" members.

At the very end of his life, James extends his thinking in *Varieties* about mystical states of fusion, absorption, unity. He is not so content to conclude that they are ineffable. He wants to know more about them. What about the cognitive power of trance states? What if there are modes of knowing that fully wakeful, distanced, analytical, focused consciousness cannot even imagine? Only dogma supposes this to be impossible—secular dogma refusing to be aware of itself. Do we better understand the terrible coldness and loneliness of contemporary intellectual life when we suppose we have shut ourselves off from the communion of all things in its sacred power?

James speculations of 1909 place him at the forefront of the speculations of the 1990s. Conventional modes of individuation within conventionalized contexts of objectification and world history are not as secure in their broad ambitions as they once were. One body individuated within its envelope of skin and containing one mind may be an idea useful in certain contexts, but limited. Quantum physics disturbs conventional ideas about the localization of bodies, and even suggests that influences between bodies of certain sorts separated in space may be instantaneous. What if the speed of light as it traverses between bodies is not the absolute it was once thought? And Rupert Sheldrake's ideas about "the morphogenic field" shouldn't be dismissed out of hand. He suggests that mimetic bonding may occur between things of certain sorts simultaneously over great distances.[9]

I think it would be unpragmatic and ahistorical to suppose that the conventional contexts of world history and personal history are best abandoned. As James (and Peirce) knew, to question effectively we must leave most of our habitual modes of thought unquestioned. Where else could we stand to question? But we must ask how the old and the new can be coordinated. If concepts are a "coordinate realm," how could they coordinate the archaic context woven in prereflective, archaic, numinous experience, on the one hand, and, on the other, conventional contexts woven in retrospection (however rapid)? Must we reconceptualize concepts themselves? Or, following Heidegger, for example, seek a mode of meditative thinking "more rigorous than the conceptual"?

James does not supply the answers. But he opens our minds and hearts and helps propel and guide our questioning. He puts us on the scent of what lured him in the last years of his life, "wild beasts of the philosophic desert."[10]

James M. Edie: A Biographical Sketch

James M. Edie, Professor Emeritus of Philosophy at Northwestern University, was born in Grand Forks, North Dakota, on 3 November 1927. After completing college preparatory studies at Saint James Academy in Grand Forks, he attended Saint John's University, a Benedictine monastic college belonging to Saint John's Abbey in Collegeville, Minnesota, where he received his B.A. with honors in classics and philosophy in 1949.

After spending a year at the Saint John's School of Theology, he completed higher theological studies at the Athenaeum Anselmianum in Rome (S.T.B. 1952; S.T.L. 1954). In Rome he also spent one year at the Pontificio Collegium Russicum, attached to the Pontifical Institute for Oriental Studies, taking courses in Russian, Slavonic and Byzantine liturgy and theology.

From 1954 to 1958 he attended the Institut Superieure de Philosophie at the University of Louvain in Belgium, where he received the degrees of Ph.B. (1955), Ph.L. (1957), and Ph.D. (1958, "*avec la plus grande distinction*").

At Louvain he concentrated both in the history of medieval philosophy and in contemporary European philosophy. His principal professor for medieval studies was Fernand Van Steenberghen at Louvain; he also spent some time at the University of Poitiers in 1956, where Etienne Gilson directed the summer institute in medieval studies. In contemporary European philosophy his professors, connected with the original Husserl Archives as well as the Institut Supérieure de Philosophie, were Georges Van Riet, Albert Dondeyne, Herman-Leo Van Breda, Alpohonse De Waelhens, and others. During this time he also occasionally commuted to Paris to hear Merleau-Ponty at the Collège de France.

From 1959 to 1961 he taught as Assistant, then Associate Professor of Philosophy at Hobart and William Smith Colleges in New York. In the fall of 1961, at the request of the Chairman of the Department, John Wild, he joined the Department of Philosophy at Northwestern University as an

Assistant Professor. Edie spent almost his entire career at Northwestern, rising to the rank of Associate Professor (1965) and Full Professor (1971). For six years during the 1970s he chaired the Department and helped build up its current strengths in contemporary European philosophy.

Edie pioneered the introduction of phenomenology and existential philosophy into the United States, as a translator, editor, philosopher, and one of the founders of the Society for Phenomenology and Existential Philosophy. Together with John Wild he convened the first committee which founded the Society at Northwestern in the fall of 1962. The following year, again with John Wild, he helped establish the Northwestern University Press Series in Phenomenology and Existential Philosophy which, apart from a hiatus of some years (1974–88, when it was published by the Indiana University Press), continues at Northwestern to the present. While serving as General Editor of this series, Edie oversaw the publication of upwards of 125 titles, many of them translations of important European sources and other major works by some of the world's best known philosophers in this tradition.

He has authored four books, *Speaking and Meaning: The Phenomenology of Language*, *The Phenomenology of Edmund Husserl: A Critical Commentary*, *William James and Phenomenology*, and *Merleau-Ponty's Philosophy of Language: From Structuralism to Dialectics*, and, as editor and contributor, published some nine others. His bibliography follows below.

In retirement he continues to write on contemporary philosophy, especially the existential philosophy of the theater, and on the history of medieval philosophy, with the forthcoming publication of a work on the development of the concept of "Christian Philosophy" in the middle ages.

Bibliography of James M. Edie

Books and Contributions to Books (as Author or Editor and Contributor)

What Is Phenomenology? Essays by Pierre Thévénaz. Edited and translated with an Introduction by James M. Edie. Quadrangle Books, 1962.

In Praise of Philosophy, by Maurice Merleau-Ponty. Translated with an Introduction by John Wild and James M. Edie. Northwestern University Press, 1963.

Christianity and Existentialism. Six essays by William Earle, James M. Edie ("Faith as Existential Choice: The Punic Fathers," and "The Absence of God: Heidegger and Tillich"), and John Wild. Northwestern University Press, 1964.

The Primacy of Perception and Other Essays, by Maurice Merleau-Ponty. Edited with an Introduction by James M. Edie. Northwestern University Press, 1964.

Russian Philosophy, 3 volumes. Edited with an Introduction and commentary by James M. Edie, James P. Scanlan, and Mary-Barbara Zeldin. Quadrangle Books, 1965. Republished by the University of Tennessee Press, 1976.

Invitation to Phenomenology. Edited with an Introduction by James M. Edie. Quadrangle Books, 1965.

Phenomenology in America. Edited with an Introduction by James M. Edie. Quadrangle Books, 1967.

New Essays in Phenomenology. Edited with an Introduction by James M. Edie. Quadrangle Books, 1969.

Patterns of the Life-World. Essays in Honor of John Wild. Edited with an Introduction by James M. Edie, Francis Parker, and Calvin O. Schrag. Northwestern University Press, 1970.

Speaking and Meaning: The Phenomenology of Language. Indiana University Press, 1976. Japanese translation, Iwanami, Gendai Sensho, 1981.

The Phenomenology of Edmund Husserl: A Critical Commentary. Indiana University Press, 1987.

William James and Phenomenology. Indiana University Press, 1987.

Merleau-Ponty's Philosophy of Language: From Structuralism to Dialectics. Current Continental Research. The University Press of America, 1987.

Articles

"Expression and Metaphor." *Philosophy and Phenomenological Research* (1963), 538–61.

"Recent Work in Phenomenology." *American Philosophical Quarterly* (1964), 115–28.

"Transcendental Phenomenology and Existentialism." *Philosophy and Phenomenological Research* (1964), 52–63. Anthologized in *Phenomenology*, ed. Joseph Kockelmans. Doubleday, 1967. 237–51.

"Notes on the Philosophical Anthropology of William James." 110–32. See also, *Proceedings* of the Thirteenth International Congress of Philosophy, Mexico City, 1963.

"Phenomenology and Psychiatry: The Need for a Subjective Method in the Scientific Study of Human Behavior." In *Conditio Humano, Erwin W. Straus on his 75th Birthday*. Springer, 1966. 55–73.

"Phenomenology as Rigorous Science." *International Philosophical Quarterly* (1967), 21–30.

"Sartre as Phenomenologist and as Existential Psychoanalyst." In *Phenomenology and Existentialism.* Edited by Edward Lee and Maurice Mandelbaum. Johns Hopkins University Press, 1967. 139–78.

"William James and the Phenomenology of Religious Experience." In *American Philosophy and the Future.* Edited by Michael Novak. Scribner's, 1968. 247–69.

Review Article: "Merleau-Ponty, Existentialist of the Social World." *Journal of Value Inquiry* (1968), 216–25.

"William James and the Phenomenological Thesis of the Primacy of Perception." *Proceedings* of the Fourteenth International Congress of Philosophy, Vienna, September 1968.

"Descartes and the Phenomenological Problem of the Embodiment of Consciousness." In *Cartesian Essays: A Collection of Critical Studies.* Edited by Bernd Magnus and James B. Wilbur. Nijhoff, 1969. 91–115.

"Vico and Existential Philosophy." In *Giambattista Vico.* Edited by Hayden V. White, Isaiah Berlin, Max H. Fisch, and Elio Gianturco. The Johns Hopkins University Press, 1969. 483–95.

"Necessary Truth and Perception: William James on the Structure of Experience." In *New Essays in Phenomenology.* Quadrangle, 1969. 233–55.

"William James and Phenomenology." *Review of Metaphysics* (1970), 481–526.

"Can Grammar Be Thought?" In *Patterns of the Life-World.* Northwestern University Press, 1970. 313–45.

"The Levels and Objectivity of Meaning." In *The Future of Metaphysics.* Edited by Robert Wood. Quadrangle Books, 1970. 121–49.

"Ontology without Metaphysics?" In *The Future of Metaphysics.* Edited by Robert Wood. Quadrangle Books, 1970. 77–97.

Review Article: "Maurice Merleau-Ponty, *Humanism and Terror.*" *Journal of Value Inquiry* (1970), 314–20.

"The Problem of Enactment." *Journal of Aesthetics and Art Criticism* (1971), 303–18.

"Husserl's Conception of The Grammatical and Contemporary Linguistics." In *Life-World and Consciousness, Essays for Aron Gurwitsch.* Edited by Lester E. Embree. Northwestern University Press, 1972. 233–61. Also in *The Journal of Philosophical Linguistics.* Edited by William Cobb (1971), 34–71. Anthologized in *Readings on Edmund Husserl's Logical Investigations.* Edited by J. N. Mohanty. Nijhoff, 1977. 137–61.

"Was Merleau-Ponty a Structuralist?" In *Semiotica* (1971). Edited by Thomas A. Sebeok. 297–323.

Review Article: "Etienne Gilson, *Linguistique et Philosophie.*" *Journal of the History of Philosophy* (1971), 116–25.

"Preface" to Bruce Wilshire, *William James: The Essential Writings.* Harper and Row, 1971. ix–xv.

"Revolution in Philosophy: What is Phenomenology?" *Southwestern Journal of Philosophy* (1971), 73–91.

"Introduction" to Gaston Berger, *The Cogito in Husserl's Philosophy.* Northwestern University Press, 1972. ix–xxvii.

"The Genesis of a Phenomenological Theory of the Experience of Personal Identity: William James on Consciousness and the Self." *Man and World* (1973), 322–40.

"Foreword" to Maurice Merleau-Ponty, *Consciousness and the Acquisition of Language.* Translated by Hugh J. Silverman. Northwestern University Press, 1973. ix–xl.

"The Present Status of the Phenomenology of Language" (The Fifth Lexington Conference). *Language and Language Disturbances.* Edited by Erwin W. Straus. Duquesne University Press, 1974. 247–67.

Review Article: "J. N. Mohanty, *The Concept of Intentionality.*" *Southwestern Journal of Philosophy* (1974), 205–18.

"Phenomenology in America: 1974." *Journal of the British Society for Phenomenology* (1974), 199–211.

"Identity and Metaphor: A Phenomenological Theory of Polysemy." *Journal of the British Society for Phenomenology* (1975), 32–41.

"John Wild's Interpretation of William James' Theory of the Free Act." *Man and World* (1975), 136–40.

"Husserl's Conception of the Ideality of Language." *Humanitas* (1975), 201–17.

"The Current Significance of Merleau-Ponty's Contribution to the Philosophy of Language." *Journal of the History of Philosophy* (1975), 385–98. Anthologized in *Dialogues in Phenomenology.* Edited by Don Ihde and Richard Zaner. Nijhoff, 1975. 247–68.

"La pertinence actuelle de la conception husserlienne de l'idealité du langage." In *Sens et existence en hommage a Paul Ricoeur.* Edited by G. Madison. Paris, Editions de Seuil, 1975. 107–23. Spanish translation in *Sentido y Existencia.* Spain: Estella (Navarra), 1976.

"Appearance and Reality: An Essay on the Philosophy of the Theater." *Philosophy and Literature* (1980), 3–17. Anthologized in *Phenomenology: Dialogues and Bridges.* Edited by Ronald Bruzina and Bruce Wilshire. State University of New York Press, 1982. 339–52.

"The Meaning and Development of Merleau-Ponty's Concept of Structure." *Research in Phenomenology* (1980), 39–57. Anthologized in *Merleau-Ponty: Perception, Structure, Language.* Edited by John Sallis. Humanities Press, 1981. 39–57.

"Phenomenology in America, 1984." *Research in Phenomenology* (1984), 233–46.

"The Roots of the Existentialist Theory of Freedom in *Ideas I.*" In *Husserl Studies* (1984), 242–61.

"The Hidden Dialectic in Edmund Husserl's Phenomenology." In *Philosophy and Science in Phenomenological Perspective.* Edited by K. K. Cho. Martinus Nijhoff, 1984. 75–84. Also in *Philosophy and Culture.* Volume 4. Montreal, 1988.

"Merleau-Ponty: The Triumph of Dialectics over Structuralism." *Man and World,* Special Issue: Phenomenology and the Human Sciences (1984), 299–312.

"A Mess of Existentialist Pottage: The Phenomenological Existentialism of William Earle." In *The Life of the Transcendental Ego: Essays in Honor of William Earle.* Edited by Edward S. Casey and Don Morano. State University of New York Press, 1986. 19–28.

"The Orders of Reality: A Phenomenological Interpretation of the Doctrine of the Analogy of Being." *Man and World* (1986), 155–77.

"John Wild and Phenomenology." Edited by Calvin Schrag and Eugene Kaelin. *Analecta Husserliana* (1989), 85–97.

"Self Presentation: James M. Edie." Edited by Calvin Schrag and Eugene Kaelin. *Analecta Husserliana* (1989), 207–11.

"Husserl versus Derrida." *Human Studies* (1990), 103–18. Also in *Phenomenology East and West.* Edited by F. M. Kirkland and D. P. Chattopadhyaya. Kluwer, 1993. 157–76.

"On Confronting Species-Specific Skepticism as We Near the End of the Twentieth Century." *Man and World* (1992), 313–39. Also in International Gurwitsch Memorial Symposium. Edited by J. Claude Evans.

"The Question of the Transcendental Ego: Sartre's Critique of Husserl." *Journal of the British Society for Phenomenology* (1993), 104–20. Also in *The Question of Hermeneutics,* (Festschrift for Joseph A. Kockelmans). Edited by T. J. Stapleton. Kluwer Academic Publisher, 1994. 127–51.

"The Philosophical Framework of Sartre's Theory of the Theater." *Man and World* (1994), 415–44. Also in *The Prism of the Self,* Festschrift for Maurice Natanson. Edited by Steven G. Crowell. Kluwer Academic Publisher, 1995. 231–53.

"The Phenomenology of the Theater." *Encyclopedia of Phenomenology.* Edited by Lester E. Embree.

"Phenomenology in America." With Calvin O. Schrag, et al. *Encyclopedia of Phenomenology.* Edited by Lester E. Embree.

Discussions

Discussion in *Phenomenology: Pure and Applied* (The First Lexington Conference). Edited by Erwin W. Straus. Duquesne University Press, 1964. 189–95.

Discussion (with Walter Douglas, Timothy Duggan, and John Wild) of Maurice Merleau-Ponty, *In Praise of Philosophy*. *Pacific Philosophy Forum* (1964), 93–104.

Commentary on "Man as an Actor," *Phenomenology of Will and Action* (The Second Lexington Conference). Edited by Erwin W. Straus and Richard M. Griffith. Duquesne University Press, 1968. 221–28, 231–32.

Discussions in *The Languages of Criticism and the Sciences of Man*. Edited by Richard Macksey and Eugenio Donato. The John Hopkins University Press, 1970. 33, 76, passim.

Discussion in *The Phenomenology of Memory* (The Third Lexington Conference). Edited by Erwin W. Straus and Richard M. Griffith. Duquesne University Press, 1970. 158–62, 170–73, 185, 195, 201, 203.

Three Discussions in *On Heidegger and Language*. Edited by Joseph Kockelmans. Northwestern University Press, 1972. 139–41, 220–28, 265–67.

Book Reviews

Maurice Dupuy, *La philosophie de Max Scheler*, and *La philosophie de la religion chez Max Scheler*. In *Philosophy and Phenomenological Research* (1961), 587–88.

Georges Vallin, *L'etre er l'individualite*. In *Philosophy and Phenomenological Research* (1962), 431–33.

Andre de Murault, *L'idee de la phenomenologie*. In *Philosophy and Phenomenological Research* (1961), 278–81.

Giambattista Vico, *The New Science*. In *Italica* (1962), 147–49.

Alexander Koyre, *Etudes d'histoire de la pensee philosophique*. In *Philosophy and Phenomenological Research* (1963), 294–95.

Anna-Teresa Tymieniecka, *Phenomenology and Science in Contemporary European Thought*. *Philosophy and Phenomenological Research* (1963), 290–92.

Husserl et la pensee moderne. Edited by H. L. Van Breda. *Journal of the History of Philosophy* (1964), 123–25.

Magda King, *Heidegger's Philosophy*. *The Journal of Bible and Religion* (1965), 201–2.

Aron Gurwitsch, *The Field of Consciousness*. *The New Scholasticism* (1967), 273–77.

J. N. Mohanty, *Edmund Husserl's Theory of Meaning*. *International Philosophical Quarterly* (1967), 673–75.

Richard Zaner, *The Problem of Embodiment*. *Journal of the History of Philosophy* (1967), 301–5.

Robert Sokolowski, *The Formation of Husserl's Concept of Constitution*. *Journal of the History of Philosophy* (1967), 184–87.

Paul Ricoeur, *Edmund Husserl: An Analysis of His Phenomenology*. *Journal of Philosophy* (1968), 403–9.

Frederick Olafson, *Principles and Persons: An Ethical Interpretation of Existentialism*. *Journal of Philosophy* (1968), 456–62.

The Blue Clown. Dialogues by Augusto Centeno y Rilova and Donald Sutherland. University of Nebraska Press, 1971. *Journal of Aesthetics and Art Criticism* (1972), 418–20.

Ghyslain Charron, *Du Langage. The Thomist* (1973), 807–11.
Essays on Russian Intellectual History. Edited by Fuhrmann, Bock, and Twarog. *Journal of the History of Philosophy* (1973), 563–64.
Marxism and Religion in Eastern Europe. Edited by De George and Scanlan. Sovietica Series, *Southwestern Journal of Philosophy* (1979), 208–11.
Klaus Boer, *Maurice Merleau-Ponty: Die Entwicklung seines Strukturdenkens. Man and World* (1981), 437–39.
Sandra B. Rosenthal and Patrick L. Bourgeois, *Pragmatism and Phenomenology: A Philosophic Encounter. Transactions of the Charles S. Pierce Society* (1981), 276–79.
Two Centuries of American Philosophy. Edited by Peter Caws. *Philosophical Topics* (1980), 200–205.
Theodor W. Adorno, *Against Epistemology: A Metacritique, Studies in Husserl and Phenomenological Antinomies.* Translated by Willis Domingo. *Husserl Studies* (1984), 315–20.
Stephen Light, *Shuzo Kuki and Jean-Paul Sartre.* Foreword by Michael Rybalka. *Nous* (1990), 196–98.
Hugh J. Silverman, *Inscriptions: Between Phenomenology and Structuralism. International Studies in Philosophy* (1991), 138–39.

Notes

Introduction: The Shipwreck of Apodicticity?

1. In *Logical Investigations*, J. N. Findlay, trans. (London: Routledge, 1976), 135ff. Husserl distinguishes "'logical," "noetic" and "metaphysical"' forms of skepticism. "Logical" skepticism denies certain laws pertaining essentially to "theoretical unity"; such laws concern the notions "of truth, of proposition, of object, of property, of relation, etc." "Noetic" skepticism denies the ideal conditions of self-evidence whose roots lie in the form of subjectivity as such "and not in factual conditions" rooted in the individual judging subject. Lastly, "metaphysical" skepticism denies objective knowledge of the real world. Husserl wants to distinguish sharply this last form of skepticism from the two above-mentioned varieties and he generally does not concern himself with it, an important mistake in my opinion.

2. The idea of a self-inflicted "shipwreck" of Husserl's quest for "absolute" foundations is due to Ludwig Landgrede's famous article "Husserls Abschied vom Cartesianismus," *Philosophische Rundschau* 9 (1962). Reprinted in *The Phenomenology of Husserl*, ed. R. O. Elveton (Chicago: Quadrangle Books, 1970), 259–306. My introduction also owes a great deal to Paul Ricoeur's "Phenomenologie et hermeneutique," *Phänomenologische Forschungen* 1 (1975). Reprinted in *Hermeneutics and the Human Sciences*, ed. John B. Thompson (Cambridge: Cambridge University Press, 1981), 101–28. Subsequent references to Ricoeur's article will be to the English translation (*HHS*) cited by page references given parenthetically in the text.

3. Heidegger makes essentially this point in *Being and Time*. See *Being and Time*, trans. Macquarrie and Robinson (New York: Harper and Row, 1962), 270f.

4. Landgrebe points out that in the *Ideas* Husserl introduces the phenomenological reduction as an "affair of our perfect freedom" (*Ideas*, Boyce Gibson translation, 46), and in *Erste Philosophie* (63), he presents the move from the natural attitude to the reduction as a decision. See Landgrebe, "Husserls Abschied," 264. Also in *Cartesian Meditations* Husserl talks of making a new beginning in philosophy, a beginning that begins "with the *decision* of philosophers." See *Cartesian Meditations*, trans. Dorian Cairns (The Hague: Martinus Nijhoff, 1973), 7 (emphasis added). Hereafter cited as *CM*.

5. See, e.g., *CM*, 39ff.

6. Husserl was aware of this general problem with his program, for in *CM*, after introducing the apodictic evidence for the *ego cogito*, Husserl writes:

> In fact, doubt arises immediately. For example; Does not transcendental subjectivity at any given moment include its past as an inseparable part, which is accessible only by way of memory? But can apodictic evidence be claimed for memory? Surely it would be wrong to deny the apodicticity of "I am" on the ground that the evidence of memory is not apodictic. . . . Nevertheless, in view of such questions, the problem of the range covered by our apodictic evidence becomes urgent. (*CM*, 22)

7. *Husserliana* VI (The Hague: Martinus Nijhoff, 1954), 508.

8. Cf., *CM*, 22, where Husserl points out that "*adequacy* and apodicticity of evidence *need not go hand in hand*" (Husserl's emphasis). I would argue that this distinction is even more pertinent to the defense of the laws of logic.

9. Edie's *Speaking and Meaning: The Phenomenology of Language* is a good case in point, as is *William James and Phenomenology*. See the bibliography of Professor Edie's writing for further references.

10. Marvin Farber quotes a letter from Husserl on his own development, in which Husserl confesses that "[a]s a young beginner I naturally read much, including classics and contemporary literature of the 1870s to the 1890s. I liked the critical-skeptical point of view, since I myself did not see firm ground anywhere." See Marvin Farber, *The Foundation of Phenomenology* (Albany: State University of New York Press, 1943), 17.

Chapter 1: On Confronting Species-Specific Skepticism

1. A first version of this paper was read at the International Aron Gurwitsch Memorial Symposium at the New School in New York on 8 November 1991.

2. Maurice Merleau-Ponty, *The Visible and the Invisible*, trans. Alphonso Lingis (Evanston: Northwestern University Press, 1968), 103, 105, 121.

3. The year 1859, the year of the birth of Edmund Husserl, John Dewey, and Henri Bergson, is a convenient year by which to date, of course arbitrarily, the beginning of "contemporary" philosophy as distinct from the "modern" conflicts between Continental Rationalism and British Empiricism which issued in the German Idealism of Kant, Fichte, and Hegel. Besides being the period of Darwin and Spencer, it was also the period of the very beginnings of positivism in France, Britain, Germany and, finally, of both logical positivism and phenomenology at the University of Vienna. What all of the "contemporary" movements in philosophy (whether phenomenology, logical positivism, pragmatism, Bergsonism, naturalism, operationalism, or other "isms") have in common is a rejection of speculative metaphysics in the aftermath of Hegel and a return to experience, *zu den Sachen selbst!*

4. Ernst Mayr, *Toward a New Philosophy of Biology* (Cambridge: Harvard University Press, 1988), 70. I wish here to thank my colleague, David Hull, who

shared with me some of his research materials and his opinions on the search for extraterrestrial intelligence (the SETI project).

5. Ibid., 70–71. See also, George Gaylord Simpson, *This View of Life: The World of an Evolutionist* (New York: Harcourt, Brace and World, 1964), 259ff., on the possibility and/or probability of humanoid forms on the other planets ("which must exist in large numbers") in the universe similar enough to ours that life, at least, must have existed and may still exist. He is not optimistic about intelligent life, since the "mutations" and "recombinations" that took place in the evolution of man as the "ultimate twig" of an extremely complicated evolutionary process on this planet are essentially "nonrepeatable" here and, since this evolutionary development is the only one we are capable of knowing and studying, it does not seem that we should assume that it is a probable scenario elsewhere. However, there are some exobiologists who, basing themselves on various very conjectural, computerized projections and extrapolations, are more optimistic.

6. In this regard it is notable that, after initially launching a program of "Cartesian linguistics," which seemed to take up the work of the Cartesian rationalists of Port-Royal, and even Husserl's project of a pure, a priori grammar, Chomsky and his school now interpret Descartes's "innate ideas"—which, in their Chomskian sense, can be taken to postulate the forms or rules of human "competence" predisposed to acquire language and to follow a universal, "depth" grammar which could account (through various transformational rules) for the "surface" grammars of all the natural languages—as being something embedded in the DNA code in some way, and thus a product of the evolution of this species on this planet. Chomsky's is a "naturalized" Descartes.

7. In its generality this is an *old* theme in the history of philosophy. Averroes thought that the "separated" mind thought independently of human individuals in such wise that the individual, singular man should not say "I think" or "you think" but "it thinks" in us. William James also toyed with the theme of the evanescence of consciousness. He wrote in the first chapter of his *Essays in Radical Empiricism* (New York: Longmans, Green and Co., 1912) that he had mistrusted consciousness for over twenty years and had begun to suggest its nonexistence to his students. When consciousness has become a bare *Bewusstsein überhaupt* "it has evaporated to [the] estate of pure diaphaneity" and is, he wrote, "on the point of disappearing altogether." "It is the name of a nonentity, and has no right to a place among first principles" (2–3). It does, however, stand for a "function," namely "pure experience." Some might even take Sartre's and Gurwitsch's theory of a nonegological consciousness up here as some kind of parallel, but since in that theory consciousness is "the being of nothingness," that through which "nothingness" comes into the world through "nihilating" processes of having objects as "otherwise" than they are given, it is probably not relevant to include them among the "death of the subject" philosophers.

8. Strictly speaking, Derrida has written only two truly philosophical books, with sustained argument, namely: *Edmund Husserl's Origin of Geometry: An Introduction*, trans. John P. Leavey, Jr., and Nicholas Hays (Stony Brook: State University of New York Press, 1978), and *Speech and Phenomena*, trans. David B. Allison

(Evanston: Northwestern University Press, 1973). There are a few passages in *De la grammatologie,* and perhaps also in *Glas,* which might also qualify as philosophical discourse in the usual sense.

9. James M. Edie, "Husserl versus Derrida," *Human Studies* (1990), 103–18.

10. This is my own reading of Heidegger, but I would like to acknowledge my indebtedness to the reflections of Mikel Dufrenne (*Pour l'homme* [Paris: Editions du Seuil, 1968], 21–25) and Arion Lothar Kelkel (*Heidegger* [Seghers, 1973], 108ff.).

11. Richard Rorty, *Philosophy and the Mirror of Nature* (New Jersey: Princeton University Press, 1979), 5. Though he claims to be "historicist," Rorty is not a very good historian. Certainly the historical influence of Husserl in the twentieth century has been greater and led to much more diversified accomplishments in philosophy that those of Rorty's peculiar triad: think only of Merleau-Ponty, Sartre, Ingarden, Ricoeur, Gurwitsch, Heidegger himself, not to mention lesser, but important, thinkers. Rorty's Heidegger is always seen through Dewey's eyes. When Husserl is mentioned, his name is nearly always coupled with his partner "transcendentalist" Russell, as William James is elsewhere coupled with Nietzsche. We don't know exactly what Russell might say about this coupling, but we do know that James considered half of everything Nietzsche wrote to be "the sick shriekings of a dying rat" (*Varieties of Religions Experience* [New York: Mentor Books, 1958], 47). From an historical perspective, one could transpose and invert the famous statement of Erasmus (as well as of Pico de la Mirandola) in his *De Transitu Hellinismi ad Christianismum* concerning Aristotle and his Christian interpreters, "Without Thomas, Aristotle would have been silent" (*Sine Thoma, mutus esset Aristoteles*), into: "Without Husserl, there would have been no Heidegger."

12. Rorty, *Philosophy and the Mirror of Nature,* 360ff.

13. In "The End of Philosophy?" *The New York Review of Books,* 19 March 1981, 46.

14. In bringing Derrida into the discussion, it is important to refer the reader to the recent work of J. Claude Evans, *Strategies of Deconstruction: Derrida and the Myth of the Voice* (Minneapolis: University of Minnesota Press, 1991). This is certainly the best, most magisterial and insightful book on Derrida from a philosophical point of view up to now. Evans spends almost as much time and space following Derrida's arguments one by one as Husserl did on his psychologistic skeptics in the *Logical Investigations.*

15. Rorty, *Philosophy and the Mirror of Nature,* 266.

16. Ibid., 372. Note the word "degenerate." I submit that Rorty's *Philosophy and the Mirror of Nature* should never be read without the corrective essay written by J. N. Mohanty, "Rorty, Phenomenology and Transcendental Philosophy," *Journal of the British Society for Phenomenology* (January 1983), 91–98.

17. Derrida, *Speech and Phenomena,* 103.

18. Jacques Derrida, *Of Grammatology,* trans. Gayatri Spivak (Baltimore: The Johns Hopkins University Press, 1974), 165ff. See also John R. Searle, "The Word Turned Upside Down," *New York Review of Books,* 27 October 1983, 74ff. There is, however, no doubt that we need to be sensitive to the perennial attraction and

force of the nonfoundationalist, "conversationalist" theory of truth which has cropped up throughout the history of philosophy, as Professor Richard Bernstein reminded me in discussing this paper. Whether it is Protagoras, Phyrro and Sextus Empiricus after Plato and Aristotle, Peter Damian after Augustine, Ockham after Aquinas, the British empiricists after Cartesian rationalism, Marx, Spencer, and Mill after Kant and Hegel, or Heidegger, Derrida and Rorty after Husserl and Frege, every time a great "foundationalist" philosopher has established the *same* a priori, absolutely coercive, necessary, and universally valid norms of thought on a firm conceptual foundation, there has been a "skeptical" reaction which bears structural similarities to all the other relativisms and skepticisms which have appeared in history. It is as if philosophers are almost doomed to repeat these arguments and bring forth this basic subject matter and the problems it involves and keep it before their minds again in each successive generation. Neither side expects to *convince* the other side, but each to *refute* the other definitively. Like Doctor Johnson, we can only say: "I can give you an argument; I cannot give you understanding." But we must bear in mind the fact that the "foundationalists" always come back to essentially the *same* logical forms (without, of course, denying the historical development of logic and mathematics) and, if we have any speculative bent at all, we have to ask ourselves whether they may not have discovered which forms must be true for any possible intelligence. Our laws of physics, chemistry, and perhaps even biology, though conclusions of empirical science on this planet, are formulated mathematically and are taken to be observed throughout the universe. Only a short time ago no man had seen the other side of the moon, though most suspected it would look much like the side which was always visible. We know that this assumption was correct because our space technology now permits men to go around to the other side and look. There was no a priori reason against it before; it just could not de facto be done; it was not a logical but a physical impossibility. In the same way the laws governing falling bodies, of Newtonian physics, of Einsteinian relativity theory are taken to hold not only for this species on this planet, but for the solar system as a whole and for intergalactic probes as well. Since all these technologies depend on mathematical forms (which are not conditioned *in their meaning* by species-bound conditions), and since mathematics is either a branch of logic or a kind of universal logical thinking that does not (like the formulae of formal logic) need to be translated into natural languages to be understood, does this consideration not add weight to the foundationalist argument of the independence of logical forms—independent of any particular empirical locations, conditions, or circumstances?

19. Richard Rorty, "Genteel Syntheses, Professional Analyses, Transcendentalist Culture," in *Two Centuries of Philosophy in America*, ed. Peter Caws (London: Blackwell, 1980), 238–39.

20. *The London Review of Books*, June 1980, 15–16.

21. Rorty, *Philosophy and the Mirror of Nature*, 33.

22. Mohanty, "Rorty, Phenomenology and Transcendental Philosophy," 96.

23. Ibid., 97. Mohanty here makes reference to Apel and Habermas.

24. Simpson, *This View of Life*, 254.

25. Though we have but "one instance" of the evolutionary process which led to true "higher intelligence" before us, namely the emergence of homo sapiens on this planet (even though the difficulty, or probable impossibility, of replicating this process elsewhere is rightly daunting to the exobiologist), this one instance will not deter the phenomenologist as such from examining the *essence* of what it is to manifest "higher intelligence" and what would be required for communication among various species of intelligent life. After all, as Husserl argued in *Ideas*, in the *Cartesian Meditations*, and elsewhere, we have in our own experience but one existential example or instance of what an ego-life actually is, namely our own experiencing. Nevertheless, if every "instance" must exemplify all the essential characteristics of its "essence," of what it is to be an ego-life (i.e., a consciousness that perceives, imagines, remembers, has emotions, thinks and reasons and through these "acts" constitutes the "world of objects" which we call the unified lifeworld), we can establish eidetically, through the method of free variation, the necessary structures without which consciousness would not be consciousness (of the world, of itself, of others).

26. It is a cliché of Scholastic logic that from the fact that something is the case it is valid to infer that it is possible for it to be, whereas one can never infer from the mere conceptual possibility of something to its actual existence. *De esse ad posse valet illatio*; *de posse ad esse non valet illatio.*

27. Mayr, *Toward a New Philosophy of Biology*, 73.

28. The best treatment of the "teleological" elements in Husserl's thought is by Andre de Muralt, *The Idea of Phenomenology: Husserlian Exemplarism*, trans. Garry L. Breckon (Evanston: Northwestern University Press, 1974). For Husserl the concrete, existing thing is a "factual example" of its idea or essence, while the idea is the "ideal exemplar" of its object. Suppose a given science in its actual, imperfect, historical state. Its "essential" character requires a continual tendency toward greater and greater precision, comprehensiveness, and certitude. In its actual state any given science is essentially relative to a state of greater perfection which awaits it in the future; science is always in an intermediate, developing state between a less perfect and a more perfect state. The completely realized and perfected state of a science is an ideal goal (telos or idea); it is, in fact, an "open" or "infinite" idea. The real, factual state of development of any given science gives its meaning to the "idea" of that science, and of science in general, but at the same time the "ideal" of science alone makes it possible to understand the "real" as an intermediate stage in the realization of the idea. This is the universal principle of the mutual exemplarity of the real and the ideal throughout the whole of Husserlian phenomenology. See also, James M. Edie, *Edmund Husserl's Phenomenology: A Critical Commentary* (Bloomington: Indiana University Press, 1987), 143–51; and Stephan Strasser, "Das Gottesproblem in der Spätphilosophie Edmund Husserls," *Philosophisches Jahrbuch* 67, 130–42, in which Strasser argues that the idea of God is, for Husserl, the final absolute reality which is both a theoretical "idea" and a practical "telos" working itself out in the innate drive of mankind to come to absolute and final knowledge. He concludes that Husserl's exemplarism is

based on a teleological conception, a "*Gottesbegriff*," both immanent within and transcendent to human striving. But it would certainly be prudent to stop short of making Husserl sound like Whitehead or Teilhard de Chardin. Nevertheless, if there is a personal, intelligent God, he is bound by the laws of logic no less than we are.

29. Anthropologists like Benjamin Whorff once claimed that languages like those of the Hopi Indians would enable them, with their relativistic verbs for time and place, to understand the relativity theory of Einstein better than we can in English, forgetting that the language of relativity theory is not any natural language but the language of mathematics, which is the same in all places and at all times. One of Heidegger's disciples, Johannes Lohmann, once argued that "the logic and grammar" of Chinese is essentially different from "the logic and grammar" of the Indo-European languages. See "M. Heidegger's *Ontological Difference* and Language," in *On Heidegger and Language*, ed. Joseph J. Kockelmans (Evanston: Northwestern University Press, 1972), 303–63. But this is easily refuted by the fact that native speakers of French have had no trouble at all teaching Chinese seminarians (in a seminary in Chentu Province prior to 1949) the logic of Aristotle in Chinese (see my reply to Lohmann in the same volume, 220–28). It is true that formal logic proceeds in a binary, either-or manner. It is the only "language," for instance, our computers can "understand" or follow. Various cultures divide up the world differently on the surface level of their ordinary speech. For the Orientals there are the four passing sights, the three vows, the eight-fold path, the four noble truths, the six elements of true religion, the seventeen great goings forth, etc., whereas for the Medieval Western Latins there were the twelve degrees of true humility, the seven deadly sins, the nine choirs of angels, the ten commandments, etc., but I strongly suspect that as the Japanese and the Chinese, no less than the Western Europeans, become more reliant on computers, they will drop any resistance they may residually have to either-or logic, including the logic and grammatical studies of Aristotle and Leibniz. There are some four thousand natural languages still spoken on earth, but there is only one "pure logical grammar."

30. In this connection, see James M. Edie, *Speaking and Meaning* (Bloomington: Indiana University Press, 1976), 45–50ff, as it deals with Husserl's conception of "pure logical grammar" from the "Fourth Logical Investigation" and *Formal and Transcendental Logic*. It is, moreover, worth pointing out in this connection that the ancient Greek realization by Socrates, Plato and Aristotle that the true domain of philosophy is "the conceptual" (*logoi*), and that it is the purpose of philosophy to distinguish and separate out the a priori in any realm of discourse and investigation, was maintained throughout the whole Western tradition until the dawn of the modern era in the seventeenth century. During the years just preceding the foundation of the University of Paris, at the time of the Latin thinkers Abelard and Gundissalinus, there was a lot of speculation on the proper divisions and ordering of the sciences under metaphysics and logic. It was a commonplace thesis to be defended in the cathedral schools and elsewhere that "there is no science which is not a part of philosophy," *nulla est scientia quae philosophiae non*

sit aliqua pars (see Fernand Van Stenberghen, *The Philosophical Movement in the Thirteenth Century* [Edinburgh: Thomas Nelson, 1955], 26ff.). The reason for this was that all the "lower" sciences like agronomy and architecture were "subordinate sciences" which took their first principles from "higher sciences," just as music and optics take their first principles from the "higher science" of mathematics and, ultimately, all sciences derive their first principles of demonstration from the "first science" which is metaphysics. In this sense, as Question 1 of the *Summa Theologiae* of Thomas Aquinas shows us, even theology is a "subordinated" science which is argumentative and demonstrative based ultimately on the higher *scientia Dei et beatorum.* It would be interesting to examine the historical relationship of the individual sciences. (Etienne Gilson has done some of this in his *The Unity of Philosophical Experience* [New York: Scribner's, 1950].) In antiquity and the middle ages, medical specialists like Galen and Avicenna felt it necessary, in order to write treatises on medicine or healing, to deal first with logic, epistemology, and metaphysics in order to properly order their researches and guarantee their validity; as we know Galen even invented a new form of syllogism. In the days of Newton, physics was not only still a part of philosophy but also of natural theology. It is as if the various nonphilosophical sciences and disciplines were all originally conceived as parts of philosophy until, having progressed to a sufficient stage of maturity to develop their own distinctive methodologies, were able to be prosecuted by scientists who no longer studied philosophy or the problems of logic *ex professo.*

31. It would not do to go into or follow the detail that Husserl himself goes into in the *Prolegomena.* An excellent summary is given for those who want a short-cut in Marvin Farber, *The Foundation of Phenomenology* (New York: Paine-Whitman, 1962), to whose very illuminating insights I have been indebted ever since I began teaching phenomenology. See especially, in the present connection, 112–24 (summary of refutation of skepticism).

32. I have several times, in articles finally all reassembled together in *William James and Phenomenology* (Bloomington: Indiana University Press, 1987), tried to explain the sense in which Husserl was indebted to James in his refutation of psychologism, but not all my readers seem to grasp the central point (as in the review of this book by William James Earle, *Canadian Philosophical Reviews* [1988], 260–65). Earle is willing to agree (263) that James rejected the atomism and associationism of Locke and Hume in their theories of perception, but he does not concede that this amounts to the same kind of phenomenological reduction that was operated by the Gestalt psychologist and others and which I (and others) have tried to explain in detail. But the main point is not merely James's rejection of "the mind-stuff" theory, but his recognition of the proper nature of "the object of thought" (what Husserl called the *noema*) and its central importance for mental life. There is no sameness, no repeatability in the real world, and therefore no sameness in the flow of acts and states of consciousness which are subject to the law of irreversible temporal sequence in which the experiencing subject is at each instant of time not only in a new position but in a new and different state of preparation, expectation, accumulation of past experience, etc., than at any other instant in time. What can be "got again" and held before the mind

in different acts of consciousness, at different times, and by other experiencers as well, is "the object of thought," the "meaning" (William James *The Principles of Psychology*, vol. 1 [New York: Holt, 1890], 460–62, and vol. 2, 641–44; see also chapters 1 and 2 of *William James and Phenomenology*). This is the true basis for James's and Husserl's refutation of psychologism. For instance when an ideal truth, such as the Pythagorean Theorem, is first established, it is seen to be true that the geometrical relationships on which it is based had been true all along, even though the final truth itself had never been stated in language. But, once stated, the same truth can be thought again and again by millions of other subjects through centuries of time, it can be fitted into new contexts that Pythagoras could never have foreseen (such as non-Euclidean geometries), but it never turns out to have been simply false (though certain presuppositions which had been latent had to be brought out) and certainly not unthinkable again and again by the same and other consciousnesses. In short, the content of an act of consciousness (James's "object of thought") is *never* identifiable with mental acts themselves, which are necessarily and always part of the real flow of history, the Heraclitean flux.

33. It is, I trust, clear that Husserl was not the first or the only philosopher in history to see himself obliged to refute species-specific skepticism. Saint Augustine also, at the beginning of his philosophical life, felt himself "blocked" by skepticism or "probabilism" and devoted his *first* philosophical dialogue to the problem in *Against the Academics.* He is appalled by the "levity of these Greeklings" (the skeptics) who deny the possibility of being able to assent to anything at all with certainty, who can *believe* (in probabilities) but never *know.* On the basis of the logical principle of disjunction he produces a plethora of a priori arguments, which make no appeal to future experience, but which can be known to be indubitably true simply by understanding the meanings of the terms involved, such as that there is either one world or more than one world. And then he asks them whether or not they exist and they *seem* to perceive the world. When they answer that they *seem* to exist and perceive the world, he answers that: what *seems to you to exist* "I call *that* appearance the *world.*" And he continues: "If you are asleep, does the world which you now see exist? . . . that three times three makes nine, and that this is the squaring of rational numbers, would be true even though the whole human race were snoring!" (Augustine, *Against the Academics,* trans. John. O'Meara [New York: Newman, 1951], 124–26). In his later, more mature, dialogue on free will, he uses similar arguments to establish the basis for a "Christian philosophy" (*philosophia Christiana*), which would establish the "believed" truths about the existence of God and the immortality of the soul with the certitude of "knowledge." He first establishes that there are norms or rules of thought such that we must think *according to* them even without thinking *about* them, since they rule our minds in a coercive, objective, and "immutable" way. Our minds are mutable; the truth is not. "I will show you something," he says, "more sublime than our minds and reason. Behold, it is truth!" He even goes on to state, rhapsodically, that "this truth itself is our God" (basing himself on the words of the Lord: "I am the truth"), but we need not follow him into his religious conclusions to appreciate his line of argument (Augustine, *The Problem of Free Choice,* trans. Dom Mark Pontifex [New York: Newman, 1955], 114–17; see

also John A. Mourant, *Introduction to the Philosophy of Saint Augustine* [Pennsylvania State University Press, 1964], 101). This concern for the formal and material a prioris that govern experience in Augustine is no doubt the reason Husserl felt somehow disposed in his favor, as his quotation from Augustine's *De Vera Religione* at the conclusion of *Cartesian Meditations* attests.

34. There are other historical philosophers who made analyses that remind us of Husserl. One was the Arab philosopher Avicenna, who distinguished three possible "states" of meanings—namely, meanings in themselves, simply entertained by the mind as such (*in se*); meanings as known by the mind in acts of consciousness (*in intellectu*); and, finally, meanings as real things that instantiate meanings in the real world and to which ideal meanings can be taken to refer (*in re*). This tripartite distinction between meanings, acts of thinking, and acts of reference had a profound influence as we know on the Latin Scholastics like Aquinas, and especially John Duns Scotus, in their theories of knowledge. Husserl does not, quite naturally, mention Avicenna, but he does mention Leibniz in the *Prolegomena*, and recognizes the distinction he made between "truths of fact" and "truths of reason" as serving as a possible basis for the same argument he is making against skepticism.

35. Plato also (*Meno*, 75b) considered these relationships to be "materially" a priori: there cannot be brightness without color, or color without surface, or surface without extension. One cannot be present without the other as "parts" of a whole, even though they belong to different "logical" categories (see Edie, *Edmund Husserl's Phenomenology*, 43–44). Or see Aquinas, *In Physicorum Aristotelis Librum Secundum*, cap. 2, lec. 3:

> Multa sunt conjuncta secundum rem, quorum unum non est de intellectu alterius: sicut album et musicum conjunguntur in aliquo subjecto, et tamen unum non est de intellectu alterius, et ideo unum separatim intelligi potest sine alio. Et hoc est unum intellectum esse abstractum ab alio. Manifestum est autem quod posteriora non sunt de intellectu priorum, sed e converso; unde priora possunt intelligi sine posterioribus, et non e converso. Sicut patet quod animal est prius homine, et homo prius hoc homine (nam homo se habet ex additione ad animal, et hic homo ex additione ad hominem): et propter hoc homo non est de intellectu animalis, nec Socrates de intellectu hominis.

Thus, if there is Socrates, there is a man; if there is a man, there is a rational animal; if there is a rational animal, there is an animal; if there is an animal, there is a living being; if there is a living being, there is a being (and not nothing); but, in all this, we have not here said anything about the *real* world, but only about the necessary a priori relationships of concepts which are implied in our *experience* of the real world in order to make it intelligible. Thus, wherever there is real experience, the possibility of a priori rules of knowledge, both formal and "material," come into play.

36. Primarily in Husserl, and later in Merleau-Ponty, the "phenomenology of perception" was the first starting point and the most frequently employed example to illustrate the phenomenological investigation of the lifeworld from

an eidetic point of view. Husserl's posthumous work, *Experience and Judgment* (ed. Ludwig Landgrebe [Evanston: Northwestern University Press, 1973]) and his earlier *Formal and Transcendental Logic* (trans. Dorion Cairns [The Hague: Nijhoff, 1969]) pose the question and give Husserl's answer about how the structures of predicative thought can be seen to be "founded" in prepredicative, perceptual consciousness. What most clearly distinguishes Husserl's phenomenology from logical positivism (with which movement it was contemporaneous and which *also* issued from Vienna) was that even though both believed that conceptual thought based on the rules of logic had somehow to be brought back to perceptual experience (remember the slogans on which we were brought up of the "empirical criterion of meaning" or "the empirical criterion of truth"?) only Husserl provided a theoretical framework for the "founding" of higher orders of experience like thinking in the foundational, underlying experience of preconceptual and prereflexive perceiving. The positivists, from Hume onwards, accepted the whole of formal logic, and then proclaimed that all meaning and truth had to be "reduced" to sense experience, juxtaposing the two without ever even posing the question of how logical thought could arise from perception.

37. Mohanty, "Rorty, Phenomenology and Transcendental Philosophy," 94–95.

38. This is discussed particularly in *Formal and Transcendental Logic.* See also, Edie, *Edmund Husserl's Phenomenology*, chapter 8: "The Hidden Dialectic in Edmund Husserl's Phenomenology," 116ff.

39. Edmund Husserl, *Logical Investigations*, vol. 2, trans. J. N. Findlay (New York: Humanities Press, 1970), 518.

40. Edie, *Speaking and Meaning*, 63, 209, with reference to Chomsky, Russell, and Wittgenstein as well as Husserl.

41. Maurice Merleau-Ponty, *The Primacy of Perception and Other Essays*, ed. James M. Edie (Evanston: Northwestern University Press, 1964), 10 (italics mine). In the title essay of the same collection, "The Primacy of Perception," Merleau-Ponty makes the same universal and objective claim for perception as the "founding term" of thought:

> If a friend and I are standing before a landscape and I attempt to show my friend something which I see and which he does not yet see, we cannot account for it by saying that I see something in my own world and that I attempt, by sending verbal messages, to give rise to an analogous perception in the world of my friend. There are not two numerically distinct worlds plus a mediating language which alone would bring us together. There is—and I know it very well if I become impatient with him—a demand that what I see be seen by him also.

What I see, from where I stand is *objectively there* for any observer who would stand where I am standing. It makes no difference if I might later turn out to be mistaken; right now my perception imposes an objective demand that what I see can be seen by anyone. "The thing imposes itself not as true for every intellect, but as real for every subject who is standing where I am" (17). Merleau-Ponty's purpose in this essay is to examine "the relation between intellectual consciousness and perceptual consciousness" (19), and yet, in this very essay, he admits that he likes to be thought of as a "skeptic" in the literal sense of the word: one who goes to see, who looks around, who practices *skepsis.* In his later writings on linguistic structuralism, between 1949 and 1959, he took up the problem of the relationships that obtain between perceptual consciousness and language. As was his wont, given the dialectical cast of his mind, he insisted on two contradictories, namely that there was the *possibility* of the universality of communication based on "algorithmic" rules (*The Prose of the World,* trans. John O'Neill [Evanston: Northwestern University Press, 1973], 115ff.) of thought and language, but at the same time he seems to have feared and denigrated Husserl's "pure logical grammar" and to want to suggest, almost as a precursor of Derrida and Rorty, that the only universality necessary was to be found in the *existential* and "oblique passage from a given language that I speak . . . to another language that I learn" (*Signs,* trans. Richard McCleary [Evanston: Northwestern University Press, 1964], 87). See also my foreword to Merleau-Ponty's *Consciousness and the Acquisition of Language,* trans. Hugh J. Silverman (Evanston: Northwestern University Press, 1973), xxviiff.; and also my monograph on *Merleau-Ponty's Philosophy of Language* (Washington, D.C.: University Press of America, 1987), 50ff., 80ff. Merleau-Ponty—because of this inner contradiction in his thought which tore him between Husserl's logic and its realization in a form of structural linguistics, on the one hand, and his commitment to an existentialism of communication, on the other—could never bring himself to finish what was to have been, in his own words, his most important work, *The Prose of the World,* but simply abandoned it around 1959, put in a drawer to be published only posthumously by Claude Lefort, and sought solace, after a philosophical breakdown, in the unfinished remnants of the last pages of *The Visible and the Invisible,* which remind some of the kind of incoherent "babble" for which Aristotle reproached Heraclitus, or which we find in Kant's *Opus Posthumum.*

Chapter 2: Thoughts on Phenomenology and Skepticism

1. See the entire *Prolegomena to Pure Logic,* vol. 1 of Husserl's *Logical Investigations,* trans. J. N. Findlay (New York: Humanities Press, 1970); chapter 7; "Psychologism as Skeptical Relativism," is especially pertinent.

2. Edmund Husserl, *Formale and Transzendentale Logik,* ed. Paul Janssen, in *Husserliana* XVII (The Hague: Martinus Nijhoff, 1974), 159.

3. Edmund Husserl, *Erste Philosophie,* part 1, ed. Rudolf Boehm, in *Husserliana* VII (The Hague: Martinus Nijhoff, 1956), chapter 3. See also, *Erste Philosophie,* part 2, ed. Rudolf Boehm, in *Husserliana* VIII (The Hague: Martinus Nijhoff, 1959), sec. 30, 20.

4. Sextus Empiricus, *Outlines of Pyrrhonism,* trans. R. G. Bury (Boston: Harvard University Press, 1967), book 1, chapter 7. I have modified slightly the translation of all my quotations from Sextus. Edmund Husserl, *Ideas Pertaining to*

a Pure Phenomenology and to a Phenomenological Philosophy, book 1, trans. F. Kersten (The Hague: Martinus Nijhoff, 1982), sec. 24.

5. Sextus Empiricus, *Outlines*, book 1, chapter 4; Husserl, *Ideas I*, secs. 31–32.

6. Sextus Empiricus, *Outlines*, book 1, chapter 4.

7. Ibid., book 1, chapter 10.

8. Ibid., book 1, chapter 13; and chapter 14, sec. 118.

9. Husserl did not only make general promises about the possibility of such descriptive analyses, but provided many concrete examples, and in this he has been imitated by many writers who work in his tradition. See, e.g., Robert Sokolowski, *Pictures, Quotations, and Distinctions: Fourteen Essays in Phenomenology* (Notre Dame: University of Notre Dame Press, 1992).

10. Husserl, *Ideas I*, sec. 24.

11. On the claims to apodicticity, see ibid., sec. 137; and *Cartesian Meditations*, trans. Dorion Cairns (The Hague: Martinus Nijhoff, 1973), secs. 6–9.

12. The absence or occlusion in evidences given to phenomenological reflection is based on vagueness, not on inaccessibility. See Robert Sokolowski, *Husserlian Meditations: How Words Present Things* (Evanston: Northwestern University Press, 1974), secs. 82–89.

13. Sextus Empiricus, *Outlines*, book 1, chapter 20.

14. Ibid., ad finem.

15. Samuel Beckett, *Murphy* (New York: Grove Weidenfeld, 1957), chapter 6.

16. The correlation between subject and object is very clearly expressed as the theme for philosophy in *The Crisis of European Sciences and Transcendental Phenomenology*, trans. David Carr (Evanston: Northwestern University Press, 1970), sec. 41. See also, sec. 53, 181, where Husserl says that the epoché give us "the attitude above the subject-object correlation which belongs to the world and thus the attitude of focus upon the transcendental subject-object correlation."

17. Thus, in *The Crisis of European Sciences*, 14, Husserl says we are "in the greatest danger of drowning in the skeptical deluge" because of the naivety of the modern mind, and he says that his phenomenology is "certain of having overcome all previous naivetés, and thus all skepticism, through the radicalness of its new beginning." At the other extreme, in *Ideas I*, sec. 62, he says that his critical phenomenology overcomes the "dogmatism" of sciences carried out in the natural attitude. Both skepticism and dogmatism are ersatz philosophies that do not recognize the distinction between the natural and the philosophical attitudes and try to handle philosophical issues from an inappropriate angle.

Chapter 3: The Epistemological Significance of Husserl's Theory of Intentionality

1. E. Husserl, *Cartesian Meditations* (The Hague: Martinus Nijhoff, 1960), 5.

2. Husserl wrote in a letter to Gurwitsch on 15 April 1932: "Only with regard to some passages I could imagine that you have not ultimately penetrated the

complete bearing of the reduction, that is, the total revolution which it purports for the idea and method of philosophy over and against the total tradition." Reprinted in *Life-World and Consciousness*, ed. L. Embree (Evanston: Northwestern University Press, 1972), translation by Embree, emphasis mine.

3. See, e.g., R. McIntyre, "Intending and Referring," in *Husserl, Intentionality and Cognitive Science*, ed. H. Dreyfus and H. Hall (Cambridge: M.I.T. Press, 1982).

4. *Cartesian Meditations* is perhaps the paradigm case here, but certainly not alone in demonstrating Husserl's incredible emphasis on method. Of its five meditations, four are devoted to introducing, explicating, and discussing issues arising out of the explicating of the reduction. Only the final meditation actually tries to solve a philosophical problem. And the speed with which Husserl carries out that final task is such that interpreters are still arguing about exactly what the problem was and exactly how Husserl's "Fifth Cartesian Meditation" is supposed to solve it.

5. E. Husserl, *Logical Investigations*, vol. 1 (New York: Humanities Press, 1970), 217.

6. See T. Clarke, "The Legacy of Skepticism," *Journal of Philosophy* 69 (1972), 754–57.

7. Husserl, *Cartesian Meditations*, 24.

8. E. Husserl, *The Crisis of European Sciences and Transcendental Phenomenology*, trans. D. Carr (Evanston: Northwestern University Press, 1970), 21–56.

9. See H. Hall, "The 'Fifth Meditation' and Husserl's Cartesianism," *Man and World* 12 (1979).

10. See Clarke, "The Legacy of Skepticism."

Chapter 4: Association in Husserl's Phenomenology

1. For what follows, see W. Spanier and K. H. Stacker, "Assoziation," in *Historisches Wörterbuch der Philosophie*, vol. 1 (Basel: Schwabe, 1971ff.), 548–53; and Sir William Hamilton, "Contributions Toward a History of the Doctrine of Mental Suggestion or Association," in *The Works of Thomas Reid*, 2 vols., ed. William Hamilton, with Notes and Supplementary Dissertations (Edinburgh: James Thin, 1895), vol. 2, 889–910. See also, S. T. Coleridge, "On the Law of Association: Its History Traced from Aristotle to Hartley," in *Biographia Literaria* (London, 1871), also in Coleridge, *Aesthetic Essays*, ed. J. Shawcross (Oxford: The Clarendon Press, 1907), 58–73.

2. See Elmar Holenstein, *Phänomenologie der Assoziation: Zu Struktur und Funktion eines Grundprinzips der passiven Genesis bei E. Husserl* (The Hague: Nijhoff, 1972), 6–13, 17–31, 230–344.

3. Ibid., 277–78. See also, 118–31 for the origin of this notion.

4. Ibid., 278.

5. Ibid., 280–81.

6. Ibid., 282.

7. Ibid., 321–27.

8. Ibid., 7ff.

9. Edmund Husserl, *Analysen zur passiven Synthesis Aus Vorlesungs und Forschungsmanuskripten, 1918–1926*, ed. Margot Fleischer (The Hague: Nijhoff, 1966), 77, 28–29.

10. Edmund Husserl, *Cartesian Meditations*, trans. Dorion Cairns (The Hague: Nijhoff, 1960), 65–83; Iso Kern, "Statische and genetische Konstitution," in Bernet, Kern, Marbach, *Edmund Husserl: Darstellung seines Denkens* (Hamburg: Felix Meiner, 1989), 181–89.

11. For what follows, see Edmund Husserl, *Analysen zur Passiven Synthesis*, 117–91. Page numbers in the text refer to this book.

12. David Hume, *An Enquiry Concerning Human Understanding*, sec. 1, iii, iv, v, xii.

13. Immanuel Kant, *Critique of Pure Reason*, A, ix.

14. Edmund Husserl, *The Crisis of European Sciences and Transcendental Phenomenology*, trans. David Carr (Evanston: Northwestern University Press, 1970), 82–90.

15. Martin Heidegger, *Zollikoner Seminare*, ed. Medard Boss (Frankfurt am Main: Klostermann, 1987), 105–46, and passim.

16. Cf. my essay, "Reflections on the 'Foundations' of Psychology and Psychoanalysis" (forthcoming).

Chapter 5: On Derrida's Reading of Husserl

1. J. Derrida, *Speech and Phenomena*, trans. David Allison (Bloomington: Indiana University Press, 1973), 88; henceforth referred to as *SP*.

2. J. Derrida, *Margins of Philosophy*, trans. by Alan Bass (Chicago: University of Chicago Press, 1982), 158.

3. Cf. J. Caputo, "The Economy of Signs in Husserl and Derrida: From Uselessness to Full Employment," in *Deconstruction and Philosophy: The Texts of Jacques Derrida*, ed. J. Sallis (Chicago: University of Chicago Press, 1987), 99–113, esp. 100–101.

4. Cf. Caputo, ibid., 104–5.

5. This review appeared in *Les études philosophiques* (1965), 617–19.

6. *SP*, 82.

7. Cf. P. Ricoeur, *Husserl: An Analysis of His Phenomenology*, trans. E. G. Ballard and Lester E. Embree (Evanston: Northwestern University Press, 1967), esp. 29–30.

8. *SP*, 34.

9. Ricoeur also suggests this translation. See his *Husserl*, 216.

10. *SP*, 35.

11. Derrida, *Margins*, 117.

12. Ibid., 118. However, in a later context, Derrida appears to be saying "Er [Husserl] warf Heidegger—*zu Recht, wie ich glaube*—vor, die Phänomenologie anthropologisiert zu haben" (see *Die Krise der Phänomenologie und die Pragmatic des Wissenschaftsfortschritts*, ed. Michael Benedikt and Rudolf Berger [Wien: Österreische Staatsdruckerei, 1986], 177; italics mine).

13. Cf. my comments on this text in "Consciousness and Existence: Remarks on the Relation between Husserl and Heidegger," *Man and World* 2 (1978), 324–35; reprinted in my *The Possibility of Transcendental Philosophy* (The Hague: Martinus Nijhoff, 1985), 155–65.

14. E. Husserl, *Logical Investigations*, vol. 1, trans. J. N. Findlay (New York: Humanities Press, 1970), "First Investigation," sec. 15.

15. J. Derrida, *Limited Inc* (Evanston: Northwestern University Press, 1988), 58.

16. M. Merleau-Ponty, *Phenomenology of Perception*, trans. Colin Smith (London: Kegan Paul, 1962), 71.

17. Derrida, *Limited Inc*, 116.

18. *SP*, 52.

19. *SP*, 53.

20. Derrida, *Limited Inc*, 77.

21. Ibid., 60.

22. Ibid., 79.

23. Ibid., 136.

24. J. Derrida, *Husserls Weg in die Geschichte am Leitfaden der Geometrie*, trans. R. Hentschel and A. Knop (München: Wilhelm Fink Verlag, 1987).

25. E. Husserl, *The Crisis of European Sciences and Transcendental Phenomenology*, trans. D. Carr (Evanston: Northwestern University Press, 1970), 358.

26. Ibid., 360–61.

27. Ibid., 361.

28. Derrida, *Husserls Weg*, 183.

29. Husserl, *Logical Investigations*, vol. 1, 23.

30. *SP*, 43.

31. E. Husserl, *Philosophie der Arithmetik*, in *Husserliana* XII, 243.

32. David Wood recognizes this. See his *An Introduction to Derrida* (Thetford: The Thetford Press, 1985).

33. *SP*, 55.

34. J. Derrida, "Genesis und Struktur in die Phänomenologie," in *Die Schrift und die Differenz*, trans. R. Gash (Frankfurt am Main: Suhrkamp, 1972), esp. 243.

35. Thus, e.g., Husserl writes: "*Die Tatsachen, die der Historismus geltend macht, brauchen wir demnach nicht erst in irgendwelche kristischen Erwägungen zu ziehen*" (*Krisis, Husserliana* CI, 383).

36. "*Dabei haben wir uns jeder Bindung an die faktisch geltende historische Welt enthoben*" (*Krisis*, 383).

37. Ibid., 380.

38. Ibid., 386.

39. Derrida, *Husserls Weg*, 126.

40. Ibid., 135.

41. Ibid., 145–46, 161–62, 192n.

42. Ibid., 193n., 192.

43. E. Ströker, *Husserl's Transcendental Phenomenology*, trans. Lee Hardy (Stanford: Stanford University Press, 1993).

44. Ibid., 182n.

45. Ibid., 183.

46. Ibid., 184.

47. Ibid.

48. This distinction between transcendent fact and transcendental fact is nicely made by Karl-Heinz Lembeck in *Gegenstand und Geschichte: Geschichtswissenschaftstheorie in Husserls Phänomenologie* (Dordrecht: Kluwer Academic Publishers, 1988), see esp. chapter 6.

49. E. Husserl, *Cartesian Meditations*, trans. D. Cairns (The Hague: Martinus Nijhoff, 1973), sec. 64.

50. J. Derrida, "Antwort an Apel," *Zeitmitschrift: Journal für Aesthetik* 3 (Summer 1987), 7–85, 79.

51. Ibid., 83.

Chapter 6: Husserl's Critique of Relativism

1. Some of the works defending such positions include: Walter Truett Anderson, *Reality Isn't What It Used to Be* (San Francisco: Harper and Row, 1990); Jean Baudrillard, "La guerre du Golfe n'a pas eu lieu," *Liberation* (29 March 1991); Baudrillard, "The Reality Gulf," *The Guardian* (11 January 1991); Tom Bridges, "Modern Political Theory and the Multivocity of Postmodern Critical Discourses," *Inquiry: Critical Thinking Across the Disciplines* 8, no. 1 (September 1991); Stanley Fish, *Is There a Text in This Class?* (Cambridge: Harvard University Press, 1980); Richard Rorty, *Objectivity, Relativism, and Truth* (Cambridge: Cambridge University Press, 1991); Barry W. Sarchett, "What's All the Fuss About This Postmodernist Stuff?" in *Morality and Moral Controversies*, 3d ed., ed. John Arthur (Englewood Cliffs, N.J.: Prentice Hall, 1993); Anne Seller, "Realism versus Relativism: Towards a Politically Adequate Epistemology," in *Feminist Perspectives in Philosophy*, ed. Morwenna Griffiths and Margaret Whitford (Bloomington: Indiana University Press, 1988); and Barbara Herrnstein Smith, *Contingencies of Value* (Cambridge: Harvard University Press, 1991). There are, of course, thousands of others.

2. Edmund Husserl, "Prolegomena to Pure Logic," in *Logical Investigations*, vol. 1, trans. J. N. Findlay (New York: Humanities Press, 1970). See esp. secs. 17–51 on "psychologism," which he classifies as "a skeptical relativism."

3. The most relevant text in this connection is Jacques Derrida, *Speech and Phenomena*, trans. David Allison (Evanston: Northwestern University Press, 1973). But for a powerful critique of Derrida's reading of Husserl, see J. Claude Evans, *Strategies of Deconstruction* (Minneapolis: University of Minnesota Press, 1991).

4. James M. Edie, "What Is Phenomenology?" in his *Edmund Husserl's Phenomenology: A Critical Commentary* (Bloomington: Indiana University Press, 1987), 1–21. As this is my first mention of Professor Edie, whom we are honoring in this volume, perhaps this would be an appropriate time for me to express to him my own personal appreciation and thanks. I was a student of Professor Edie's at Northwestern University, where he directed my doctoral dissertation. Should I succeed in making any cogent and worthwhile points in this essay, or in any other of my writings, I know that the credit deserves to go to the teachers from whom I learned, among which James Edie would rank very high indeed. My errors and confusions, on the other hand, undoubtedly reveal only my failure to learn from him as much as I should have.

5. On the other hand, Husserl's arguments against relativism are given sustained and detailed attention in Gail Soffer, *Husserl and the Question of Relativism* (Dordrecht: Kluwer, 1991).

6. Bridges, "Modern Political Theory," 3, 7.

7. For example, see *Logical Investigations*, esp. secs. 32, 35, 36; *Ideas Pertaining to a Pure Phenomenology and to a Phenomenological Philosophy*, book 1, trans. F. Kersten (The Hague: Martinus Nihhoff, 1982), secs. 20, and 79; *Experience and Judgment*, trans. James S. Churchill and Karl Ameriks (Evanston: Northwestern University Press, 1973), 392–93; "Philosophy as Rigorous Science," in *Phenomenology and the Crisis of Philosophy*, trans. Quentin Lauer (New York: Harper Torchbooks, 1965), 122–47; and *The Crisis of European Sciences and Transcendental Phenomenology*, trans. David Carr (Evanston: Northwestern University Press, 1970), sec. 6. This is but a small sample.

8. Husserl, *Ideas Pertaining to a Pure Phenomenology*, sec. 79, 185.

9. This is Smith's strategy in *Contingencies of Value*. But for a critique of Smith on precisely this point, see David L. Roochnik, "Can the Relativist Avoid Refuting Herself?" *Philosophy and Literature* 14, no. 1 (April 1990), 92–98.

10. Husserl, *Logical Investigations*, sec. 35.

11. James M. Edie, "Husserl versus Derrida," *Human Studies* 13 (1990), 116.

12. G. B. Madison, "Merleau-Ponty's Destruction of Logocentrism," in *Merleau-Ponty Vivant*, ed. M. C. Dillon (Albany: State University of New York Press, 1991), 135.

13. Patrick Colm Hogan, *The Politics of Interpretation* (New York: Oxford University Press, 1990), 35.

14. See esp. *The Crisis of European Sciences*; Husserl, "Philosophy and the Crisis of European Man," in *Phenomenology and the Crisis of Philosophy*; Husserl, *Vorlesungen über Ethik und Wertlehre, 1908–1914*, ed. Ulrich Melle (Dordrecht: Kluwer, 1988); and Edie, *Edmund Husserl's Phenomenology*, 72.

15. See, e.g., Jean-Paul Sartre, *Truth and Existence*, trans. Adrian van den Hoven (Chicago: University of Chicago Press, 1992).

16. The idea that we should theorize according to our experiencing seems to me quite faithful to the radically experientialist thrust of Husserl's phenomenology.

17. I am grateful to David Turpin for the information about what transpired at this antiwar meeting.

18. See the "Prolegomena" to the *Logical Investigations.*

19. Here I am giving a variation on an example given in Roderick M. Chisolm, *Theory of Knowledge* (Englewood Cliffs, N.J.: Prentice-Hall, 1966), 79.

20. And, as Edie points out, "[o]ur greater novelists and other thinkers, like Dostoevsky, Kierkegaard and Nietzsche, have always known that human beings not only can, but almost always do, hold and act on contradictory impulses and beliefs" ("On Confronting Species-Specific Skepticism as We Near the End of the Twentieth Century," *Man and World* 25 [1992], 326; reprinted in this volume).

21. As Gottlob Frege puts it, "It would be strange if the most exact of all the sciences had to seek support from psychology, which is still feeling its way none too surely" (*Foundations of Arithmetic* [Oxford: Basil Blackwell, 1950], 38).

22. Perhaps the reason why this fallacy is so common is that thinkers, once they notice the undeniable fact that individual acts of thinking are in some sense historically conditioned, tend to confuse these acts of thinking with their contents—the objects of thought. From the fact that the former (e.g., individual *acts* of judging that 2 + 2 = 4) are particular and unrepeatable, it does not follow that the latter (e.g., 2 + 2 = 4) are. Edie explains this clearly in several places. See, e.g., "On Confronting Species-Specific Skepticism," 317, 336n., 31.

23. See esp. part 1 of *Ideas Pertaining to a Pure Phenomenology.*

24. Erazim Kohák, *Idea and Experience* (Chicago: University of Chicago Press, 1978), 16.

25. It must be conceded that we do, of course, err in our judgments of essential truth, sometimes in particular confusing the necessarily true with the merely culturally familiar. But this consideration is not sufficient to sustain Bridge's conclusions.

26. In this way we can attempt to avoid the reductionistic tendencies of both dogmatism and skepticism, a task which, it is somewhat embarrassing to admit at this late date in history, we have yet to complete.

27. Among the points needing to be considered are these, as articulated by Jean Grimshaw: "The experience of gender, of being a man or a woman, inflects much if not all of people's lives. . . . But even if one is always a man or a woman, one is never *just* a man or a woman. One is young or old, sick or healthy, married or unmarried, a parent or not a parent, employed or unemployed, middle class or working class, rich or poor, black or white, and so forth. . . . Experience does not come neatly in segments, such that it is always possible to abstract what in one's experience is due to 'being a woman' " (*Philosophy and Feminist Thinking* [Minneapolis: University of Minnesota Press, 1986], 84–85).

Chapter 7: The Constitutional Problematics of Nonrelativity or How to Dump Garbage in Nobody's Backyard

1. For an analysis of propositional truth as a species coordinate with pictorial and indicational adequacy, cf. Lester Embree, "The Problem of Representational

Adequacy," in *The Prism of the Self*, ed. Steven Galt Crowell (Dordrecht: Kluwer, 1995), 59–70.

2. Lester Embree, "Phenomenology of Action for Ecosystemic Health or How to Tend One's Own Garden," in *Environmental Philosophy and Environmental Activism*, ed. Don Marietta and Lester Embree (Lanham: Rowman and Littlefield, 1995), 51–66.

3. Cf. Alfred Schutz, "The Well-Informed Citizen: An Essay on the Social Distribution of Knowledge," in Alfred Schutz, *Collected Papers*, vol. 2, ed. Arvid Brodersen (The Hague: Martinus Nijhoff, 1964).

4. Cf. Lester Embree, "Some Noetico-Noematic Analyses of Action and Practical Life," in *The Phenomenology of the Noema*, ed. John Drummond and Lester Embree (Dordrecht: Kluwer Academic Publishers, 1992), 157–210.

5. Cf. *Confronting Environmental Racism: Voices from the Grassroots*, ed. Robert D. Bullard (Boston: South End Press, 1993).

Chapter 8: The Desire of Reason: A Plea for a "Practical" Response to Skepticism

1. See Bruce Wilshire's "Edie's Hard-Nosed James and the Retrieval of the Sacred" for a brief discussion of this possibility and further references.

2. Edmund Husserl, *The Crisis of European Sciences and Transcendental Phenomenology*, trans. David Carr, (Evanston: Northwestern University Press, 1970), 18. Subsequent references to the *Crisis* will be given in parenthesis in the text.

3. For the failure of science to present such a language, see Joseph Rouse, *Knowledge and Power: Toward a Political Philosophy of Science* (Ithaca: Cornell University Press, 1987).

4. Nagel is a good example of someone outside the phenomenological tradition who defends the claim that intentional states cannot be understood in physical terms. See Thomas Nagel, "What Is It Like to be a Bat?" in *Mortal Questions* (Cambridge: Cambridge University Press, 1979), 175ff. John Searle's *Intentionality* would be another case that argues for the nonreducibility of intentional states to physical causes but also argues paradoxically that mental states are identical to brain phenomena. See Searle, *Intentionality* (Cambridge: Cambridge University Press, 1983), 262ff.

5. That Husserl thought that science must aspire to systematic unity is clear from statements like the following:

> If we live through and recognize the presence of inner precepts, singly or in groups, we have knowledge but are far removed from science. . . . A group of isolated bits of chemical knowledge would certainly not justify talk of a science of chemistry. More plainly is required, i.e. systematic coherence in the theoretical sense, which means finding grounds for one's knowing and suitably combining and arranging the sequence of such groundings. . . . The investigation and

> setting forth of truths must, therefore, likewise be systematic, it must reflect the systematic connections of those truths and must use the latter as a ladder to progress and penetrate from the knowledge given to or already gained by us to even higher regions of the realm of truth. (*Logical Investigations*, vol. 1, trans. J. N. Findlay [London: Routledge, 1976], 62; hereafter cited as *LI*)

6. *LI*, 60, 61.

7. *LI*, 13.

8. Edmund Husserl, *Ideas Pertaining to a Pure Phenomenology and to Phenomenological Philosophy*, trans. F. Kersten (The Hague: Martinus Nijhoff, 1983), 113. This is a position he never finally renounces, even in the *Crisis*.

9. Ibid., 111.

10. Paul Ricoeur has made this problem a focal point for his analysis of Husserl's phenomenology. See Paul Ricoeur, *Husserl: An Analysis of His Phenomenology* (Evanston: Northwestern University Press, 1967).

11. Compare Paul Natorp's comments on the publication of Husserl's *Prolegomena to Pure Logic*, vol. 1 of the *Logical Investigations*.

> There also remains unresolved in Husserl, the *opposition* between formal and material, apriori and empirical . . . or to put it in one word and at the same time in his own terminology: the ideal and the real. . . . The "real" remains an uncomprehended, irrational surd; the question about the *relation*, the inner epistemological and also the *logical* bond between the two is not at all raised but with their sharp and pure *separation* the problem is laid to rest. And therefore in spite of all the extraordinary lucidity of each special logical discussion—I venture to say—the reader is left with a certain logical dissatisfaction.

Even in 1901 this question dogged Husserl, as it has continued to do so in every subsequent generation of his readers. This quote is from Natorp's "On the Question of Logical Method," republished in *Readings on Edmund Husserl's Logical Investigations*, ed. J. N. Mohanty (The Hague: Martinus Nijhoff, 1977), 65. It originally appeared in *Kant-Studien* 6 (1901).

12. See Robert Sokolowski, "Thoughts on Phenomenology and Skepticism," in this volume.

13. This is particularly true of the *Cartesian Meditations* with its solipsistic account of evidence and a radical idealism that leads Husserl to assert "the world to be inseparable from transcendental subjectivity, which constitutes *actuality of being and sense*" (*Cartesian Meditations*, trans. D. Cairns [The Hague: Martinus Nijhoff, 1973], 62; my emphasis). This tendency to see constitution in "creative" terms is only one tendency among others in Husserl's statements about constitution. However, it is a recurrent tendency, never finally reconciled with accounts of constitution which make more modest plausible claims. See Eugen Fink, "Die phänomenologische Philosophie Edmund Husserls in der gegenwärtigen Kritik," *Kant-Studien* 38 (1933), for an account of constitution which emphasizes its creative world-founding character, an interpretation which Husserl himself unequivocally endorsed in the preface to this article.

14. Even in the *Cartesian Meditations*, Husserl's most radically idealist work, he can claim that "[p]henomenological explication does nothing else—and this can never be emphasized too much—but explicate the sense that the world has for all of us prior to all philosophy and which manifestly our experience gives to it. This sense can be analyzed [*enthüllt*] by philosophy, but never modified [*geändert*] by it. And in each actual experience it is surrounded—for essential reasons and not because of our weakness—with horizons in need of clarification" (177). And the *Logical Investigations* seem even more clearly realist in their intentions: "The system peculiar to science, i.e. to true and correct science is not our own invention but it is present in things, where we simply find or discover it" (*LI*, 62).

15. I agree with Ricoeur that "Husserl's phenomenology labors under two requirements. First, there is an idealistic exigency which expresses itself in the theme of consitution. This is the work [*Leistung*], the 'doing' of consciousness. Secondly, there is an intuitionistic requirement antedating the phenomenological reduction which is expressed in the dictum of the *Logical Investigations* '*zu den Sachen selbst.*' " Thus, it is the case that "two possible senses of constitution intermingle throughout Husserl's work: first, to constitute is to unfold the implicit claiming . . . and second, to constitute is to recognize and distinguish the irreducible types of 'seeing,' of fulfillment by the originary" (Ricoeur, *Husserl*, 102). I doubt, however, that these two tendencies are ever reconciled in Husserl's thought, nor do they ever come to a kind of happy coexistence.

16. Martha Nussbaum, *The Fragility of Goodness* (Cambridge: Cambridge University Press, 1986), see esp. chapters 4 and 5.

17. For a helpful discussion of Montaigne's humanistic skepticism as an alternative to Descartes's (and most of modern philosophy's) antipathy to skepticism, see Stephen Toulmin, *Cosmopolis: The Hidden Agenda of Modernity* (Chicago: University of Chicago Press, 1990), 36–44.

18. As Errol Harris reminds us below in "Skepticism and Dialectic," ancient skeptics often described their arguments as a way of achieving a certain state of mind, *ataraxia*. They see their arguments as a technique for bringing about a desirable psychological state. For a more extended discussion, see Martha Nussbaum, *The Therapy of Desire* (Princeton: Princeton University Press, 1994), 280–315.

19. See David Detmer's essay in this volume for more discussion of this possibility.

20. See my "Prejudice, Reason and Force," *Philosophy* 63 (1988), 231–53.

21. Husserl has sometimes been accused of making these mistakes, or ones like them, because his response to National Socialism was to write the *Crisis*. Nowhere does he suggest that his response is the only responsible response or that it is sufficient to overcome Nazism. See Tom Rockmore's essay in this volume, where Husserl is accused of seeing philosophy as a sufficient response to Nazism.

22. A source from which I have drawn this connection between eros and metaphysics is Stanley Rosen's work, particularly, *The Quarrel Between Philosophy and Poetry* (New York: Routledge, 1988).

23. I agree with Sokolowski's "realistic" criticism of Husserl's one-sided, idealistic account of constitution. For Sokolowski,

> constitution is not simply the evolution of subjectivity (the idealist extreme), nor only the evolution of reality as a closed process independent of consciousness (the empiricist position), but the development of reality and subjectivity in their fundamental relationship to one another. . . . [Thus] intentionality is essentially oriented to discovering the real world, and so this real world is a necessary correlate to consciousness. Reality thus gives consciousness its sense. (Robert Sokolowski, *The Formation of Husserl's Concept of Constitution* [The Hague: Martinus Nijhoff, 1964], 218–20)

24. Since Ricoeur's publication of his work on Husserl there has been an ever-increasing tendency—despite Ricoeur's attempt at a more balanced approach—to see Husserlian constitution in a voluntaristic light. It is no wonder that the major sources of skepticism today often come from French intellectual circles. See J. N. Mohanty's article in this volume for further discussion.

Chapter 9: Meditations of a Russian Neo-Husserlian: Gustav Shpet's "The Skeptic and His Soul"

1. I have profited greatly from the helpful criticisms and suggestions of Stephen Cassedy, Philip T. Grier and Tom Rockmore.

2. Further details are provided by Alexander Haardt in *Husserl in Russland: Phänomenologie der Sprache und Kunst bei Gustav Shpet und Alesksej Losev* (Munich: Fink, 1993), part 1, and also, more briefly, in his "Gustav Shpet's *Appearance and Sense* and Phenomenology in Russia," in Gustav Shpet, *Appearance and Sense: Phenomenology as the Fundamental Science and Its Problems,* trans. Thomas Nemeth (Dordrecht: Kluwer, 1991), xvii–xxxi.

3. *Logicheskie issledovaniia. Chast' pervaia. Prolegomeny k chistoi logike,* trans. F. A. Bershtein, ed. with intro. by S. L. Frank (St. Petersburg, 1909). This is an "authorized" translation only in the sense that Husserl gave his permission to undertake it, not in the sense that he was able to check the adequacy of the translation.

4. "Filosofiia kak strogaia nauka," *Logos: Mezhdunarodnyi ezhegodnik po filosofii i kul'ture. Russkoe izdanie* (*Logos: An International Yearbook of Philosophy and Culture. Russian Edition*), Moscow, no. 1 (1911), 1–56.

5. For example, in N. O. Lossky's *Obosnovanie intuitivizma: Propedevticheskaia teoriia znaniia* (St. Peterburg, 1906); trans. Natalie Duddington as *The Intuitive Basis of Knowledge: An Epistemological Inquiry* (London: Macmillan, 1919). See esp. chapter 7.

6. Cf. G. Lants, "Gusserl' i psikhologisty nashikh dnei" ("Husserl and the Contemporary Defenders of Psychologism"), *Voprosy filosofii i psikhologii,* no. 98 (1909).

7. Boris Jakovenko, "Filosofiia Ed. Gusserlia" ("The Philosophy of Edmund Husserl"), in *Teoriia poznaniia,* t. 1 (*The Theory of Knowledge,* vol. 1) (St. Petersburg, 1913), 74–146.

8. *Iavlenie i smysl: Fenomenologiia kak osnovnaia nauka i ee problemy* (Moscow: Hermes, 1914). For the English translation, see n.2, above.

9. Lev Shestov, "*Memento Mori*: Po povodu teorii poznaniia Edmunda Gusserlia" ("*Memento Mori*: On Edmund Husserl's Theory of Knowledge"), *Voprosy filosofii i psikhologii,* nos. 139–40 (1917), 1–68. When it was published in a French translation by B. de Schloezer nine years later, this article served to introduce Husserl's work to a French audience. Cf. "*Memento Mori*: A propos de la théorie de la connaissance d'Edmund Husserl," *Revue philosophique* 101 (1926), 5–62.

10. Edmund Husserl, *Briefwechsel,* 10 vols., ed. Karl Schuhmann with Elisabeth Schuhmann, "Husserliana: Documenta" (Dordrecht: Kluwer, 1994), vol. 6, 371–76. Unfortunately, Shestov's letters to Husserl have not been preserved.

11. *Briefwechsel,* vol. 6, 371; italics added. The letter is dated 3 July 1929.

12. "Pamiati velikogo filosofa: Edmund Gusserl'," *Russkie zapiski* (Paris), no. 12 (1938), 126–45; no. 1 (1939), 107–16. Translated (with minor abridgments) by George L. Kline as "In Memory of a Great Philosopher: Edmund Husserl," in *Russian Philosophy,* vol. 3, ed. James M. Edie, et al. (Chicago: Quadrangle, 1965; Knoxville: University of Tennessee Press, 1976, 1984), 248–76.

13. The appalling story of Shpet's final days was not made public until 1989, when his grandson, the late M. K. Polivanov, was permitted to examine the secret police archives in Tomsk and reported his findings in "O sud'be G. G. Shpeta" ("On G. G. Shpet's Fate"), *Voprosy filosofii,* no. 6 (1990), 160–64. I have drawn biographical details from this source as well as from two essays by Elena V. Pasternak, Shpet's granddaughter: "Pamiati Gustava Gustavovicha Shpeta" ("In Memory of Gustav Gustavovich Shpet"), *Voprosy filosofii,* no. 11 (1988), 72–76, and her partly overlapping introductory essay in G. G. Shpet, *Socheniniia,* ed. E. V. Antonova (Moscow: Pravda, 1989), 3–8. I have also drawn details from articles published by A. A. Mitiushin (1988, 1989) and K. A. Svas'ian (1990), and from several of the contributions to *Shpetovskie chteniia* (*Lectures on Shpet*) (Tomsk, 1991).

14. Its title is *Germenevtika i ee problemy* (*Hermeneutics and Its Problems*). The first three-quarters of the Russian text, edited by Mitiushin, was published in the Moscow yearbook *Kontekst* in 1989, 1990, and 1991. The final quarter of the text, edited by Elena Pasternak, appeared in *Kontekst* in 1992. A German translation, from Shpet's manuscript, by Alexander Haardt and the late Erika Freiberger, edited by Haardt and Roland Daube-Schackat, was published recently: *Die Hermeneutik und ihre Probleme* (Freiburg/Munich, 1993). An English version, also translated from Shpet's manuscript, by Freiberger, edited by George L. Kline, is forthcoming.

15. All three of the texts dating from 1922–27, just listed, were included in the 1989 Moscow edition of Shpet's *Sochineniia.* His rather unusual expression *etnicheskaia psikhologiia* names that branch of social psychology which deals with a people or peoples, an ethnic group or ethnic groups. The German equivalent of the Greek *ethnos* is *Volk,* and the established German academic term for the discipline Shpet has in mind (as he was well aware) is *Völkerpsychologie.*

16. Among émigré authors, see V. V. Zenkovsky, *Istoriia russkoi filosofii,* vol. 2 (Paris: YMCA, 1950), 370, 372; translated by George L. Kline as *A History of*

Russian Philosophy, vol. 2 (New York: Columbia University Press, 1953), 830, 832. Among Soviet authors, see A. F. Losev in his *Posleslovie* (Afterword) to the Russian translation of Arthur Huebscher's *Contemporary Thinkers* (Moscow, 1962), 337, and V. F. Asmus in *Filosofskaia entsiklopediia,* vol. 5 (Moscow, 1970), 519.

17. Husserl, *Briefwechsel,* vol. 3, 525–44.

18. To the best of my knowledge, none of Husserl's six letters to Shpet has ever been quoted or translated. Shpet's letters to Husserl have been quoted and translated only sparingly and in very brief excerpts. Thus, three sentences from Shpet's letter of 11 March 1914 were quoted in German (from the Louvain Husserl Archive) in Elmar Holenstein, *Linguistik Semiotik Hermeneutik: Plädoyers für eine strukturale Phänomenologie* (Frankfurt am Main, 1976), 15. These same three sentences were also quoted in German by Alexander Haardt in *Husserl in Russland,* 60 (this letter, however, is misdated as 4 May 1914). These same sentences, slightly abridged, are quoted in English translation in Haardt's "Gustav Shpet's *Appearance and Sense,*" in *Appearance and Sense,* xx. Haardt also quotes two sentences from Shpet's letter of 23 November 1913 (*Husserl in Russland,* 78); the same two sentences appear in English in his "Gustav Shpet's *Appearance and Sense,*" xxii. In his *Husserl in Russland,* Haardt also quotes three sentences from Shpet's letter of 14 December 1913 (111) and one sentence from his letter of 10 June 1918 (114n.323). He also paraphrases a sentence from Shpet's letter of 4 May 1914 (98n.266).

19. Letter of 15 March 1914; *Briefwechsel,* vol. 3, 536.

20. Ibid., 527–28. Shpet signed all of his letters to Husserl "GvonSpett."

21. Ibid., 257.

22. Husserl's expression is *Exemplar des fertigen Werkes* (ibid., 528). It is not clear whether this refers to the fully revised but not yet published text of vol. 2, or to the already published second edition of that work. It would seem that two months (from late August to late October) would be too short a time for actual publication. In any case, the *Vorwort* to the second edition is dated "October 1913," and the year of publication of both vol. 1 and vol. 2 is given as 1913. Shpet, writing from Paris on 14 December, thanks Husserl for sending him the two volumes; so it appears that the book was published earlier that month (see ibid., 529, and editorial note, 529n.9).

23. Ibid., 542; emphasis added.

24. Ibid., 536.

25. Ibid., 531, 537.

26. Ibid., 536.

27. Ibid., 542. There is no evidence that this visit ever took place, or indeed that Shpet ever again traveled outside Russia or the Soviet Union after his return to Moscow from Paris late in 1913. His planned trip to Germany may have been put off because of the imminent threat of war. In any case, the First World War interrupted the Husserl-Shpet correspondence for more than four years.

28. Ibid., 529.

29. Ibid., 528. In this letter Shpet does not make his attitude toward "presentationalism" and "representationalism" explicit, perhaps assuming that Husserl

already knows what it is. His positive attitude toward the former first becomes clear in *Appearance and Sense,* where Shpet asserts that "firmly establishing a presentationalism [*prezentativizm*] for our consciousness of everything that exists" is central to the phenomenological project (*Appearance and Sense,* 170; translation revised). Shpet's negative attitude toward the second becomes clearest, perhaps, in "The Skeptic and His Soul," to be discussed in sec. IV, below.

30. In fact, Shpet refers quite frequently to Plato, as an exemplar of "affirmative philosophy," in both *Appearance and Sense* and "The Skeptic and His Soul."

31. *Briefwechsel,* vol. 3, 528–29.

32. As it turned out, the "Sixth Investigation" (in vol. 2, part 2 of the revised edition of the *Logical Investigations*) was only "partially revised" and did not appear until 1921. In his letter of 29 December Husserl says that he has not been able to work as rapidly or productively as he had earlier, and that as a result the publication of vol. 2, part 2, has been put off "for several months." Nearly seven years later, in the Foreword (October 1920) to that volume, he blamed the further delay on his heavy teaching schedule at Freiburg (where he had been since April 1916), as well as on the difficulties of the war and immediate postwar period (see *Logische Untersuchungen,* vol. 2, part 2, iii). What he does not mention, but his wife Malvine conveys with great dignity as well as poignancy in her letter of 20 September 1918 to Shpet's wife, is that their twenty-year-old son Wolfgang, an officer in the German Army, had been killed in the Battle of Verdun in March 1916. Their other son, who had been seriously wounded, was already back in action (*Briefwechsel,* vol. 3, 543).

33. Shpet refers to the passage at vol. 2, 19 (sec. 7 of the Introduction), which corresponds to *Husserliana* XIX/1, 24.

34. *Briefwechsel,* vol. 3, 529–31.

35. Husserl wrote only "*Wiss*" at this point; the editors, who regularly fill out his abbreviations, put "*Wissenschaft.*" However, since the word "*Wissenschaft*" does not occur elsewhere in this paragraph, whereas the word "*Wissenschaftlichkeit*" occurs twice, I have chosen to read Husserl's "*Wiss*" as "*Wissenschaftlichkeit.*"

36. Ibid., 532.

37. Ibid.

38. Ibid., 531.

39. Ibid., 540. At this time Shpet was thirty-five, Husserl's age in 1894. In an unsent draft of the last part of this letter, Husserl couched his warning in less confessional terms, but terms that were more flattering to Shpet: "Take care of your health, don't overwork. Given your great seriousness and your outstanding gifts of intuition, you cannot fail to be successful in phenomenology [*kann es Ihnen an phänomenologischen Erfolgen nicht fehlen*]" (*Briefwechsel,* vol. 3, 599).

40. Ibid., 533, 533n.18. Husserl had sent Bergson a copy of *Ideas I* and Bergson had responded with a friendly note (dated 15 August 1913) in which he addressed Husserl as "*très honoré Collègue,*" referred to *Ideas I* as a "*très important ouvrage,*" and assured him of the "*haute estime*" in which he held his work generally (*Briefwechsel,* vol. 6, 11).

41. *Briefwechsel,* vol. 3, 533–35.

42. Ibid., 538.

43. Ibid., 536.

44. Ibid., 539–40.

45. Ibid., 541; ellipses in the original.

46. This copy is held in Husserl's library in Louvain. See editorial note, ibid., 528n.8.

47. A typical production by an ideologist is Iuli Martov, "Marks s Kantom, Kant s Gindenburgom" ("Marx with Kant, Kant with Hindenburg"), *Letopis'*, no. 3 (1916), in which the Menshevik author attacked such Russian "Kantian Marxists" as Berdyaev for associating Marx with Kant and tried to discredit Kant by associating his views and values with those of Prussian General Paul von Hindenburg, at that time supreme commander of the armed forces of the central powers in the East. A typical production by a philosopher is Vladimir Ern, "Ot Kanta k Kruppu" ("From Kant to Krupp"), in his book *Mech i krest* (*The Sword and the Cross*) (Moscow, 1915), in which the neo-Slavophile author associated Kant's philosophy with the German "military-industrial complex" of the day.

48. *Briefwechsel*, vol. 3, 542–43.

49. Ibid., 543.

50. See Hegel, *Phänomenologie des Geistes*, ed. J. Hoffmeister (Hamburg: Meiner, 1952), 154–58; *Phenomenology of Spirit*, trans. A. V. Miller (Oxford University Press, 1977), secs. 202–6; *Vorlesungen über die Geschichte der Philosophie*, vol. 18, ed. H. Glockner (Stuttgart: Frommanns, 1928), 538–86; *Lectures on the History of Philosophy*, vol. 2, trans. Elisabeth S. Haldane and Frances H. Simson (London: Kegan Paul, 1894), 328–73. See Husserl, *Logische Untersuchungen*, vol. 1: *Prolegomena zur reinen Logik*, 2d ed. (Halle: Niemeyer, 1913), chapter 7, 110–54; *Logical Investigations*, vol. 1: *Prolegomena to Pure Logic*, trans. J. N. Findlay (London: Routledge, 1970), chapter 7, 135–67.

51. B. N. Poizner, "Skeptik v otsenke Shpeta i vnutrenniaia forma tvorchestva" ("Shpet's Evaluation of the Skeptic, and the Inner Form of Creativity"), in *Shpetovskie chteniia v Tomske 1991* (*Lectures on Shpet in Tomsk* 1991) (Tomsk: Izdatel'stvo Tomskogo universiteta, 1991), 89, 95.

52. See "Skeptik i ego dusha" ("The Skeptic and His Soul"), *Mysl' i slovo* (1919), 113. In the remainder of sec. IV references to this essay will be by page number in parentheses in the text. (This essay was reprinted in *Filosofskie nauki*, no. 9 [Moscow, 1991], 85–136.)

53. For the ten earlier tropes, see "Aenesidemus," in *Encyclopedia of Philosophy*, vol. 1, ed. Paul Edwards (New York: Macmillan/Free Press, 1967). For the five later tropes, see "Agrippa" in the same volume. For ancient skepticism generally, see "Sextus Empiricus," in ibid., vol. 7. For a concise and intelligent summary of all fifteen *tropoi*, see Errol E. Harris, "Skepticism and Dialectic," in this volume.

54. See Hegel, "Relationship of Skepticism to Philosophy" (1802), trans. H. S. Harris, in *Between Kant and Hegel: Texts in the Development of Post-Kantian Idealism*, trans. and annotated by George di Giovanni and H. S. Harris (Albany: State University of New York Press, 1985), 313–62. For a helpful commentary, see Michael N. Forster, *Hegel and Skepticism* (Cambridge: Harvard University Press, 1989).

55. Hegel, *Vorlesungen,* vol. 18, 553; *Lectures,* vol. 2, 344.

56. Husserl, *Logische Untersuchungen,* vol. 1, 110; *Logical Investigations,* vol. 1, 135.

57. Cf., "Montaigne or the Skeptic" (1850), in *The Collected Works of Ralph Waldo Emerson,* vol. 4, ed. Wallace E. Williams and Douglas E. Wilson (Cambridge: Belknap Press, 1987), 97; italics added.

58. This may be viewed as a variation on the Hegelian theme that skepticism, as a complete negation of otherness, is the "realization" of that of which stoicism, as an "incomplete negation of otherness," is only the concept. See *Phänomenologie des Geistes,* 154; *Phenomenology of Spirit,* secs. 201–2. Presumably, Shpet would wish to qualify Hegel's remark about "complete negation"; at least, he denies that the skeptic is a nihilist or seriously opposed to *anything* (111).

59. Hegel, *Vorlesungen,* vol. 18, 539; *Lectures,* vol. 2, 329; emphasis added.

60. Cf. Nietzsche: "*Vorausgesetzt, dass die Wahrheit ein Weib ist . . .*" ("Supposing truth is a woman . . ."), *Jenseits von Gut und Böse,* in *Werke in drei Bänden,* 2d ed., vol. 2, ed. K. Schlechta (Munich: Hanser, 1960), 565; *Beyond Good and Evil,* trans. Walter Kaufmann (New York: Vintage, 1966), 2. The word "truth," which of course is genderless in modern English, is grammatically feminine in Russian (*istina*), German (*Wahrheit*), and Greek (*alētheia*)—as Shpet, Nietzsche, and Plato, respectively, were well aware.

61. *Vnutrenniaia forma slova: Etiudy i variatsii na temy Gumbol'ta* (*The Inner Form of the Word: Studies and Variations on Themes from Humboldt*) (Moscow, 1927), 155.

Chapter 10: Skepticism and Dialectic

1. Cf. Hegel, *Vorlesungen über die Geschichte de Philosophie,* in *Werke,* vol. 20, (Suhrkamp Verlag, 1978), 127. In a footnote, reference is made here to Spinoza's *Principia philosophiae Cartesianae.* See Van Vloten and Land, *Benedicti de Spinoza Opera,* vol. 4 (The Hague: Nijhoff, 1914), 110.

2. Cf. David Hume, *Treatise of Human Nature,* book I, part 2, sec. 7.

3. Ibid., book I, Appendix.

4. Hegel, *Vorlesungen über die Geschichte der Philosophie,* in *Werke,* vol. 20, 269.

5. Ibid., 386.

6. Ibid., *Werke,* vol. 18, 188 (E. S. Haldane's translation).

7. There is, of course, a sense in which Ground is a provisional definition of the Absolute (as is every other category), and as such (qua ground of all finitude) does not involve the false infinite.

8. Hegel, *Enzyklopädie,* sec. 111, *Zusatz* (Wallace's translation).

9. Cf., *Recognition: Fichte and Hegel on the Other* (Albany: State University of New York Press, 1992), 101f.

10. Cf. my *Formal, Transcendental, and Dialectical Thinking: Logic and Reality* (Albany: State University of New York Press, 1987), chapter 5, and *L'idee*

de phenomenologie, l'exemplarisme husserlien, trans. G. L. Breckon as *The Idea of Phenomenology: Husserlian Exemplarism* (Evanston: Northwestern University Press, 1974).

11. Cf. Jacques Derrida, *De la grammatologie* (Paris: Les Éditions de Minuit, 1967), 38; *Of Grammatology*, trans. Gayatri Chakravorty Spivak (Baltimore: The Johns Hopkins University Press, 1976), 23.

12. Jacques Derrida, *Positions* (Paris: Les Éditions de Minuit, 1972), 78, n.22; trans. Alan Bass (London: Athlone, 1981), 104, n.31.

13. Cf. my discussion in *The Reality of Time* (Albany: State University of New York Press, 1988), 121–31, and Gillian Rose's critique in *The Dialectic of Nihilism* (Oxford: Basil Blackwell, 1984–87), chapters 7, 8, 9.

Chapter 11: The Phenomenological Tradition and the End of History

1. See David Carr, "Husserl's *Crisis* and the Problem of History," *Southwestern Journal of Philosophy* 5, no. 3 (1974), 127–48; and *Phenomenology and the Problem of History* (Evanston: Northwestern University Press, 1974). James Edie was the editor of the series in which both this book and Carr's translation of the *Crisis* appeared.

2. "Un entretien avec Emmanuel Levinas," *Le Monde*, Tuesday, 2 June 1992, 2, my trans. Since this was written, Emmanuel Levinas has died (in December 1995).

3. It should be observed, for the record, that Merleau-Ponty's conclusions in the two works in question (as we were both aware during our discussion) differ greatly from one another. In the earlier one, he was very much inclined to "give the benefit of the doubt" to Communist Party claims about, for example, the "objective guilt" of some purge trial members—or at the very least to explore the meanings of such claims while provisionally taking them at face value. By the time of writing *Adventures of the Dialectic*, on the other hand, Merleau-Ponty had become convinced that history was moving along essentially unchartable paths, and any rate not along the path alleged and prescribed by the Communist Party.

4. James Edie, *Edmund Husserl's Phenomenology* (Bloomington: Indiana University Press, 1987), 120.

5. William McBride, *Sartre's Political Theory* (Bloomington: Indiana University Press, 1991).

6. This is a point particularly stressed by Ludwig Landgrebe, *Phänomenologie und Praxis* (Freiburg: Alber, 1976). Carr, from a slightly different perspective, points out the ultimate ambiguity in Husserl's use of "*Lebenswelt*" as both a perceptual and a cultural referent.

7. Edmund Husserl, *Die Krisis der europäischen Wissenschaften und die transzendentale Phänomenologie*, ed. Walter Biemel (The Hague: Martinus Nijhoff, 1954), 347 (in the appendix text, "Die Krisis des europäischen Menschentums und die

Philosophie"); my translation. *The Crisis of European Sciences and Transcendental Phenomenology*, trans. David Carr (Evanston: Northwestern University Press, 1990).

8. Ibid., 14.

9. Paul Ricoeur, *Husserl: An Analysis of His Phenomenology*, E. G. Ballard and L. E. Embree (Evanston: Northwestern University Press, 1967), 156.

10. Husserl, *Die Krisis*, 15.

11. See George Leaman, *Heidegger im Kontext* (Hamburg: Argument-Verlag, 1993), for one more collection of convincing documentary proof to this effect.

12. Husserl, *Die Krisis*, 380 (in the appendix text known as "Vom Ursprung der Geometrie," originally published by Eugen Fink in the *Revue Internationale de Philosophie* in 1939). A rough translation is: "History is, from the beginning, nothing other than the living movement of the togetherness and reciprocity of original meaning-formation and meaning-sedimentation."

13. Ibid., 381. It should be noted, for what it is worth, that I am steering clear, in my discussions both of Husserl and of Sartre, of the obsession with distinctions among *Geschichte, Geschichtlichkeit, Historie, Historizität*, etc., or among *histoire, historicité, historialité*, etc., that have occupied a prominent place in some of the scholarly literature. While such distinctions are no doubt of some merit, they have often been made to bear an importance that does not correspond to their actual linguistic usages, whether in German or in French. I owe the recognition of this to Vincent von Wroblewsky, the German Sartre translator.

14. Carr, "Husserl's *Crisis*," 133.

15. Husserl, *Die Krisis*, 503 (in appendix text 26, "Stufen der Geschichtlichkeit: Erste Geschichtlichkeit").

16. Ibid., 501 (in appendix text 25, also not included in Carr's translation). Roughly, "The history of the world itself, in itself, is world history in the sense of the infinite idea."

17. Ibid., 382 (in "Vom Ursprung der Geometrie").

18. Jean Paul Sartre, *Vérité et existence* (Paris: Gallimard, 1989), iv.

19. Jean Paul Sartre, *Truth and Existence* (Chicago: University of Chicago Press, 1992).

20. It was to be some years, in fact, after the writing of *Vérité et existence* before Sartre would become fully cognizant of the importance of "lived experience." However, the notion was already at least inchoate in his writing and was being articulated by Simone De Beauvoir, whose work he presumably read: she employed it as the subtitle naming the second half of her great work, *The Second Sex*, which she was completing during the same period. See my "Sartre and Lived Experience," *Research in Phenomenology* 11 (1981), 75–89.

21. As the *Cahiers pour une morale*, composed at the same time or just a little earlier, show, he was then developing a strong theoretical interest in Hegel and Marx, which would eventuate in, above all, the *Critique de la raison dialectique*.

22. Sartre, *Vérité et existence*, 29.

23. Ibid., 31–33, my translation. (Many even-numbered pages in this part of the published text are reserved for marginal notes; hence, "31–33" for two short sentences.)

24. Ibid., 39–41. This is the only reference to Husserl in the text proper; there is also one marginal reference, itself of only marginal importance.

25. Ibid., 107.

26. Ibid., 57–58, my translation. This is an interesting departure from the standard pragmatist conception of truth, to which in many respects—as a marginal reference by Sartre to James's *Pragmatism* confirms—some of these ideas can usefully be compared.

27. Ibid., 127; my translation.

28. Ibid., 29.

29. One is reminded here of Sartre's famous quarrel, several years later, with Albert Camus over the theories of the latter's *The Rebel.* At one point in his reply to Camus, Sartre says: " 'Has history a meaning?' you ask, 'has it an end?' For me, it is the *question* that is meaningless: for history, outside of man who makes it, is only an abstract and motionless concept, about which one cannot either say that it has an end or that it does not" ("Réponse à Albert Camus," *Situations,* vol. 4 [Paris: Gallimard, 1964], 124; my translation).

30. Sartre, *Vérité et existence,* 132; my translation.

31. See in particular my "Sartre's Philosophy of History," *Eros* 8, no. 1 (June 1981), 71–81, where I strongly urge this, as well as in *Sartre's Political Theory,* 161–70 and elsewhere, most of which was completed before the publication of *Vérité et existence.*

32. Sartre, *Vérité et existence,* 74.

33. Ibid., 132.

34. James Edie, "On Confronting Species-Specific Skepticism as We Near the End of the Twentieth Century," *Man and World* 25 (1992), 330; reprinted in this volume. The citation from Merleau-Ponty is taken from *The Primacy of Perception and Other Essays,* ed. Edie (Evanston: Northwestern University Press, 1964).

35. I am thinking here especially of a very good essay by that title, "Existential Universals," written by the late, lamented Head of the Purdue Philosophy Department, Richard Grabau, that appeared in *An Invitation to Phenomenology,* ed. James Edie (New York: Quadrangle, 1965), 147–60.

36. James Edie, "The Question of the Transcendental Ego: Sartre's Critique of Husserl," manuscript prepared for a *Festschrift* for Joseph Kockelmans, ed. Tim Stapleton (forthcoming).

37. Sartre, "L'universel singulier," in *Situations,* vol. 9 (Paris: Gallimard, 1972), 152–90. I discuss this paper at some length in "Sartre's Debts to Kierkegaard: A Partial Reckoning," to appear in *Kierkegaard in Post/Modernity,* ed. Martin Matustík and Merold Westphal (Bloomington: Indiana University Press, 1995), 18–42.

38. *Russian Philosophy,* 3 vols., ed. James M. Edie, James P. Scanlan, and Mary-Barbara Zeldin, with the collaboration of George L. Kline (Chicago: Quadrangle, 1965).

39. See especially my article, "La philosophie politique sartrienne d' aprés le deuxiéme tome de la *Critique de la raison dialectique,*" in *Gli scritti postumi di Sartre,*

ed. Giovanni Invitto and Aniello Montano (Genova: Casa Editrice Marietti, 1993), 227–38.

40. Sartre, *Vérité et existence,* 130.

41. Francis Fukuyama, *The End of History and the Last Man* (New York: Free Press, 1992).

Chapter 12: A Crisis of Reason? Husserl, Heidegger, and National Socialism

1. Richard J. Bernstein, *Beyond Objectivism and Relativism: Science, Hermeneutics, and Praxis* (Philadelphia: University of Pennsylvania Press, 1983), 11.

2. See Immanuel Kant, *Critique of Pure Reason,* trans. Norman Kemp Smith (London and New York: Macmillan and St. Martin's Press, 1961), B 370, 310.

3. See Iris Murdoch, *The Fire and the Sun: Why Plato Banished the Artists* (Oxford: Clarendon Press, 1971), 31.

4. See Kant, *Critique of Pure Reason,* B 866–67, 657–58.

5. See "On the Proverb: That May Be True in Theory But Is of No Practical Use," in Immanuel Kant, *Perpetual Peace and Other Essays,* trans. Ted Humphrey (Indianapolis: Hackett, 1983), 61–92.

6. I am relying here principally on Herbert Spiegelberg, *The Phenomenological Movement: A Historical Introduction* (The Hague: Martinus Nijhoff, 1982), 339–47.

7. See Walter Biemel, "Husserl's *Encyclopedia Brittanica* Article and Heidegger's Remarks Thereon," in *Husserl: Expositions and Appraisals,* ed. Frederick Elliston and Peter McCormick (Notre Dame: University of Notre Dame Press, 1977), 286–303.

8. See "My Way to Phenomenology," in Martin Heidegger, *On Time and Being,* trans. Joan Stambaugh (New York: Harper and Row, 1972), 74–82.

9. See Edmund Husserl, *The Phenomenology of Internal Time-Consciousness,* ed. Martin Heidegger, trans. James S. Churchill (Bloomington: Indiana University Press, 1966).

10. See Martin Heidegger, *Being and Time,* trans. John Macquarrie and Edward Robinson (New York: Harper and Row, 1962), 62.

11. See ibid., 62.

12. See ibid., sec. 32, 188–95.

13. See the "Nachwort" to *Ideen,* cited in Spiegelberg, *The Phenomenological Movement,* 345.

14. See "The Discourse on Method," in *The Philosophical Works of Descartes,* trans. Elizabeth S. Haldane and G. R. T. Ross (London: Cambridge University Press, 1970), 1.

15. Maurice Merleau-Ponty, *The Primacy of Perception and Other Essays,* trans. James M. Edie (Evanston: Northwestern University Press, 1964), 43.

16. See Tom Rockmore, "The Concept of Crisis and the Unity of Husserl's Position," in *Phenomenology and the Human Sciences,* ed. J. N. Mohanty (Dordrecht: Martinus Nijhoff, 1985), 5–19.

17. See Iso Kern, *Husserl und Kant* (The Hague: Martinus Nijhoff, 1964): "Die fundamentale Gemeinschaft liegt hier wohl in der Idee der Philosophie als einer streng wissenschaftlichen und reflexiven 'Kritik' der Vernunftprinzipien mit dem Ziel des Vernünftigwerdens der Vernunft und der Errichtung einer endgültigen Metaphysik" (422).

18. See "Epistemology Naturalized," in W. V. Quine, *Ontological Relativity and Other Essays* (New York: Columbia University Press, 1969), 69–90.

19. Edmund Husserl, *Ideas: General Introduction to Pure Phenomenology*, trans. W. R. Boyce Gibson (New York: Collier, 1962), 166.

20. See Edmund Husserl, *Logical Investigations*, vol. 1, trans. J. N. Findlay (New York: Humanities Press, 1970), 145.

21. According to Heidegger, Kant uncritically appropriates Descartes's position. See Heidegger, *Being and Time*, 45.

22. Edmund Husserl, *Formal and Transcendental Logic*, trans. Dorion Cairns (The Hague: Martinus Nijhoff, 1969), 16.

23. See "Philosophy as Rigorous Science," in Edmund Husserl, *Phenomenology and the Crisis of Philosophy*, trans. Quentin Lauer (New York: Harper and Row, 1965), 71.

24. See Edmund Husserl, *The Crisis of European Sciences and Transcendental Phenomenology*, trans. David Carr (Evanston: Northwestern University Press, 1970), 3.

25. See ibid., 389.

26. Ibid., 17; his emphases.

27. Ibid., 12; his emphases.

28. See Heidegger, *Being and Time*, sec. 44, 256–73.

29. See ibid., sec. 32, 188–95.

30. See ibid., 29.

31. Ibid., 1.

32. See ibid., 35.

33. Ibid., 62.

34. See Martin Heidegger, *Introduction to Metaphysics*, trans. Ralph Manheim (New Haven: Yale University Press, 1977), 38–39; see also 199.

35. See chapter 5: "Nazism and the *Beiträge zur Philosophie*," in Tom Rockmore, *On Heidegger's Nazism and Philosophy* (Berkeley: University of California Press, 1992), 176–203.

36. See Martin Heidegger, *Beiträge zur Philosophie*, ed. Friedrich-Wilhelm von Hermann (Frankfurt: Vittorio Klostermann, 1989), 11.

37. See chapter 1: "Revealing Concealed Nazism," in Rockmore, *On Heidegger's Nazism and Philosophy*, 15–28.

38. See Jaspers's *Gutachten*, written for the Oehlker's commission, cited in Hugo Ott, *Martin Heidegger: Unterwegs zu seiner Biographie* (Frankfurt: Campus, 1988), 317.

39. Edmund Husserl, *Phenomenology and the Crisis of Philosophy*, trans. Quentin Lauer (New York: Harper, 1965), 149.

40. Ibid., 153.

41. Ibid., 149.

42. Ibid., 192.

43. Husserl, *The Crisis of European Sciences*, 6.

44. See "Den Führer führen? Heidegger und kein Ende," in Otto Pöggeler, *Neue Wege mit Heidegger* (Freiburg: Karl Alber, 1992), 203–54.

45. See Heidegger, *Introduction to Metaphysics*, 57.

46. See ibid., 38.

47. Ibid., 199.

48. See Zygmunt Bauman, *Modernity and the Holocaust* (Ithaca: Cornell University Press, 1989). For discussion, see Alan Milchman and Alan Rosenberg, " Review of Bauman, *Modernity and the Holocaust*," in *Holocaust and Genocide Studies* 5, no. 3 (1990), 337–42.

49. See Karl Löwith, *Mein Leben in Deutschland vor und nach 1933: Ein Bericht* (Stuttgart, 1986).

50. "Technology and modern science gave us the tools that in the twentieth century made mass destruction possible." Alan Rosenberg and Paul Marcus, "The Holocaust as a Test of Philosophy," in *Echoes from the Holocaust: Philosophical Reflections on A Dark Time*, ed. Alan Rosenberg and Gerard Myers (Philadelphia: Temple University Press, 1988), 209.

51. See "Letter on Humanism," in Martin Heidegger, *Basic Writings*, trans. David Farrell Krell (New York: Harper and Row, 1977), 239–40.

Chapter 13: Edie's Hard-Nosed James and the Retrieval of the Sacred

1. See "Notes on the Philosophical Anthropology of William James," the opening pages. Edie has published at least four major essays on James. They are reprinted in his *William James and Phenomenology* (Bloomington: Indiana University Press, 1987), and in this form I allude to them in this paper.

2. William James, *The Principles of Psychology*, vol. 2 (New York: Dover Books, 1950 [1890]), 641ff.

3. "The Philosophical Framework of Sartre's Theory of the Theatre," to appear in a Festschrift for Maurice Natanson.

4. See William James, "The Place of Affectional Facts in a World of Pure Experience," in *A Pluralistic Universe.* I use the 1942 edition, bound together with *Essays in Radical Empiricism.*

5. See William James, *A Pluralistic Universe*, "The Continuity of Experience," 288ff.

6. William James, *A Pluralistic Universe*, "Bergson and Intellectualism," 262.

7. *Orion: Nature Quarterly*, "In Animals We Find Ourselves" (Spring 1990).

8. James, "The Place of Affectional Facts," 85.

9. See Rupert Sheldrate, *A New Science of Life* (Los Angeles: J. P. Tarcher, 1981), and *The Presence of the Past: Morphic Resonance and the Habits of Nature*, (London: Collins, 1988).

10. James, *A Pluralistic Universe*, 299, 330.

Contributors

David J. Detmer
Associate Professor of Philosophy
Purdue University-Calument

James M. Edie
Professor Emeritus of Philosophy
Northwestern University

Lester Embree
Professor of Philosophy
Florida Atlantic University

Harrison Hall
Professor of Philosophy
University of Delaware

Errol E. Harris
Professor Emeritus of Philosophy
Northwestern University

George L. Kline
Professor Emeritus of Philosophy
Bryn Mawr College

Joseph J. Kockelmans
Professor of Philosophy
Pennsylvania State University

William L. McBride
Professor of Philosophy
Purdue University

J. N. Mohanty
Professor of Philosophy
Temple University

Tom Rockmore
Professor of Philosophy
Duquesne University

Robert Sokolowski
Professor of Philosophy
Catholic University of America

Brice R. Wachterhauser
Associate Professor of Philosophy
St. Joseph's University

Bruce Wilshire
Professor of Philosophy
Rutgers University